S0-AEL-645

HELLAS

Your pedigree has left a stamp
upon your looks that makes one
take you for the sons of kings,
those sceptred favorites of Zeus,
for no mean folk could breed
such men as you are.

Homer, Odyssey, Book IV

HELLAS
THE CIVILIZATIONS
OF ANCIENT GREECE

KEITH BRANIGAN
MICHAEL VICKERS

Foreword by
JOHN BOARDMAN

McGRAW-HILL BOOK COMPANY

NEW YORK ST. LOUIS SAN FRANCISCO

CONTENTS

DEDICATION

For Alun, Holly and Tania
and Gerald and Sophie

A McGraw-Hill Co-Publication

Copyright © 1980 by McGraw-Hill Book
Company (UK) Limited, Maidenhead,
England. All rights reserved. No part
of this publication may be reproduced,
stored in a retrieval system, or transmitted in any form or by any means,
electronic, mechanical, photocopying,
recording, or otherwise, without the
prior written permission of the
publisher.

Library of Congress Cataloging
in Publication Data
BRANIGAN, KEITH.
   Hellas, the civilizations of ancient
Greece.

   1. Civilization, Greek.
   I. VICKERS, MICHAEL J.,
   joint author. II. Title.
DF77.B83   938   80-18306
ISBN 0-07-007229-9

Designer:
CHARLES WHITEHOUSE

Editor:
DAVID BAKER

Managing Editor:
FRANCINE PEETERS

Picture Procuration:
ROSARIA PASQUARIELLO

Production Manager:
FRANZ GISLER

Graphic Artist:
FRANZ CORAY

Printed by:
RÉUNIES, LAUSANNE,
SWITZERLAND

Bound by:
CHARLES BUSENHART, LAUSANNE

Composition by:
WEBER AG, BIEL, SWITZERLAND

Printed in Switzerland

The beginnings of Aegean civilization, in farming communities dating
to 6000 B.C., led to the development of town life, crafts, writing. By
2000 B.C. there emerged in Crete a
brilliant palace civilization which
flourished as a maritime power for
five centuries.

Contacts with the eastern Mediterranean brought a quickening to
mainland Greek civilization from the
eighth century B.C.: greater wealth,
colonies, new fighting methods,
more individual liberty, artistic developments, the rise of the city-state.

From the seventeenth century B.C. the Greek mainland saw the heyday of Mycenaean civilization, in an era of warfare and heroic prowess, of small kingdoms ruled from fortified citadels. There followed a long Dark Age, the period of the Trojan War.

Her defeat of the Persians in 479 B.C. left Athens in a commanding political and economical position. The city contributed decisively to classical Greek art, architecture, literature, and thought. Even in decline, Athens left an enduring legacy.

Geographers, when they come to
deal with those parts of the
earth which they know nothing
about, crowd them into the
margins of their maps with the
explanation, "Beyond this lie
sandy, waterless deserts," or
"trackless swamps," or
"Scythian snows," or "ice-locked
sea." Now that I have
reached the end of those periods
in which theories can be tested
by argument or where history can
find a solid foundation in fact,
I might very well follow their
example and say of those
remoter ages, "All that lies beyond are prodigies and fables,
the province of poets and roman-
cers, where nothing is certain
or credible."

However... let us hope that I
shall succeed in purifying fable,
and make her submit to reason and take on the appearance
of history.

Plutarch, "Life of Theseus"

FOREWORD

Fact and fiction are strongly interwoven in our views of ancient Greece. This is a book about fact—tempered by that exercise of the imagination which every historian and archaeologist is bound to call upon in attempting to present a coherent picture of a period or culture for which the evidence is necessarily so incomplete. It is written by scholars as well at home with excavation and objects as with text and theory. The Bronze Age world of the non-Greek Minoans and the Greek Mycenaeans has been revealed by the spade and is virtually mute. The world of the resurgent Greece of the Age of Iron is opened to us by the same sources but becomes yet more strongly defined through the words of poets, historians, statesmen, and generals (sometimes all one and the same man) preserved for us by the appreciative scholarship of antiquity. We are learning again, though slowly, the educative value of the visual image, the "icon" in its broader sense. For much of antiquity it was a prime purveyor of culture and instruction. We use it perforce (and abundantly in this book) to present the evidence of antiquity and guide our understanding of a place and people infinitely remote yet acknowledged as ultimate inspiration of Western culture.

So much is fact. The fiction which adds the color and grips the imagination stems from many sources. Some of it is purely emotive, based on roseate interpretations of Greece, mainly by poets and artists of the nineteenth century, who worked too on the imaginations of scholars and archaeologists. Whether or not we have "read Classics," our education has been influenced by generations to whom some Classical texts meant as much as the Bible. Their view of Greek antiquity was an admirable but inaccurate one and it is easier today to shake it off. But we have become more insidiously affected by the representational arts inspired by antiquity, from the Renaissance to photography, and it is more difficult, if not impossible, to shake off this influence and judge afresh the achievements of those who pioneered realism and the subtler expressions of emotion and narrative in the arts.

A book such as this is not a work of fiction, but it has not been only the attitudes of recent generations which have hampered our clear view of the facts. The pace of new discoveries has meant that classical archaeologists, quicker than most scholars, have learnt to change their minds in the face of new evidence. Moreover, the imaginative play with the past was already at work in antiquity and colored the quality of life. No other period so clearly shows how a culture might depend for its inspiration as much on its opinion of itself and its past, as on its ability to invent and plan for the future. The Greeks did not "live in the past"—this is the hallmark of a type of decadence we can recognize today—but their literature and art are informed by an awareness of a past in which their forefathers walked with the gods, which they could turn to as a model and inspiration. Hence their insistent and subtle use of myth. What the scholar of today can do is match the truth of their past, the achievements of the Minoan and Mycenaean world, with their own views of their Heroic Age, and add to this a fuller understanding of the brilliance and humanity of their later achievements. It is hard to say which, the fact or the fiction, is the more remarkable or the more fruitful, but both have contributed so much to the development of Western civilization that they deserve our respect and study in their own right as much as for the challenge they present to the tawdry anti-heroism of our own day.

JOHN BOARDMAN

THREE CIVILIZATIONS

In the mid-nineteenth century, *Greek Civilization* could mean but one thing—the civilization which flourished in classical Greece between about 500 and 350 B.C. By 1900 it was clear that Greece had spawned not one but three civilizations, each with its own distinctive flavor, yet all revealing a common reaction to the natural environment in which they were nourished.

The Minoan civilization of Crete, which emerged about 2000 B.C., is still something of an enigma. It was clearly a palace-based civilization, with four or five principal palatial centers controlling, or at least organizing, agricultural production and the distribution and storage of agricultural surplus. The same palaces also employed many different craftsmen and appear to have regulated internal exchange and overseas trade. Minoan ritual and ceremony was apparently focused on the palaces.

craftsmen combine workmanship of the highest quality with individualism, warmth, and exuberance. Whatever the power exerted by the palaces, nowhere in Minoan civilization does one sense oppression or excessive authoritarianism.

When Minoan civilization was abruptly swept away in the mid-fifteenth century B.C., its preeminent position in the Aegean was assumed by the civilization of Mycenae which had emerged some two centuries earlier. Much of its inspiration in arts and crafts, in overseas commerce, and in administration and its system of writing came from Crete, but it matured into a distinctive civilization in its own right. Like Minoan civilization, that of Mycenae was palace-based, but the control exercised by the palaces appears to have been much tighter and more pervading than in Crete. From the Linear B tablets emerges an impression that

The classical Greeks saw "Hellas" as a new civilization distinct from its Aegean antecedents. But moderns tend to see the history of the region in antiquity as far more of a continuum. An idea of the 2,000-year span covered by this book, and of the underlying continuity linking the Hellenic civilizations, can be seen in this series of statues of the male form. *Left to right, this page:* An early Minoan worshipper, clay statuette from Crete,

    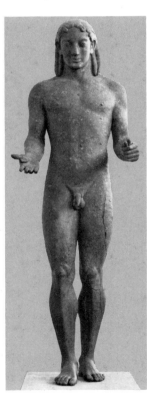

ca. 1950 B.C. Already more realistic is the saluting figure from the heyday of Minoan civilization, ca. 1600 B.C. From Delphi comes the third figure, a kouros by Polymedes, ca. 590 B.C., typifying archaic art. The flute player from Samos dates to the late sixth century, as does the last figure on this page, the bronze "Apollo" from the Piraeus, 525 B.C.

Yet despite the impression of considerable control and organization of almost every aspect of life in Crete from the palaces, Minoan civilization retains an inherent spirit of individualism and freedom. In the densely packed towns around the palaces fashionable houses with frescoes and porticoes jostle for space with smaller houses and workshops. Neither the palaces nor the towns themselves are surrounded by defenses. The products of the Minoan

the activities of every craftsman and craftswoman in the kingdom were controlled by the state. The impression of an authoritarian regime is heightened by the massive defenses which protect the citadels and palaces of the rulers, and by the ample evidence of a warrior elite which kept a close control on the supply of arms and armor, and of the raw materials to make them. Against such a background, it would not be surprising if state rivalries and ambitions played a part

in the collapse of Mycenaean civilization around 1200 B.C.

Through the ensuing "Dark Age," the tradition of an Age of Heroes survived to form the basis of early Greek poetry and drama when the Greeks began to acquire the skills of civilization again in the seventh and sixth centuries B.C. The full glory of the classical civilization which blossomed in the fifth century—its passion for the arts and sciences, its genius in the fields of architecture and sculpture, its eager exploration of the world beyond the Aegean, and so much more—need not be examined here, for it is demonstrated in words and pictures later in this book. What should be emphasized here is the amazing unity of the Greek world at this time. Classical Greece was a myriad of small city-states, many with their own systems of law and government, and their own standards of weights and measures, and all

Classical sculpture shows a steady development toward greater fluidity and freedom of movement, along with progressive refinement and enrichment in the treatment of surfaces. The earliest examples, like the Charioteer from Delphi *(large figure at left)*, ca. 475 B.C., are relatively staid and static, still showing affinities with archaic models of the preceding centuries. The last three figures shown here, all in marble, from the

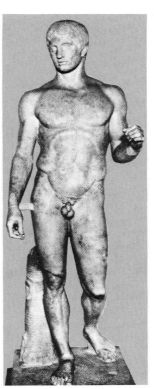

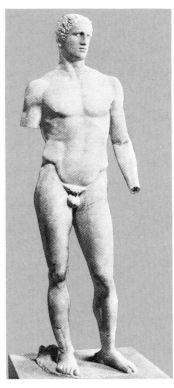

with a fervent belief in their own independence. Yet not only throughout the Aegean, but through the Greek colonies of the Mediterranean, there were bonds of race, language, religion, and above all culture, which united all these states and their peoples into a single civilization—Hellas. Despite their many differences, the civilizations of Crete, Mycenae, and classical Greece show a common response to the environment they shared.

fourth century B.C., depict classical art in its full flowering. The last of them *(above)* dates to 336 B.C., close to the death of Alexander the Great, the generally accepted terminal date for classical Hellenic civilization.

9

MACEDONIA

CHALCIDICE

Mt. Olympus

EPIRUS

CORCYRA

THESSALY

IONIAN SEA

EUBOEA

AETOLIA   Delphi   Chalcis
                     Orchomenos
ITHACA   Eretr

                    Thebes
CEPHALLENIA   ACHAEA   BOEOTIA
                         Eleusis   Athe
                    Megara
ELIS   Piraeus
       ARCADIA   Corinth   ATTICA

Olympia   Argos Mycenae
                  Tiryns ARGOLID

        PELOPONNESE

   MESSENIA   Sparta

Pylos   LACONIA

                    CYTHERA

THE LAND AND THE SEA

Greece is not one country but many—its
many regions and islands kept apart by
mountain ranges and deep seas. For
convenience we can speak briefly of
perhaps six principal regions. In the
north are Macedonia and Thessaly, with
large, fertile plains suitable for the cultivation of cereals. Central and southern
Greece—Boeotia, Attica, the Argolid,
and the Peloponnese—are characterized by small plains, deeply indented
coastline, and rugged mountains. Here
vines and olives are grown, and sheep
and goats grazed on the lower mountain
slopes. To the west, mountains shut off
Epirus and the Ionian islands from the
rest of mainland Greece. To the east, the
Aegean Sea provides not so much a
barrier but rather an avenue of communication first with the islands of the
Cyclades, and further east with the islands and adjacent coast of western
Turkey. Finally, to the south, is the

largest of all the islands—Crete—a
hundred and fifty miles long, with small
coastal plains, some fine bays, and a
mountainous backbone which runs
from east to west.

Despite many differences of climate,
soils, terrain, and natural resources between these regions, there are certain
common factors which played an important part in the shaping of the civilizations of ancient Greece. The terrain
makes the mainland difficult to unite,
while the many bays and inlets make the
sea the natural means of communication
and draw the Cyclades, Crete, and the
islands of the east Aegean into closer
contact with the mainland. A shortage
of mineral resources, together with the
constant use of sea communications,
encourages overseas trade and exploration. Yet the sea and the mountain
ranges to the north protect Greece from
easy attack from outside.

BLACK SEA

SEA OF
MARMARA

THASOS

HELLESPONT

LEMNOS
• Poliochni
Troy •

MYSIA

LESBOS
• Mytilene

AEGEAN SEA

CHIOS

Smyrna •   • Sardis

LYDIA

Ephesus •
ANDROS   SAMOS Magnesia

SYROS

DELOS   Miletus •

PAROS   NAXOS   IONIA

CYCLADES   CARIA

MELOS   Halicarnassus •

COS

THERA   LYCIA

RHODES

SEA OF CRETE

CRETE
Knossos •   Mallia •
Ayia Triadha • Phaistos •   Zakro •

THE SURVIVING TESTIMONY

The civilization of Greece, unlike that of Crete and Mycenae, never became a "lost civilization": it was known and admired, and often emulated, by civilizations which succeeded it, right through to our own times. Throughout the ages, visible testimony to the skill, craftsmanship, artistry, and intellectual brilliance of the ancient Greeks has been preserved in fair abundance. The Greek experience has provided the tangible foundations on which the civilizations of the Western world have been established.

This is particularly true of Greek thought, which has survived to us as drama, history, poetry, and philosophy. In the tragedies of

Silver coins, issued from the end of the seventh century B.C. onward, are useful sources of evidence for Greek commerce as well as dating agents for the archaeologist.

The works of important Greek authors only survive in much later copies. One of the finest such manuscripts is a fourth-century A.D. copy of the *Iliad (above right)*, which in addition to the text is richly illustrated with scenes of the Trojan War.

Aeschylus, the comedies of Aristophanes, and the philosophy of Plato and Aristotle, there survive not only great works of drama and literature, but also vivid insights into the thoughts and attitudes of the ancient Greeks. The same can be said of the histories of Herodotus and Thucydides, and the epic poems of Homer and Hesiod. All of these provide invaluable testimony to the very spirit of Greek civilization.

So too, in their way, do painted Greek vases and sculpture. From the neat, stylized severity of Geometric vases of the ninth and eighth centuries B.C., through the colorful, orientalized Corinthian styles of the seventh and sixth, to the refined artistry of the black-and red-figured vases produced by Athenian master potters and painters, the full flavor of ancient Greece has been there to sample and savor throughout the centuries. Through surviving Roman copies of the great works of Greek sculpture—the discobolus of Myron, the doryphorus of Polyclitus, and the Aphrodite of Praxiteles—the Greek search for perfection and truth can still be perceived and experienced.

But the painted vases, in particular, do much more than convey the spirit of Greek civilization; they form an enormous picture gallery illustrating almost every aspect of Greek life. Scenes from Greek mythology, drama, and legend are numerous and an invaluable supplement to the written word,

evidence available to us. Alongside the elegant words of the poets, philosophers, and playwrights, we have the more mundane witness of inscriptions on stone recording such things as public decrees, dedications, and epitaphs. Some of the most fascinating documents are indeed the simplest of all—the *ostraka* or potsherds on which the people of Athens wrote the names of those politicians they wished to send into exile for ten years. From the Athenian Agora have come *ostraka* bearing the names of such powerful men as Themistocles and Aristides, both banished by the people.

The famous Venus de Milo *(left)* should more accurately be known as the Aphrodite of Melos, being a late Hellenistic sculpture of around 200 B.C. Most Greek sculpture is known to us through the many Roman copies of original masterpieces.

Far fewer Greek inscriptions survive than Roman ones, but those that do are often fine examples of craftsmanship, like this example from Epidaurus, which records in great detail how one Antiochus was cured of his illness.

but especially valuable are the many insights into everyday life. On the one hand we see potters, metalsmiths, and weavers at work, and on the other boxers, wrestlers, and athletes at play. Children are seen both at school and at play, and their parents at both weddings and funerals. More intimate scenes include parties, bathing, and even the use of the commode! Furthermore all of these scenes of action contain so much detail—of clothing, jewelry, furniture, tools, musical instruments, and other personal belongings—that if painted vases were the sole surviving testimony to the everyday life of the ancient Greeks, we should still know a great deal about it.

But there are, of course, other sources of

Although the Agora at Athens had been submerged beneath later buildings over the centuries, many Greek temples and other buildings have survived to bear monumental witness to the glory that was Greece. To these standing monuments, the excavations of the nineteenth and twentieth centuries have added many more. The early work of the British and French has been followed by that of the Austrians at Samothrace, the Germans at Olympia, the Greeks themselves at Eleusis, and the Americans at Olynthus and the Athenian Agora. Yet despite all this, archaeology's greatest contribution to the study of Greek civilization has been to demonstrate that it was preceded by the civilizations of Crete and Mycenae.

Of all the buildings of the ancient Greeks, their temples are best represented by surviving monuments. Some of the finest examples are found not in the Greek homeland but in southern Italy and *(above left)* in Sicily. This is the Doric temple of Concordia at Agrigento, built in the fifth century B.C.

13

ARCHAEOLOGY: THE PAST REDISCOVERED

Greek myth and legend spoke clearly about civilizations which had vanished long before Homer spoke of Knossos and Mycenae, and which had flourished a full millennium before the historians Herodotus and Pausanias wrote of them. But until the later nineteenth century there was no recognizable trace of these lost civilizations, although the locations of Knossos, Mycenae, and Troy were still known. Two men were responsible for rediscovering the Bronze Age civilizations of the Aegean.

Heinrich Schliemann was born in Germany in 1822. As a child he acquired a love of Homer and a passionate belief in the reality of the Trojan war. Family poverty, however, compelled him to start life as an errand boy, but by the age of forty he had become a very wealthy man indeed and was able to retire from commerce to devote himself to his study of Greek and his search for Troy and Mycenae.

Heinrich Schliemann, the excavator of Troy.

Schliemann's wife, Sophia, who helped him uncover the Great Treasure of Troy, is seen here wearing some of the gold jewelry.

Mycenaean civilization was rediscovered during Schliemann's excavations at Mycenae itself, particularly in the year 1876. It was then that he discovered the grave circle, enclosing the shaft graves *(below right)* in which he found the burials of the princes of Mycenae, accompanied by a wide variety of artifacts of great value and fine craftsmanship.

Among the finds in the shaft graves the most dramatic were the gold face masks which allowed Schliemann to claim that he had found the mortal remains of Agamemnon.

Schliemann's discoveries at Mycenae brought to light for the first time the work of Mycenaean goldsmiths, such as the hexagonal wooden box *(right)*, covered with embossed gold plates.

The discovery of gold signet rings and sealstones *(far right)* not only testified to the skill of the Mycenaean goldsmith and gem cutter but also provided insights into the nature of Mycenaean society, with its emphasis on religion and ritual on the one hand, and heroic combat on the other.

In April 1870, after following Homer's description of the location of Troy *verbatim*, Schliemann began to dig not at the traditionally favored site for the ancient city but some five miles to the north at a site called Hissarlik. He at once uncovered the remains of a fortified city, which in the next three years was to yield a wealth of fine objects of bronze, silver, and gold, and ample proof of a great destruction by fire. He had found Homer's Troy, and now he was anxious to move on to find his Mycenae. In 1876 he began work at Mycenae, and in November of that year found the first of the shaft graves. Others soon followed and from the immense wealth found in these tombs, and the superb gold funeral masks which overlay several of the skulls, he was convinced that he had found the graves of Agamemnon and his ancestors.

Evans' discoveries in the palace of Knossos revealed Minoan crafts, such as faience manufacture, represented here by plaques *(left)* showing wild goats and cows. The spirit of Minoan civilization, with its interest in and love of the natural world, was apparent from the first.

Though his techniques left much to be desired, and his dating both of Priam's Troy and Agamemnon's graves was wrong, he had rediscovered Mycenaean Greece. He had also hoped to excavate at Knossos, but he failed to buy the land and so it was, after five years of patient negotiation that an Englishman, Arthur Evans, came to acquire the site and begin work there in March 1900. Previous soundings had shown that a large building stood on the site, but it was Evans who, in a series of massive excavations,

brought to light the palace of Minos, discovered the written documents (in both linear A and B) which he was so desperately anxious to find, and earned himself the title of the "father of Minoan archaeology."

Elsewhere in Crete there was a proliferation of other excavations, so that within twenty years of Evans' beginning work at Knossos, Minoan civilization was better documented archaeologically than that of Mycenae. The British excavated Palaikastro and Zakro, the Americans Gournia and Mochlos, the Ital-

The discoverer of Minoan civilization, Arthur Evans, was inspired by the exhibition of Schliemann's discoveries which he saw in Athens in 1883. He was convinced that the prehistoric peoples of the Aegean must have had a system of

Evans' excavations at Knossos revealed a palace built on three or four levels, the upper portions of which

Evans partially restored on the basis of the surviving remains and the scenes depicted on frescoes found

in the palace. The building which emerged was fit for the legendary King Minos.

writing and his first visit to Crete in 1894 was for the purpose of buying seal-stones engraved with pictographic signs. On that visit he first saw Knossos, and six years later he began his great excavations there.

ians Phaistos and Ayia Triadha, the French began work on the palace of Mallia, and the Greeks excavated a whole series of important Early Bronze Age sites. Only in the 1930s did the rediscovery of Mycenaean Greece begin to catch up with the pace in Crete. New excavations at Mycenae were followed by Blegen's further work at Troy. After the war came the dramatic discoveries at Pylos, and the excavations at Lerna and Ayia Eirene on the emergence of civilization in the Aegean. The fervor of Schliemann and Evans had been replaced by the skills and techniques of modern excavation.

Perhaps the most dramatic moment in the rediscovery of Minoan civilization was when Evans' workmen uncovered the "throne of Minos" at Knossos, on 13 April 1900 *(left)*. The throne had been in place, undisturbed, for over three thousand years.

15

OLYMPIA

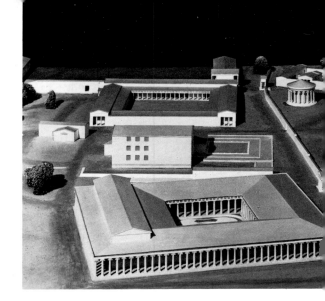

The public impact of Schliemann's excavations at Troy, and then at Mycenae, was enormous, but archaeologically Schliemann's work was soon surpassed by the German excavations at Olympia.

Unlike Troy and Mycenae, Olympia was regarded not as half-legendary but as one of the best-known and most celebrated sanctuaries of ancient Greece. Its athletic contests, held every four years, were famed throughout the Greek world, and its buildings were described in some detail by the second-century A.D. writer Pausanias. Nevertheless, although the site of this great cult center was well known, and remains of its monumental buildings littered its surface, its excavation was a major undertaking.

The excavations at Olympia were begun by the Germans, with the support of the Prussian royal family, in 1875. For six years a labor force of up to 250 men spent each excavation season clearing the soil and the debris which had accumulated over the foundations of the ancient buildings. Work began on the Temple of Zeus which was both the focus of the whole complex and also the most prominently exposed of the ruined buildings. From there it was systematically expanded to take in the other parts of the complex—the Temple of Hera, the treasuries, the exercise hall, the stoa, the hotel built by Leonidas of Naxos, and of course

Local workers and German supervisors, Olympia, 1875. Their excavation methods differed little from Schliemann's, but observation, recording, and publication were on a much higher standard.

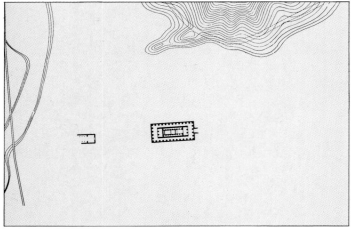

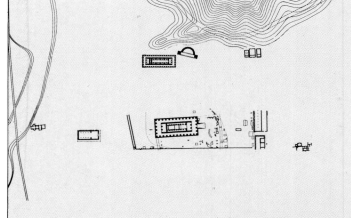

The impact of the well-organized German excavation team at Olympia can be seen in the plans of the site seen above. At the left is Olympia as it was known before excavations began; only the Temple of Zeus is clearly visible. The successive exposures of the second, third, fourth, and fifth seasons are seen to the right, showing how the whole complex of temples, treasuries, accommodation, exercise areas, and stadium was revealed.

the stadium where the games were held, along with a host of smaller buildings. This great undertaking differed from Schliemann's contemporary excavations at Troy and Mycenae in several respects.

In the first place, the excavations at Olympia were very much a team effort. Directed from Berlin by Ernst Curtius, the work on the spot was masterminded by a small team of young scholars led by Adolf Furtwängler and Wilhelm Dorpfeld. Dorpfeld generally took responsibility for the architectural remains, and Furtwängler for the objects found in the excavations. Furtwängler saw to it that all the finds were properly catalogued, and Dorpfeld ensured that the building remains were carefully observed and fully recorded. When the excavations were concluded, the German team were able to publish a detailed and fully documented

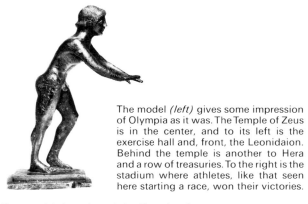

The model (left) gives some impression of Olympia as it was. The Temple of Zeus is in the center, and to its left is the exercise hall and, front, the Leonidaion. Behind the temple is another to Hera and a row of treasuries. To the right is the stadium where athletes, like that seen here starting a race, won their victories.

From amid the ruins of the Temple of Zeus, erected around 470–456 B.C., the German excavators recovered fragments of fine statuary that had once stood on the west pediment of the temple.

Collapsed drums (below) from the fluted Doric columns of the Temple of Zeus lie as they fell. These columns originally stood nearly 10 meters high.

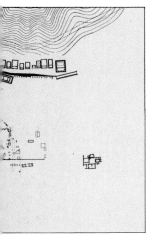

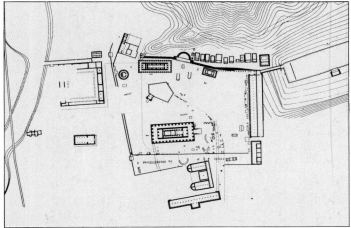

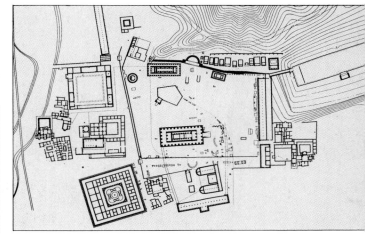

report, in no less than five volumes, which put Schliemann's publications on Troy to shame. The report revealed a proper concern for the later, Roman and Byzantine, history of the site, a careful analysis of the historical development of the various buildings, and a detailed study of all the excavated objects. Furthermore, and also in contrast to Schliemann's conduct, all the finds from the excavations were ceded to the Greeks.

Further major campaigns of excavations at Olympia have been undertaken by the Germans in the 1930s, the 1950s, and 1960s, each marked by improved techniques. Yet the excavations of the 1870s were, for their time, the most remarkable. They were by no means faultless—stratification and pottery were effectively ignored—but they were systematic, carefully observed and recorded, and fully published.

Overleaf: The excavated site of Olympia as seen today. A comparison with the reconstruction model (top of this page) shows that little actual restoration has taken place—unlike the elaborate building undertaken by Evans at Knossos in Crete.

17

A CONTINUING SEARCH

Though the civilizations of Crete, Mycenae, and classical Greece died millennia ago, our knowledge of them continues to expand year by year. Every year a wealth of new discoveries are made, both by accident and design, and each adds something new to our picture of life in ancient Greece or Crete. Some of these discoveries are of major importance of course. The careful uncovering of the earliest Minoan palace at Phaistos, the discovery and excavation of an unknown and richly furnished palace at Zakro, and the total excavation and study of a prepalatial settlement at Myrtos are three such new contributions to our knowledge of Minoan Crete. In the Cyclades we have witnessed the resurrection of the Greek Pompeii—the settlement of Akrotiri on Thera, destroyed and buried in a massive eruption around 1500 B.C. The rise of Mycenae has been illuminated by the discovery and examination of a second, earlier grave circle there, while a great deal has been learned about the administrative machinery of the Mycenaean states from the recovery of the palace archives at Pylos. Classical Greece too has shared in the wealth of new discoveries. At Olympia the German excavators have found not only the workshop of the great sculptor Phidias, but even a cup inscribed with his name. At Verghina, the Greeks have gone one better and found the tomb and mortal remains of Philip of Macedon, the father of Alexander the Great.

The manner in which all of these excavations have been conducted has been very different to that of Schliemann's excavations at Troy. Excavation has become a science, with the careful observation and recording of everything that is removed during the

digging. In particular the stratigraphy of the sites (the relationships between the various layers, buildings, pits, and so on) is studied with great care and interpreted with great skill, in order to piece together the course of events on the sites under investigation. Special excavation techniques have had to be devised to deal with the peculiar problems of digging in and below the volcanic debris on Thera. Similarly, underwater archaeology has become a science in itself, with its own techniques and equipment for studying and excavating the sunken remains of both harbors and shipping.

The finds made during the course of modern excavations can now be subjected to methods of study and analysis undreamt of in the time of Schliemann and Evans. Chemical analysis of pottery and obsidian has allowed the Aegean archaeologist to trace imported pottery and stone implements back to their point of origin, and thus provided completely new information about Minoan and Mycenaean trade. Similar methods applied to metalwork have given us new insights into the technological skills of the Bronze Age craftsman, and revealed the technical

The discovery of the Bronze Age settlement of Akrotiri on the island of Thera, buried beneath deep deposits of volcanic debris, has required the development of new excavation techniques and a lot of improvisation from its excavators.

Greeks arms and armor are represented by an ever-growing number of surviving pieces. The example seen here was found during the excavation of a well at Olympia, and after careful conservation has been placed on exhibition in the Olympia Museum. It is the breastplate of a hoplite soldier of the early sixth century B.C.

excavation as in survey. Recent surveys in Messenia, the Argolid, the Cyclades, and Crete, have all involved geomorphologists, geologists, soil scientists, and botanists, as well as archaeologists. The surveys have been either more intensive or involved specially devised survey techniques, and have also been multiperiod—concerned with all the traces of man and his activities from the earliest times to the present day. The picture which has emerged from these

New discoveries of fine Greek statuary are relatively rare, but are still occasionally made. Such are the Kouros and Kore seen here (left), which were found in a field near Merenda in Attica. They date to the period around 530 B.C., and the female figure was made by a sculptor called Aristion, who came from the island of Paros.

surveys has therefore been more complete in every sense than that from earlier work. We are slowly piecing together a picture of the ancient landscape, of man's settlement in it and his interaction with it, and of the way in which both the landscape and man's relationship with it has changed through time. Changes in time can now be better understood because of new dating techniques such as Carbon 14, thermoluminescence (for dating fired clay), and archaeomagnetic dating. But more fundamentally important are changes in attitude and approach among archaeologists. We are now less concerned with art history, architecture, and political history. These things are now seen to be the products of social and economic forces and processes which have previously been ignored if not unrecognized. Aegean archaeologists today, particularly those concerned with the civilizations of Crete and Mycenae and their origins, are increasingly concerned with social and economic problems. By studying these, we may eventually better understand how the Aegean civilizations began, how they worked, and what eventually caused their downfall.

Some of the work of conservation and recording entailed in modern excavations is suggested by this view of the Thera excavations. In the foreground are storage jars, carefully restored by a craftsman working from sherds; in the rear are the rows of labeled storage for the finds from the excavation.

As excavation techniques have improved, so many ancient sites in Greece have been re-visited by the archaeologists. The bronze cremation urn exposed at Eretria in Euboea, for example, was found in Swiss excavations, following earlier work by Greeks, preceded in turn by the Americans.

inventiveness of the early Aegean metalsmiths.

At the same time some types of evidence have been seriously studied for the first time only in the past decade or so. Remains of plants and animals, which can contribute so much new information about the life style not only of the prehistoric peasants but also of the classical farmer, are virtually untapped sources of evidence in the Aegean. Soil science, which used in conjunction with the testimony of animal and plant remains, can tell us much about past climates as well as farming activities, is still in its infancy in the study of ancient Greece.

At present, the greatest advances in the multidisciplinary approach to the study of the ancient Aegean has come not so much in

21

KINGS OF THE SEA

A superbly detailed painting of a Minoan ceremonial seagoing barge, propelled by oarsmen, and carrying important passengers seated beneath a sun shade on deck. The entire length of the hull is decorated with a frieze of animals including lions and dolphins. This boat is one of many depicted on a seascape found on the wall of a Minoan house on the island of Thera, and dated ca. 1500 B.C.

*In the wine-dark sea
 there lies a land
called Crete,
 a rich and lovely land,
washed by waves on every side,
 densely peopled
and boasting ninety cities.*

Homer, Odyssey

The first Aegean civilizations had their roots in the farming communities which first appeared in the seventh millennium B.C. in Thessaly, Macedonia, Crete, and other parts of the Aegean. In the third millennium B.C., some of these settlements developed into small towns where craftsmen practiced many skills, early forms of writing were in use, considerable wealth was accumulated, and social power was concentrated into fewer hands.

From such a background, the civilization of Minoan Crete emerged in the years around 2000 B.C. The palace of Knossos with its spacious central court, sweeping staircases, and huge storage magazines, was soon followed by others elsewhere in the island. In the palatial towns, skilled craftsmen worked in a wide variety of metals and stones to produce a bewildering display of beautiful objects.

The countryside was dotted with villages from which came grapes, olives, wheat, and sheep to supply the palaces and towns. Elegant villas perched on hillsides overlooked the estates they controlled, while coastal villages exploited the rich resources of the sea. From harbor towns such as Zakro, Minoan ships made voyages to all parts of the Aegean and opened up the sea routes to the east Mediterranean.

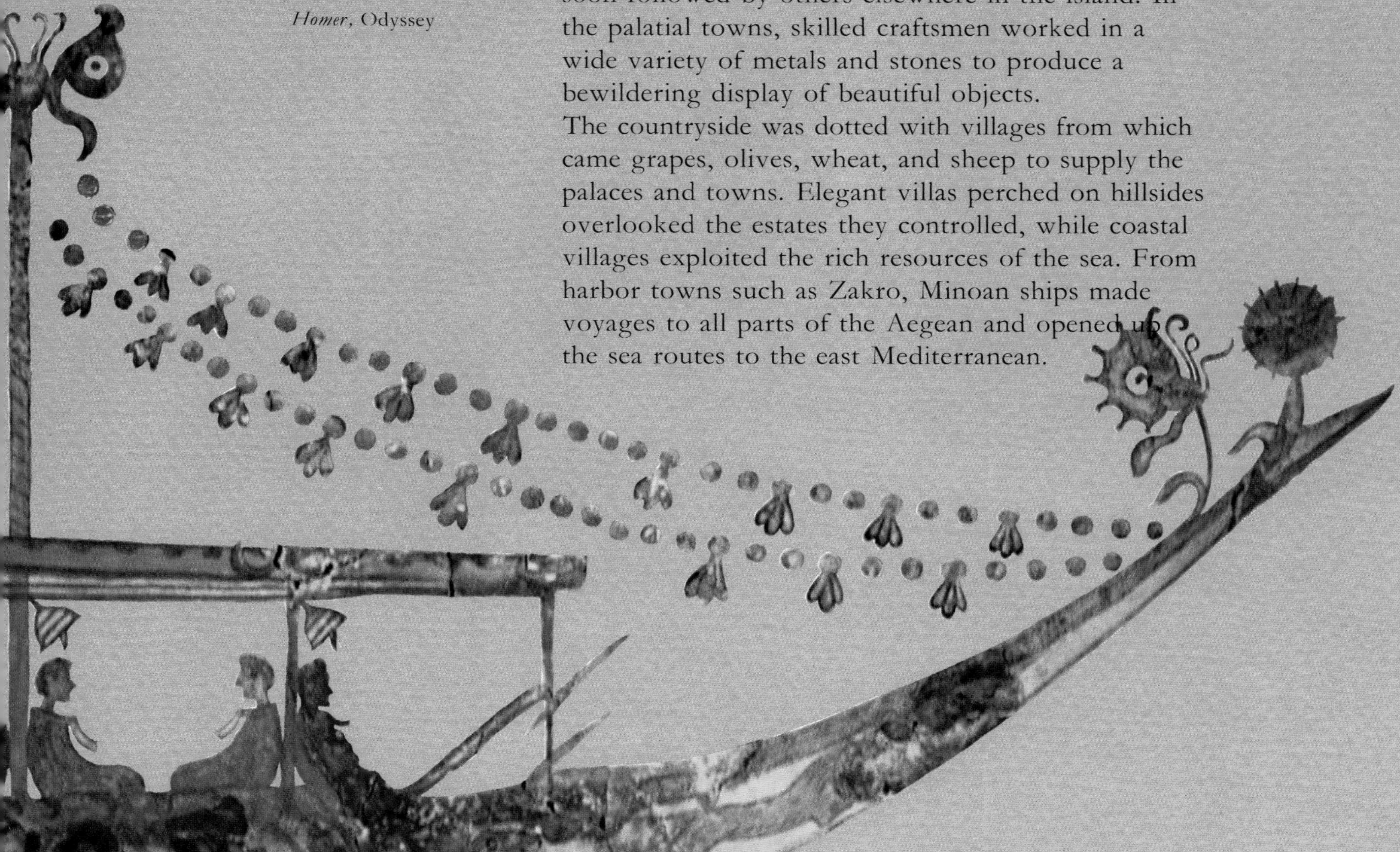

The earthquakes which have plagued Crete throughout history seem to have had little effect on Minoan prosperity, though the palaces needed repair after an earthquake around 1700 B.C. But the massive eruption of Thera soon after 1500 B.C. seems to be linked, directly or otherwise, with the destruction of Minoan civilization shortly after.

23

IN THE BEGINNING

In the first farming villages in Greece there is little sign of social distinctions, but by the fourth millennium B.C., in Thessaly at least, we see local chiefdoms emerging. In the reconstruction of the fortified village of Dhimini seen here, the crest of the settlement is dominated by an enclosed courtyard in which stands a "megaron" with a columned porch. This appears to be the home of the local chieftain, who is surrounded on the lower slopes by his retainers. The defenses are not massive, but they are complex and include many blind alleys in which attackers might find themselves trapped. Beyond the village live the mass of the peasants, who in time of war may flee to the safety of the village.

Until twenty years ago, it was thought that human occupation of Greece began in the years between 6000 and 5000 B.C. We now know that Palaeolithic hunters inhabited the country at least as early as 40,000 B.C., and very probably earlier.

They seem to have been relatively few in number, however, and it was not until some three to four thousand years after the end of the last Ice Age (around 10,000 B.C.) that significant changes in the size and the life of the population of Greece took place. Although Greece's natural food resources could have allowed the indigenous population of hunter-gatherers to develop a settled existence based on farming, all the evidence from the earliest farming settlements suggests that the growing of wheat and barley and the rearing of domesticated cattle, sheep, and pig were introduced to Greece by peoples who came to Greece with these skills, crops, and animals. They seem to have come from Anatolia—modern Turkey.

remain settled for the next three thousand years, and the pattern of life now established was destined to last in many parts of Greece for even longer.

Regional differences existed, however, and were sometimes marked. The village at Nea Nikomedia consisted of six large, more or less square huts, with walls and pitched roofs erected on a framework of oak posts and poles. The houses were well spaced out and surrounded an oblong hut of different design, in which the roof was supported by pairs of timber uprights, which also served to divide the interior into a central aisle and two naves. The discovery of five fine clay figurines and two deposits of flint knives totaling over four hundred blades, suggests that this building was indeed different to the others in the village—perhaps a shrine, less probably the home of the village chieftain. The early settlement at Knossos was quite different. Houses here were very irregular in shape, even though their rooms were usu-

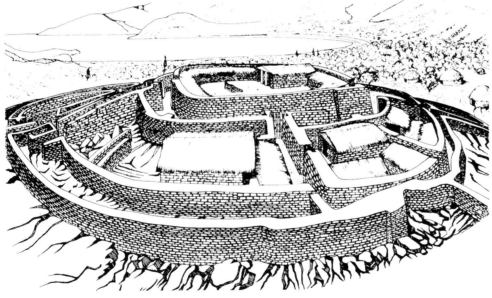

The pottery used by the early farmers of Greece varied in style, although the range of shapes was limited. Apart from plain red bowls like that seen *(above right)* from Sesklo, attractive designs were painted in red on a white or buff ground, while on Crete incised patterns were filled with white paste on dark polished surfaces.

These settlers appear to have mastered not only the skills of farming, but also of making pottery and clay figurines, and of building substantial rectangular huts of timber, wattle, clay, and mud pisé. Their settlements are widely spread, from Nea Nikomedia in Macedonia, Sesklo and Argissa in Thessaly, to Corinth and Lerna in southern Greece, and already, by 6000 B.C., to Knossos in Crete. Everywhere the family groups and hunting bands of the earlier ages were replaced by village communities with populations running into several dozens, and at some sites into three figures. Many of the sites now occupied for the first time were to

ally rectangular. Buildings were constructed not of timber but mud brick, and roofs were not pitched but flat. The different method of roofing partly reflects a different relationship between buildings, for at Knossos houses were often built onto one another, forming blocks. Between the blocks ran narrow lanes, twisting and turning around the irregular outlines of the houses and the low walls which enclosed yards outside them. We should not allow these differences in building techniques and social attitudes to obscure the underlying similarities which were now established in the pattern of life in Greece. Farmers everywhere were heavily

the Cycladic islands are now occupied and already their inhabitants are beginning to display a mastery of marbleworking, as well as the ability to exploit the rich food resources of the Aegean Sea.

By soon after 3000 B.C., civilization is visibly emerging in the Aegean, with the appearance of walled towns, craft specialists, immense concentrations of wealth, increase in social differentiation, and widespread trade and exchange. Just how, and why, this process took place when it did is still uncertain and much argued over. The crucial centuries are those around 3000 B.C., when there are signs of important developments taking place. Silver, lead, copper, and gold begin to appear sporadically in central and southern Greece, the Cyclades, and

dependent on wheat and sheep as the staple crop and animal on which their prosperity depended. Throughout Greece, the villagers showed an increased spirituality, represented by their numerous figurines and their carefully made burials. From Macedonia to Crete, the settlers showed great interest and ingenuity in working stone, bone, clay, shell, and probably wood, as they greatly increased the range of artifacts available to them.

The success of these earliest farmers in establishing a viable way of life in Greece is witnessed by the growing numbers of settlements, and their increasing size and density of population as time passes. By 4000 B.C., for example, Knossos had grown to over seven acres in size, with a population which must have run into many hundreds. In Thessaly we see the emergence of chieftains, living in fortified villages and occupying houses with columned porches and a main room with hearth—early examples of the "megaron" house used in Early Bronze Age Troy, and later in Mycenae and other Mycenaean centers, as a palace for the local king. Further north in Macedonia, contacts with southeast Europe have by now led to the appearance of copperworking and the manufacture of small gold pendants. Several of

Crete. Standardized types of stone figurines and vases in the Cyclades may point to the first craft specialists here. The spread of metalwork, and of certain distinctive types of pottery and figurines, suggests increasing contacts between the regions of the Aegean. There is an increase too in the number of settlements occupied, and in some cases a shift to more defensive locations; in others, such as Thermi, on Lesbos, there are signs of greater internal organization. Nowhere is the picture clear, but everywhere there are hints that the people of the Aegean around 3000 B.C. were on the threshold of civilization.

Religion and superstition appear to have played a prominent role in the life of the early Greek farmers. Figurines of clay are common finds in their settlements, and others were made of stone, bone, and even shell. Where it is possible to tell the sex of these figurines, they are usually female, but a few are certainly male. There is no reason to think, however, that all the female figurines represent a single deity, let alone a universal Mother Goddess. That seen here is a fourth millennium example from Knossos in Crete.

The growth of spirituality and of organized religion on the one hand, and of social ranking and leadership on the other, may well have become fused in the Aegean as they did elsewhere in the eastern Mediterranean and Near East. There is no clear evidence that this was so in the earliest farming communities, but by the third millennium B.C. the fusion was underway. This elaborate ceremonial hearth was found in the remains of a large mansion underlying the great House of the Tiles at Lerna—a building that must have been the home of a local chieftain.

Although figurines of animals were made by the first farmers, they did not become common until the third millennium B.C., and the same is true of zoomorphic vessels. This vivid portrayal of a young bird demanding food *(above left)* is a jug from Koumasa in Crete.

Overleaf: Two scenes of early Aegean settlement. The first, a landscape in the Thessalian plain, site of the richest Neolithic cultures in Greece; the River Peneios winds through the plain. The other photograph shows a landscape from the Cycladic islands, which were occupied by 4000 B.C.

25

TOWARD CIVILIZATION

The processes which can be indistinctly seen at work in the final stages of the fourth millennium B.C. in the Aegean, developed rapidly and dramatically at the beginning of the third. Although peoples all around the Aegean Sea now emerged into what, for the sake of convenience, archaeologists often call a Bronze Age, the developments taking place went far beyond the introduction of bronzeworking. There were many other technological advances, and these were closely related to important changes in social and economic organization.

It used to be thought that the rapid advances made at this time were due to the arrival of migrants from further east, but it is now clear that there is very little evidence to support this view. Although it is difficult to identify and explain the complex process of the emergence of civilization in the Aegean, there can be little doubt that significant factors in that process were the growth of population, the widespread introduction of metallurgy, the extension of trade, the provision of a stable base to the agricultural economy, and increasing social stratification. It is in the third millennium B.C. that for the first time we can clearly see the widespread adoption of both vines and olives, which together with wheat, provide the basis of the agricultural economy of the Aegean. The evidence for viticulture comes not only from the remains of grapes and vines themselves, found in Crete, the Argolid, Attica, Macedonia, and the Troad, but also from the huge increase in the numbers of cups and jugs made by the potters. Similarly, the adoption of olives as a staple crop is demonstrated as much by the appearance of oil lamps and storage jars as it is by the pruned remains of olive trees found at Myrtos in Crete, and the olive stones found elsewhere in the Aegean.

These changes in the agricultural economy owed little or nothing to the technological revolution that was sweeping the Aegean at this time. Bronzeworking, for example, though widespread, was used mainly for making tools and weapons and personal jewelry; it was scarcely used for agricultural implements at all. Carpentry, which was now provided with a fine range of tools by the bronzesmiths, produced furniture, building timber, and most important of all large boats, but there is little evidence that it produced new or improved plows. Stoneworking, which until now had been mainly concerned with producing axes and various

In the debris of the House of the Tiles at Lerna, the excavators found a deposit of clay sealings. There were well over a hundred of them, and careful study showed that originally they had been used to seal boxes, jars, and vases. The impressions of about seventy different seals were recorded, most of them, like the example seen above, abstract patterns. Since the sealings were being carefully stored on the upper floor of the building in which they were found, we assume that the designs on the seals conveyed some sort of basic information—very possibly indicating the origin or owner of the goods they had originally sealed.

The surviving foundations of the House of the Tiles at Lerna are impressive for their size and regularity, but the completed building must have been even more spectacular. The long narrow rooms which flank its principal chambers were stairwells, by which it was possible to gain access to the upper floors of this mansion. The first few stairs of each flight remain and can be seen in this view.

The purpose of the so-called frying pan on the left is uncertain, but the rich decoration on its base is important for its illustration of a Cycladic ship of about 2500 B.C. These ships, powered by perhaps twenty or thirty oarsmen, testify both to the new abilities of the Aegean carpenters, and to the increasing contact and trade that was now possible.

small tools, now concentrated more on the manufacture of superb figurines and the making of stone vases. Ivory and bone, previously used largely for pins, needles, and small implements, were now fashioned into figurines and minutely carved seals. Throughout these, and other crafts, then, we see many new products and techniques, and a spirit of invention and innovation pervades the whole field of technology.

It is not surprising, therefore, to find evidence that many of these crafts were now practiced by specialists—craftsmen who, while they may not have devoted their time exclusively to their craft, were nevertheless recognized by the communities in which they lived as the principal makers and suppliers of certain goods. Some of the intricate gold jewelry from early Troy, for example, would have taken months of skilled workmanship to produce, and elsewhere archaeologists have found the workshops of specialist bronze and silver workers, potters, and stoneworkers.

Increasing numbers of craft specialists was but one way in which society was being changed at this time. The manufacture of weapons and tools of bronze, jewelry and tableware of gold and silver, and vessels of

exotic stone, meant that it was now possible for some members of a community to accumulate a great amount of wealth in a small space. At the same time, a growing population, increasingly dependent not only on the security of food supplies but on imported raw materials such as copper, tin, obsidian, and ivory, needed to be more highly organized. In this situation the appearance of social ranking is to be expected, and in the Aegean it can be seen very clearly in some regions in the third millennium B.C. At Troy, for example, a very highly fortified citadel area contained a handful of buildings including a great hall. From an adjacent building in this complex came a rich hoard of wealth in the form of gold, silver, and electrum plate and jewelry, bronze tools and weapons, and other exotic items. At Akovitika and Lerna in the Peloponnese, great oblong buildings, much larger than anything seen before, have been excavated. The House of the Tiles at Lerna is particularly impressive, nearly 25 meters (80 feet) long, with lobbies and principal rooms, an upper story, and a tiled roof. An equally impressive building, though of less regular build and quite different plan, stood at Vasiliki in Crete. These "mansions" must surely have belonged to a social elite.

Whether such people exerted control over both local and external trade is uncertain but likely. The hoard of sealings found in the House of the Tiles at Lerna, for example, may have been kept as an "archive" of information about goods received. Long-distance trade suddenly flourished in this period, for raw materials such as tin and ivory had to come from beyond the Aegean, and copper and gold were only to be found in a small number of locations. Manufactured goods such as Minoan stone vases and Cycladic figurines and marble vases were also exchanged, and no doubt other materials which no longer survive. The appearance of large, oared ships provided both the means and the stimulation for the growth of trade and contact around the Aegean.

They also encouraged piracy in the Cyclades, and it may well be this which accounts for the many walled townships to be found in the third millennium in the Cyclades and along the coasts which fringe the Aegean. Strangely, no such defenses are to be found in Crete, and it is there that the most dramatic developments took place at the close of the period.

The purpose of the so-called frying pan on the left is uncertain, but the rich decoration on its base is important for its illustration of a Cycladic ship of about 2500 B.C. These ships, powered by perhaps twenty or thirty oarsmen, testify both to the new abilities of the Aegean carpenters, and to the increasing contact and trade that was now possible.

The stoneworkers of the Cyclades produced superb vases and figurines of marble in the third millennium B.C., and were almost certainly specialist craftsmen. Several of the figurines play musical instruments such as lyres and, here, pipes and these delightful miniature sculptures typify the new developments in both music and the visual arts.

Overleaf: Another marble Cycladic figurine depicting a musician: harpist, from Keros, third century B.C. The right-hand page shows a hedgehog-shaped painted clay vase, 2300–2100 B.C.

THE GREAT PALACES

The palaces of Crete were designed inside-out. Unlike most of the great buildings both of antiquity and the present day, the Minoan architect did not decide on the size and external appearance of his building, and then fit the required rooms into his outer shell. Rather he began at the heart of the palace—with the central court, which was an oblong, roughly half as wide as its length. The court and all other parts of the building were laid out using a standard unit of measurement, the Minoan foot of 30.36 centimeters, almost identical to the modern English foot.

From the central court the rest of the palace was laid out within the framework of an overall design. To the west of the court were ritual and ceremonial rooms, and behind these the principal stores. To the east were

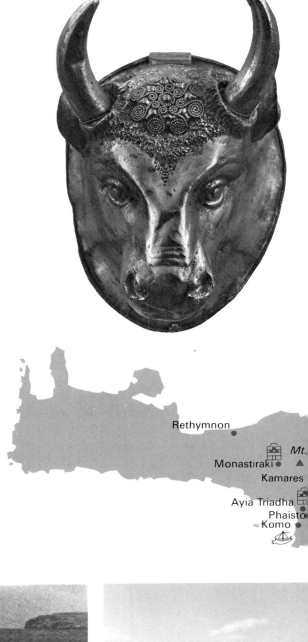

The Snake Goddess, breasts bare, displays her mastery of the reptile as she holds out her arms, around each of which a snake is entwined. She was worshipped in household shrine and rural sanctuary alike, throughout the island.

Palaces

Cities; major country villas

Port cities

Rethymnon

Monastiraki   Mt.

Kamares

Ayia Triadha

Phaisto

Komo

workshops, smaller stores, and sometimes domestic quarters. Kitchens, storerooms for pottery and food, and other workshops were usually to the north of the court, while the southern end of the building could be variously given over to workshops, stores,

and perhaps offices and archives where people and goods arriving at the palace could be recorded and checked.

But these were only the ground-floor rooms; above them rose at least one and often two more stories, while where the lay of the land permitted it, basement rooms were built below the level of the central court. While the basements tended to be used for further storage and cult rooms, the upper floors were largely devoted to reception suites, accommodation, and at least one large banqueting hall overlooking the central court. To provide access to these "state apartments" there were many staircases, several of which were deliberately broad and superbly paved, presumably to be used as processional ways for important visitors to the palace. Equally, the hundreds of rooms throughout the palace required a great deal of space to be devoted to access corridors. Finally, the erection of such a large building to a height of three and, at Knossos at least, four stories meant that further space had to be devoted to broad shafts—or light

vided an intermediate zone between the palace and the town houses at Knossos, Phaistos, and Mallia. At Knossos and Phaistos it is flanked by broad flights of stepped seating which suggest it could be used for public displays or ceremonies, while at all three palaces large grain silos are also found on the edge of the west court. It may be that grain could be dispensed to the population in times of shortage from these communal granaries.

To the townsman of Knossos or Phaistos, standing in the west court of the palace, the building would appear somewhat forbidding. The west façade at both palaces is designed to give an impression of monumental strength. Great ashlar blocks of limestone are tightly fitted together to present a blank façade, the line of which is broken only by shallow offsets and insets. These probably indicate the position of windows built into the wall on the first or second floor.

Once inside the palace, however, a visitor would find a building full of pleasing architectural effects and a great deal of color. The harshness of the stone walls was relieved in the first instance by the regular use of wooden beams running horizontally along the walls, and linked by vertical timbers. Wood was also used for columns of a

Opposite: A gold bull's head, representative of the cult of the bull which pervaded palace life. Apart from the bull games, the palace was lavishly decorated with representations of the sacred horns. According to Greek legend the bull-headed monster, the Minotaur, roamed the labyrinth at Knossos.

Minoan palaces *(below, left to right)*: The palace of Zakro, the last of the Minoan palaces to be built, was smaller and less regular in plan than the three palaces in the center of the island. Mallia stands on a small coastal plain surrounded by an extensive town and cemetery. The pillared hall at the north end of the central court supported a banqueting hall approached by a flanking staircase. The superb façade and ceremonial stairs at Phaistos overlook the west court of the palace with its raised processional ways. Phaistos was built to dominate the rich arable land of the plain of Mesara.

wells—down which the sunlight could penetrate to light the lower rooms.

Beyond the outer walls of the palace was another area which seems to have been an integral part of the palatial design—the west court. This paved area seems to have pro-

peculiarly Minoan kind which tapered from top to bottom.

However, these were not left in their natural color but were painted bright red with a black capital. These columns were used in vast numbers to allow light to penetrate to

Knossos *(above)* was the largest of all the Minoan palaces, covering an area of about 19,000 square meters. Sir Arthur Evans' restorations, intended to preserve the ruins from further collapse, manage to convey some impression of what the multi-story building once looked like.

And the chief city is Knossos,
where Minos was king—
He that for nine long years
had converse with Zeus.

Homer, Odyssey

rooms and staircases, and often were alternated with square piers to provide a pleasing visual effect.

Floors were in many areas paved either with finely worked gypsum slabs or with squared flags of limestone or banded calcite. In the more important cult and residential rooms, stone veneers were often applied to the walls too.

Most wall decoration, however, was in the form of frescoes, painted in a full range of colors and shades. Some of the frescoes depicted rituals and ceremonies which no doubt took place in the palace itself. In one, we see fashionably dressed ladies seated on

however, the frescoes also record scenes from the Minoan countryside. Rocky hillsides are shown with streams and waterfalls, lush grasses and brightly colored flowers. Hoopoes, partridges, and other birds are seen in their natural habitat or in formal friezes, while goats clamber over rocks and cats stalk their prey through the grass. On other frescoes the Minoan painters have turned to one of their favorite themes, the sea, and dolphins and fish swim across a wall.

Occasionally the art of fresco painting is combined with that of low-relief sculpting in plaster, the most famous example of

The superbly built "Royal Road" at Knossos *(below)* runs from the northwest corner of the palace toward the spacious residence known as the Little Palace. Recently, a second road of similar construction has been found to join it from the west.

A reconstruction of the west wing of the Palace of Knossos *(above, right)* shows the ceremonial staircase flanked on the right by the antechamber to the throne room, and on the left by ritual rooms.

stools, in another elegant ladies in blue dresses seem to be conversing in lowered tones, while a third shows rows of these courtiers seated in a "grandstand," presumably watching some dance or ritual in the courtyard below them. Whether or not the famous bull-jumping fresco also depicts a ritual that was practiced within the walls of the palace is still uncertain.

Alongside the scenes of life in the palaces,

which must be the so-called Priest-King from Knossos. But whether he was a priest or a king is still argued; one expert has even suggested that "he" may in fact be a woman. This plaster relief epitomizes some of our present uncertainties about the focus of power in Minoan palaces, and the relative status of men and women, priests and kings. Who then did rule the palaces, and how did they work?

The truly monumental nature of the palace of Knossos can perhaps be appreciated in this view of the masonry at the north entrance of the building. Note how prominently "the horns of consecration" are placed.

The restored north entrance of the palace of Knossos *(above)* reveals both the ashlar masonry used for important façades, and above it the coarser stonework used for interior walls. This was usually covered as here by plaster and frescoes.

HOW A PALACE WORKED

One impression which emerges very clearly from a study of the Minoan palaces is that they fulfilled a variety of quite different functions, which were all nevertheless interlinked by the Minoan system of government.

Perhaps the most obvious role of the palaces is as places for ceremony, for the great open spaces of the central and west courts and the majesty of the broad staircases and elaborately planned reception and banqueting halls immediately catch the eye. Such features were clearly designed to impress, and there can be little doubt that the courts and halls saw ceremonies which were essentially secular in nature. They may have been used to receive and entertain both officials and local dignitaries from other parts of the island and also important visitors from abroad.

But the courts at least seem likely also to have been the focus of communal rituals. The west courts and associated tiers of seats obviously provided a convenient location for ritual dances and other performances which could be attended by the population at large. At Phaistos, seating alone provided space for more than five hundred persons. The central courts, on the other hand, were presumably used for rituals attended by a more select audience, most of whom, to judge by contemporary frescoes, sat on the verandas and at the windows of the upper stories overlooking the court. On balance it still seems likely that the bull sports were held in the central courts of the palaces. Sacrifices and offerings associated with this or any other ritual performed in the central court could either be made at altar places erected in the court itself as at Zakro and Mallia, or in the shrine rooms and their sacred stores which were mainly grouped on the west of the court. These shrines, like that of the Double Axes at Knossos, were such small rooms they could clearly be entered only by one or two persons at a time, whether priestesses or worshippers.

It was usually behind these rooms that the principal storerooms of the palaces were placed, and the function of the palaces as major depositories of both food supplies and other forms of wealth is clear from the volume of storage provided. At Knossos the main magazines were originally provided with more than 400 great storage jars (pithoi) capable of holding up to 100,000 liters of grain or oil. At Mallia there was a special oil store on the east of the central court with spaces for more than 150 oil jars, each with its own drainage groove to catch spilt oil and channel it into a collection jar at the end of the row. On the other side of the court at Mallia stood a battery of eight circular silos for grain storage, holding perhaps a total of two thousand bushels of wheat or barley. Storage for valuable goods and luxury items was provided in a series of small rooms, or treasuries as Minoan archaeologists invariably label them, and possibly at Knossos by carefully lined storage cists or boxes built into the floors of the pithoi magazines. At Zakro the built chests in the treasury still contained some of the valuables kept there in Minoan times, including superbly made stone drinking chalices and imported vases from Egypt.

The Zakro chalices may well have been made in the palace itself since here, as well as at Mallia and Knossos, the workshops of stone vase makers have been found, with the unfinished and rejected products of their labors still lying on the floor. The workshops of craftsmen skilled in carving ivory and making faience have also been uncovered at Zakro. Most of the bronze cutlery and tableware used in the palaces, as well as jewelry and weaponry of bronze, would also have been made within the walls of the palaces. At Mallia a collection of bronzesmith's molds, including those for double axes, was found in the northwest of the palace, while a large smith's furnace can still be seen in the palace at Phaistos. Other craftsmen working inside the palaces included vase painters, goldsmiths, and seal carvers.

All of this craft activity, together with the storage of such large quantities of foodstuffs, meant that records had to be kept of goods moving in and out of the palaces. Record tablets were therefore maintained by scribes or clerks and have been discovered in all the main palaces. At Zakro the archives room was flanked by storerooms, a shrine, a treasury, a workshop, and a reception hall. Nowhere is the interlinking of palatial functions so well demonstrated.

Sir Arthur Evans labeled this heavily restored relief fresco "The Priest-King," with all that this implied about the nature of the Minoan rulers. Today the figure's identity is still argued over, and it has even been suggested that the figure is that of a woman.

The skillful combination of a light shaft, a staircase, and columns standing on a dwarf wall to produce an impressive visual effect and allow as much light as possible into the lower levels of the palaces is clearly seen in the interior view of the Palace of Knossos (opposite).

ANATOMY OF A PALACE

Many stone blocks in the palace of Knossos carry incised marks like the double axe above. Some may have ritual importance, others are mason's marks.

The ground plan of the palace of Knossos *(center)* shows the dozens of small rooms serving to support the floors of the spacious rooms on the first and second floors. Some impression of the palace in its heyday, with central court, its several stories, brightly painted columns, and essential light-wells, can be seen in the fanciful reconstruction below the plan.

The characteristic device of alternating a row of columns with a row of piers is seen from both within and without in the two views below.

The larger of the two Snake Goddesses *(left)* found in a storage cist in the "Temple Repositories" is 34 cm (13½ in.) high. Snakes are twined around her body and her hat.

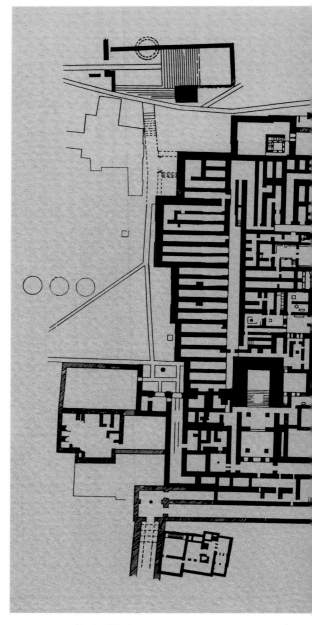

The magazines at Knossos *(below)* provided storage both for oil, in the pithoi, and dry goods and perhaps valuables in the cists in the floor.

The "throne of Minos" *(above)* may have been a priestly seat rather than a kingly one, and the throne room in which it stands was built after the collapse of Minoan civilization around 1450 B.C.

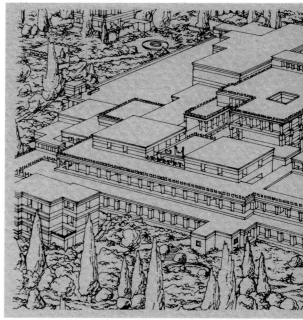

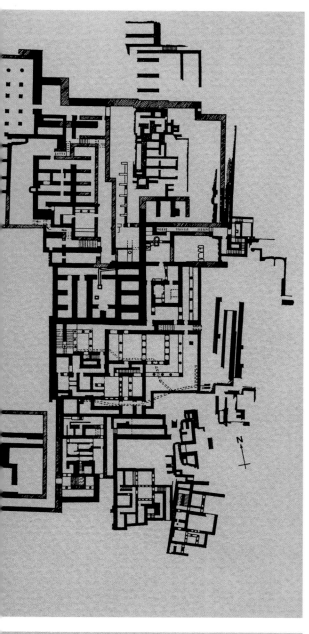

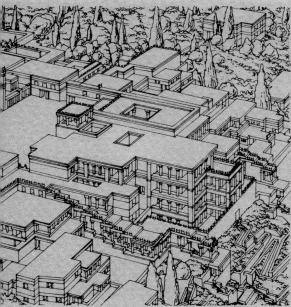

The Minoans put a great deal of thought into providing a water supply, drains, and sewers for their palaces, as can be seen in the carefully constructed water channel with settling tanks seen below.

In addition to toilets the Minoans also had small bathrooms in which clay bathtubs like that above were placed. Similar tubs were sometimes used for burials.

The illuminating effect of the light-wells is seen below, with sunlight penetrating to the basement rooms of the palace.

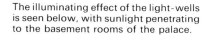

Whether the "Queen's Megaron" (below) was really occupied as a private chamber by a Minoan queen is open to speculation. Certainly the rooms would have been cold in winter.

Sealstone engravers, working with the aid of rock crystal lenses were employed in the palace workshops.

Much of the finer palace pottery was made by potters who worked for the palace alone. Above right, one example.

Other palatial craftsmen included lapidaries who produced a wide array of stone vases in attractive rocks from the island.

Palatial archives initially took the form of collections of clay sealings removed from letters, packages, and boxes which had arrived at the palace, and an archive room in the first palace at Phaistos contained about seven thousand such sealings. These sealings were impressed, while the clay was wet, with a sealstone on which a design had been carved. The design presumably conveyed information of some sort, perhaps simply the identity of the sender but possibly the name of a commodity or information about the quantity of goods being dispatched. The manufacture and use of such seals began several centuries before the appearance of the first palaces.

The earliest archive found at Knossos, however, contained a mixture of clay sealings, tablets, and labels—about eighty in all—on which information was written in a hieroglyphic script. Some of the inscriptions had been impressed with a sealstone, but others were written with a pointed implement. The individual signs of the script are mostly instantly recognizable—a bull's head, a man walking, a ship, a saw, or a double axe. The way in which the signs are combined in groups, however, and the increasingly schematic way in which some signs are drawn suggest that they were being used not just to convey ideas and as pictures of objects but also to represent sounds in the spoken language.

Some of the signs found in the hieroglyphic script also appear in the so-called Linear A script, which was that used in a third archive of tablets and sealings found in the royal villa or summer palace at Ayia Triadha near Phaistos. This script, perhaps developed initially for rapid writing in ink rather than on clay tablets, appears widely throughout Crete, although the total number of inscriptions in it is small—less than four hundred. Most of the tablets which survive seem to be accounts of one sort or another, and many of them deal with the staple products of the Minoan countryside—wheat, oil, olives, and figs. Although we cannot translate or decipher the tablets in detail, we can see that they usually begin with a group of signs perhaps indicating the name of a place or person, followed by a single sign which may show the nature of the transaction recorded—"received" or "given out." There then follows the list of goods with the quantities of each recorded, sometimes down to fractions, the final figures giving

This clay sealing of about 1700 B.C., found in the early archives of the Palace of Knossos, carries the portrait of a Minoan man with an elaborate hair style. It is possible that the hieroglyphic inscription next to him records his name.

the total quantity involved. Apart from accounts tablets of this sort, Linear A seems to have been used largely for ritual inscriptions on stone offering tables and on votive gifts.

In contrast to the widely used Linear A script, that used on the so-called Phaistos Disk occurs only once, and no other instances are found on Crete or, at present, anywhere else in the world. The script and the disk itself are unique. Dating to the seventeenth century B.C., it is a flat clay disk about 16 cm (6.4 inches) across. On each face it carries an inscription, in the form of a spiral, which has been made by pressing stamps, probably of wood, into the damp clay. The signs have been divided up into sixty-one groups, each of which is presumably a word. Many of the signs can be identified at once, but others are more problematic, and even if all the signs could be firmly identified, we should still be a long

The axe-adze is a well-known tool in the Aegean. A bronze example of about 2500 B.C. from the Greek mainland is seen alongside the sign from the Phaistos disk.

The crested head shown here has been the source of much argument. Some believe he represents the sun, others compare him with Philistine warriors, and others say he is a Carian. He also appears, however, on a Minoan double axe from Arkalokhori.

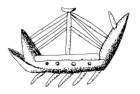

The lady is probably in mourning, her hair let down and her breasts bared. The closest parallels to this figure are found in Palestine at a later date.

Ships with a high prow and a steep, almost vertical stern, like that seen on the Phaistos disk, are not common in the Aegean although similar ones do appear on Minoan seals of about the same date.

The two sides of the Phaistos disk *(center)* carry a total of 241 signs, each of which was impressed into the clay with an individually made stamp. It has never been deciphered, and controversy still rages as to whether the disk was made in Crete, southern Turkey, or elsewhere. Some signs appear typically Cretan but others find their closest parallels in the east Mediterranean.

The Linear A script was probably first developed to enable rapid writing in ink, but few such records survive since they would have been written on parchment or papyrus. One inscription written in cuttle-fish ink survives, on the base of a vase. More commonly, though, the Linear A records survive as clay tablets like those from Ayia Triadha *(below)*.

way from deciphering what the inscription says. There have been many attempts to translate or decipher the text, including claims that it is written in Basque or Finnish, apart from others which more predictably believe it to be in Greek or a Semitic language. The form in which the inscription is written, and the way in which the signs are combined to form groups, make it likely that the disk carries a list of people or places, and that they are listed here in either a ceremonial or ritual order. This means that the disk might contain a list of tribute or tributaries, a muster of soldiers, a list of witnesses in a trial, or even the text of a hymn—all of which have been proposed at one time or another. What is quite certain is that the Phaistos Disk was never part of the office archives at Phaistos, but rather it was a prized inscription of religious rather than bureaucratic importance.

Overleaf: This vivid wall painting found in the east wing of the palace of Knossos is the clearest picture we have of the sport of bull-leaping, showing as it does two successive stages in the leap itself. In the center, a male acrobat is already somersaulting over the bull's back and will be caught by the young girl on the right. Meanwhile, at the left, a second girl is grabbing the bull's horns and appears to be rising into the air as it tosses its head. No modern acrobats have ever reenacted this sport.

MINOAN RELIGION

Many Minoan signet rings show religious scenes, but it is difficult to interpret their meaning. The female figure in the center above may be a goddess, flanked by two priestesses, one of whom raises her hands in worship while the other tends a sacred tree.

The faience Snake Goddess *(center)* was one of two found carefully stored in a cist in a sacred storeroom at Knossos. Her flounced dress is like that worn by Minoan court ladies, but her divinity is suggested by mastery of the snakes and by the animal, a leopard perhaps, seated on her head.

Opposite:
This bronze worshipper from Tylissos, central Crete, appears to be in adoration or prayer, the body stiff and knock-kneed in its imploring posture thought to be the Minoan worshipping pose.

The everyday life and government of Minoan Crete appear to have been inextricably bound up with religion and ritual. Even if Sir Arthur Evans' identification of the Priest-King fresco is now in doubt, the close relationship between the gods and government which the title implied is clearly visible in the archaeological remains.

The palaces, from which the everyday affairs of the Minoans were controlled, have yielded both architectural and artifactual evidence of the all-pervading influence of contemporary religion. In statuettes, engravings on signet rings, models, and clay sealings, we see depictions of the gods and goddesses of Minoan Crete. We still cannot be sure that all the goddesses we see are different deities, and not various aspects of a single Great Goddess, as Evans suggested. The Snake Goddess who seems to have been worshipped as the protectoress of the household is easily recognized by the snakes which she grasps in her hands, or which twine around her body. She appears to be quite distinct from the Lady of the Animals, who appears on signets flanked by rampant animals, and who might be recognized as the goddess Artemis, whose name already appears in the Bronze Age on the Linear B tablets. Other goddesses we can recognize include perhaps Eileithyia, the goddess of childbirth, and Aphrodite, who may be represented in Crete in the form of a dove, clay models of which appear in several shrines. Again the tablets record the existence of a goddess called Eileithyia, and

The Rhyton vase detail above, which depicts a Minoan hilltop shrine, is one of the most interesting finds from the Palace of Zakro. Note the "horns of consecration" at the lower right side. The shrine portal is decorated with spirals, and above there are four wild goats with imposing horns (agrimi, a type still seen today on Crete). A bird carrying prey can be seen next to the goats; and to the right of the portal stands an altar.

The massive columns in a hallway of the palace of Knossos *(above left)* resemble the pillars in underground crypts on which sacred symbols were inscribed. The shrines in several palaces also included repository boxes in the floor for offerings.

another known as the Dove Goddess, in the Bronze Age. Male deities seem to be far fewer in Crete, and only a Master of the Animals is immediately recognizable from pictures of him on signet rings and sealings. But the tablets refer to both Hermes and Poseidon, and the latter's frequent connection with bulls in later Greek religion suggests an obvious link between him and the religion of the palaces.

The importance of the bull in Minoan religion is firmly established both by the models and frescoes which depict the bull-leaping ritual, and by the many models and depictions of the horns of consecration. Frequently associated with the bull's head or the horns as a religious symbol is the double axe, possibly because it was the implement with which bull sacrifices were perpetrated. Apart from carvings and engravings of the double axe symbol, large double axes of sheet bronze, or more rarely sheet gold, were set up on wooden posts which were themselves set into large stone or clay bases. Examples found outside some of the storerooms at Knossos were presumably intended to protect the contents of the stores from theft or destruction.

Votive offerings in the form of, or depicting, double axes, horns, birds, and snakes are often found together in a single shrine in the palaces or elsewhere and suggest that even if there were several separate deities, their worship was closely interwoven. Each palace, and many of the larger town houses and country villas, had at least one small shrine

which seems to have served as a household shrine. It was usually a small, often square room with perhaps a raised bench or offering shelf along the far wall. The Household or Snake Goddess was represented either by a statuette or by ritual tubes down the sides of which ran clay loops, like snakes. The other furnishings of the shrine might include small double axes, model horns, clay birds, and a stone or clay offering table. Elsewhere in the palaces there were dark basement rooms where the massive stone piers or pillars supporting their ceilings were inscribed with sacred symbols, and particularly the double axe, and repository boxes for offerings were let into the floor. Some at least of these "pillar crypts," as Evans called them, were probably shrines. In the countryside different places of worship were established, and in some cases different deities honored within them. Crete has many caves and some of them became important centers of ritual. The cave at Psychro, and perhaps another at Arkalokhori, were probably venerated as the supposed birthplace of Zeus, known to the Minoans as Velchanos. Both caves have yielded many bronze votives as well as other offerings left there by worshippers over a period of many centuries. The Cave of Eileithyia at Amnisos, on the other hand, was dedicated to the Minoan goddess of childbirth, who here seems to have been identified with a great stalactite, around which a low wall had been built and offerings placed.

The most prolific rural shrines, however, were peak sanctuaries, so called because they were usually situated on small but prominent hilltops. Recent work has suggested that there were far more of them in the Minoan countryside than was previously imagined. Each clan or large family group

however, and included a built shrine with one or two rooms. Most of these larger sanctuaries were built on peaks overlooking important settlements, such as that on Mount Iuktas overlooking Knossos or the peak sanctuary on Prophet Elias above Mallia, and they were presumably major

The bull's head in black serpentine *(right)* is in fact a ritual vase, with a pouring hole in its mouth. In addition to serpentine, shell, jasper, rock, and crystal, were used in its manufacture, as inlays for eyes and nostrils. The horns, of gold or bronze, are a modern restoration.

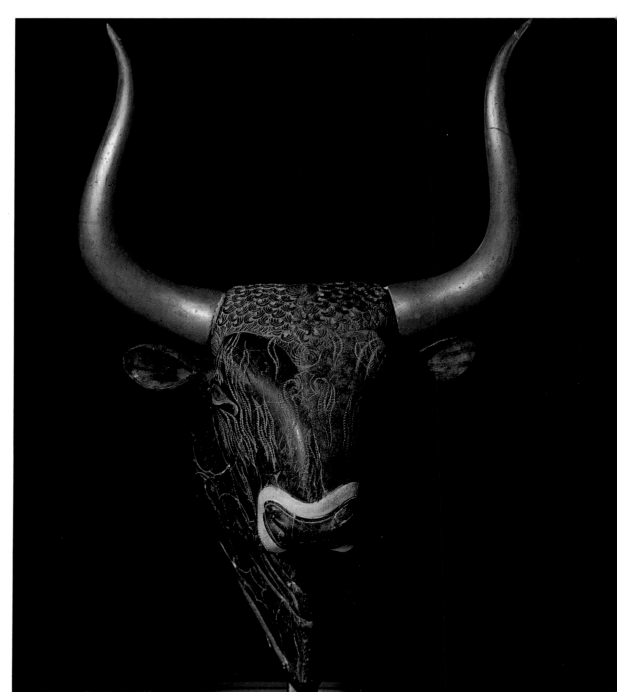

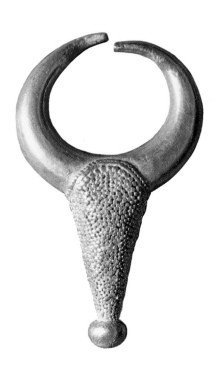

The bull's horns were a common symbol in Minoan art and were incorporated into many items of personal use, like the earring *(above)*, decorated with fine drops of gold, or granulation. From the period 1700–1400 B.C. The bull's head in this case has been treated most abstractly, in contrast to the elaborate black serpentine head at right.

may have had their own rural shrine on their land, at which they made offerings to the gods. Many such shrines were no more than the bare hilltop, with perhaps a rough wall of boulders placed around it and an area for offerings and ceremonies cleared at one side. A few were more substantial structures,

shrines to which the religious leaders of the Minoan settlements processed on the appropriate days of the year.

From these larger peak sanctuaries in particular comes some of the best evidence we have for the sort of rituals practiced by the Minoans. Large fires were lit at many peak

Dances would certainly have formed a part of palace ritual too, but more exhausting and exciting activities also seem to have had a ritual significance in the palaces. A superbly carved drinking cup showing boxing and wrestling also portrays the bull-leaping sport, and suggests that all three activities had a religious role in Crete. Certainly the prominence given to wall paintings and low-relief sculptures of tossing bulls, together with the evidence of models and seal designs, suggest that the ritual of the bull games was an important event in the Minoan calendar. Whether or not the bull-leaping was followed by the sacrifice of the hard-worked bull is uncertain, but the painted sarcophagus from Ayia Triadha certainly shows a bull sacrifice in progress. The Ayia Triadha sarcophagus is of partic-

Left: The miniature gold double axes seen here were part of a large collection of votive offerings discovered in the sacred cave at Arkalokhori, which included bronze sword blades and daggers. These axes were miniature copies of larger ones which were erected on wooden poles standing in pyramidal bases, as seen on the Ayia Triadha sarcophagus *(below).*

Our richest single source of information on Minoan religion is probably the famous painted sarcophagus from Ayia Triadha (ca. 1400 B.C.). The side panel shown here, depicting a rite or series of rites, combines several symbolic themes. In the white-background panel at the far left, a liquid is being poured into a large pot suspended between two double axes (each surmounted by a bird figure). The woman bearing two containers of liquid seems from her crown to be a

sanctuaries, and from their ashes archaeologists recover large numbers of clay figurines of people, animals, and objects. It looks as if the figurines and other clay objects were thrown into the fire in the expectation that the prayers and hopes that were embodied in them for protection and cure would be carried to the gods in the smoke. Animal bones found in the ashes may imply that sacrifices were also made here, while stone offering tables suggest that token quantities of food were also placed here by worshippers. Other rituals practiced in the countryside included harvest dances, like that seen on a carved stone vase from Ayia Triadha, and no doubt other dances of which models survive from Palaikastro and Kamilari.

ular interest not only for its scenes of Minoan ritual but because these rituals are here implicitly linked with death and burial. This connection between everyday ritual and funerary customs goes back to the pre-palatial era when double axes, and models of bulls, snake goddesses, and birds are found in tombs. In the early palace period it is seen at Arkhanes where a suite of ritual rooms, including perhaps a pillar crypt, is built around a tholos tomb. About 1600 B.C. it is embodied in the Temple Tomb at Knossos, where a place for ritual is provided alongside a place for burial. Its survival into the period after the collapse of Minoan civilization is witnessed by the sarcophagus itself, dating to about 1400 B.C.

royal figure; she walks ahead of a musician playing a lyre. In the central (dark-shaded) panel, two dark-skinned young men are carrying calves as sacrificial offerings while a third carries a small boat. Facing them, in the right-hand panel, a standing figure in a fur mantle appears to represent the deceased in whose honor the rites are being carried out. The structure behind this person, decorated in a scroll motif, could be the sarcophagus. On the other side of the sarcophagus a painting shows the sacrifice of a bull.

COUNTRY LIFE

Although Minoan Crete was a civilization organized and controlled from a small number of palatial towns, and a larger number of smaller settlements, the great majority of Minoans lived in the countryside. Indeed the towns, the palaces, and even the civilization itself, were dependent on the successful exploitation of Crete's natural resources. Wheat and barley, the staple grain crops of Crete, were grown wherever the soil was rich enough and the slope of the land gentle enough to allow them to take root. Most farms therefore had several small fields in which a simple wooden plow was used to turn the soil before planting, and from which the grain could easily be reaped in late summer using short bronze sickles which cut off the grain just below the heads. In the Mesara, where a reasonably deep fertile soil had the additional advantages of a water supply and flat terrain, much larger areas of land were devoted to cereal production.

On some land the grain was grown between and beneath the olive trees from which olives were collected both for consumption

The Harvester Vase from Ayia Triadha is a useful source of information about both Minoan agriculture and ritual, for it shows a band of villagers carrying their hayforks and their threshing sticks, singing and dancing as they celebrate the harvest. The vase, carved from black steatite, dates to about 1500 B.C.

and for pressing to produce oil. The oil presses and their low-spouted vats to allow oil to be drained off from them have been found in several rural villas and settlements. The other principal fruit tree grown in Minoan Crete was the fig. Carbonized figs themselves have survived at Zakro, but a Linear B tablet which refers to two thousand fig trees is the clearest evidence we have of the fruit's importance. Where figs and olives were not grown, the hillsides were often terraced to take vines. Wine drinking became popular in the Bronze Age in Crete, and wine jugs and chalices are common finds

At Vathypetro (right) a clue to the villa's economy is given by the discovery of a wine press, with tub, collecting bowl, overspill groove, and collection basin.

on most Minoan sites. At Zakro, pips and other residues survive to reveal the location of at least one wine press. Again, some idea of the quantities which were produced can be inferred from a single tablet from Knossos which refers to the production of fourteen thousand liters of wine.

We should not imagine the Minoan farmers, however, as specializing in the production of wheat, or olives, or grapes. The hilly character of the island, and the effect this had on the richness and the depth of the soils, meant that few if any farmers could afford to ignore the grazing land, particularly that suitable for sheep. It is clear from the Knossos tablets that sheep were by far the most numerous and important animal in the Minoan economy. More than eight hundred of the tablets from Knossos are concerned with the management of sheep. From the tablets, it appears that most of the sheep listed there, more than 100,000 of them, were kept mainly as a source of wool, although their importance as a source of meat was not of course ignored. Many of the flocks recorded will have been under the control of transhuming shepherds who moved their sheep over distances of many kilometers during different seasons of the

The extreme frequency with which clay model cattle turn up in peak sanctuaries in Crete suggests that although they were few in number, cattle were prized possessions for which protection was sought.

Fish figure prominently in Minoan art. The fine painting of a fisherman and his catch from Thera *(center)* is a colorful reminder of the importance of seafood in the Aegean diet.

Opposite:
The dominant role of sheep in the Minoan economy is neatly represented in this bowl from Palaikastro with its shepherd and flock of about two hundred sheep.

vided by all of these animals and crops was further supplemented by hunting, particularly of the wild Cretan goat, the agrimi.

All of this activity, with the exception perhaps of hunting, seems to have been highly organized by the central administration. The tablets list the agricultural produce of whole regions, such as the Mesara, on some tablets, but also refer on others to the detailed stock records of individual farms or villages. In addition, some land of course was farmed directly from the towns, and it is not unusual to find farm implements and even oil-pressing installations in town houses.

Along the coasts of the island the occupants of villas, villages, and harbor towns alike exploited the rich resources of the sea. A wide variety of fish could be caught in Minoan waters, including tunny, mullet, mackerel, and perch. Much of this fishing was carried out with hook and line from small fishing boats, clay models of which still survive. Other fish may have been speared, but net sinkers and needles thought to be for mending nets also point to attempts to catch fish in larger quantities and possibly from bigger ships. Whether or not the Minoans had also learned already to make rock-cut tanks in which to catch fish is uncertain, but many undated examples survive along the island's coasts. In addition to fish, the fishermen were also able to catch large quantities of lobster, crab, and octopus, and to collect shellfish to add variety and extra taste to the diet.

Altogether, by a combination of skill, hard work, and careful management, it was possible for the Minoans to provide themselves with a reliable and varied diet.

year, but others will have been pastured permanently within a few hours' journey of their home farm.

Goats, which utilize high pastures of little use for other purposes, were also kept in large numbers to judge by the tablets, whereas pigs and cattle were relatively minor sources of meat. The food supply pro-

This farm at Vathypetro in central Crete was equipped with a wine press, olive oil press, and several workshops and storage facilities, all of which have provided information on the workings of the Minoan farm economy.

All Minoan villas, and many town houses too, have their magazines of pithoi *(left)*. Above all else they were probably used to store olive oil.

MINOAN MASTER CRAFTSMEN

The traditions of high craftsmanship which had emerged in Crete in the third millennium B.C. were maintained in the palatial era when workshops both within and without the palaces produced a superb repertoire of stone vases, painted pottery, goldwork, and carved ivories.

The Minoan goldsmiths were concerned mainly with the production of fine jewelry and splendid tableware. Few examples of the latter survive, the most notable exceptions being the two gold cups found in a tomb on the mainland of Greece at Vapheio. Both their style and the theme of their decoration—the trapping of bulls—suggest they are Minoan masterpieces. These, and other vessels whose existence is known only from their appearance in frescoes or as clay or stone copies, were all made from sheet gold, skillfully hammered and worked in repoussé, to produce relief decoration. Minoan

they could shape and then grind and polish the vases to their finished perfection. Working in this way they produced stone vases of remarkable color and shape, some of which imitated contemporary pottery and metal vessels, but many of which were in turn imitated by Minoan potters.

The discovery of a workshop at Knossos where sealstones rather than vases were made appears to confirm that seal making and vase making were separate crafts. Certainly they used largely different types of stone, the seal carvers' favorites being red or green jasper, amethyst, orange carnelian, agate, and chalcedony. Using bronze and perhaps obsidian gravers, together with small drills and abrasives, the seal makers engraved the most exquisite miniature scenes onto surfaces no more than 3 cm (1¼ inch) across and often much less. On these tiny surfaces agile agrimi, aggressive

One of the finest products of the Minoan goldsmiths is this brooch from a royal cemetery at Mallia showing two wasps at a flower. Already, soon after 2000 B.C., the art of granulation has reached perfection.

Center: This gold cup from Vapheio is among the few Minoan gold vessels to survive. These exports to the mainland, made by Minoan craftsmen around 1500 B.C., show the rearing and trapping of bulls.

Above, far right: Kamares ware at its best is both colorful and tasteful. This superb example from Phaistos is almost eggshell thin and may well imitate contemporary metal cups, which do not survive.

gold jewelry, including necklaces, ear and finger rings, and brooches, called for different techniques. Signet rings had elaborate scenes engraved on their bezels, while earrings, beads, and brooches were decorated with fine gold wire (filigree) or tiny droplets of gold (granulation), both of which were cleverly soldered to the surface of the object. The lapidaries (stone workers) of Minoan Crete used a far wider range of materials than the metalworkers, but a more limited number of techniques. Stone-vase makers used more than twenty different rocks, including a few imported ones from both Egypt and southern Greece. Using bronze chisels, they roughly carved the outer shape of the vase and then used a bow-driven tubular drill, usually made of reed, together with an abrasive sand to bore a cylindrical core from the center of the vessel. With bronze tools, and further use of abrasives,

bulls, and delicate birds are portrayed in dynamic realism.

By contrast, the Minoan vase painters were able to work on much larger surfaces and these they decorated very often with formalized designs based on motifs from nature. The Kamares style, popular in the nineteenth and eighteenth centuries B.C., was exuberant and extrovert, with bold designs painted in red, orange, and white on a dark surface. By the later palace period more sober designs in red and brown on a buff background were favored, but one outstanding group of vases of this period are those in the Marine style, with very lifelike octopuses wriggling across their surfaces, surrounded by seaweed, coral, fish, and other marine life.

The remarkable skills of the Minoan sealstone engraver are clearly seen in these two examples. Note particularly how the subjects have been cleverly designed to fit the shape of the field on which they are engraved.

Left: One of the masterpieces of ancient craftsmanship from anywhere in the world must surely be this rock crystal scent vase from the palace of Zakro. Apart from the difficulties of hollowing out this hard stone, the skillful use of gold and bronze to hold the beads of rock crystal on the collar and handle in place is also notable.

51

TOWNS AND HARBORS

Town houses of well-to-do Minoans were likely to be two or three stories high, as these small painted tiles from Knossos suggest. The houses, which would have stood directly side by side without space between, were apparently constructed of stone and mortar combined with wood beams. The small-paned windows were only on the

upper floors; the ground level, as in Minoan palaces, was windowless. Town houses of this kind imitated the royal palaces in several other details.

These were no doubt the residences of the upper echelons of Minoan society, and the day-to-day housekeeping was most likely overseen by the fashionably dressed ladies we see in contemporary fresco paintings.

The plan of Gournia (opposite) shows the compact concentration of individual buildings in the Minoan city and the prevailingly grid-like layout. Gournia's modest size (with an estimated population of 700 in the city center) is typical of Minoan cities.

The three largest palaces of Minoan Crete were each surrounded by extensive settlements which we are right to call towns, even though they were no larger than many modern villages. The palaces which stood at their center, and at the center of smaller towns such as Zakro and Gournia too, indicate that these settlements fulfilled important administrative functions as well as being the principal places for the production and exchange of goods.

Finely paved main roads led from the palaces at Knossos, Phaistos, and Mallia into the surrounding town, and from these roads ran narrow lanes, lined with workshops and houses. In the areas close to the palace the houses were notably large, and many elements of their design and decoration—such as light-wells, porticoes, bathrooms, and frescoes—consciously imitate the palaces. Most of these houses also have their own small storage magazines, and the finds made within these buildings when they were excavated often included luxury objects made by highly skilled craftsmen.

Smaller houses of simple design and construction, and probably with but a single story, become commoner farther away from the palace buildings and presumably housed the bulk of the population, whose main occupation was farming the land around the town. Scattered throughout the towns were many workshops, some of which produced the sort of goods which were made in every town and village on the island—pottery, cloth, woodwork, and bronze tools. But other workshops in the palatial towns were used for crafts which probably had a more restricted clientele. North of the Royal Road at Knossos, for example, the remains of an ivory workshop were found, with bits of raw ivory, waste pieces, and pieces of finished ivory inlay, as well as fine bronze tools with which the pieces were carved. To

the south of the palace at Knossos another house was used by a stone lamp-maker, whose products, including at least one unfinished example, were found in his workshop. At Mallia, a modest two-story house built around a small central courtyard proved to be the home of a seal engraver. His workshop was situated on the first floor of his home, and the debris from it contained many sealstones, including broken examples, more than a hundred rough-outs, and pieces of unused steatite and rock crystal from his stock of raw materials.

Just how many people lived in the main palatial towns is difficult to estimate because we still know only tiny fragments of their overall plan. But the total areas occupied are so small that populations of less than five thousand persons seem certain. Even so, substantial areas close to the towns had to be set aside as cemetery areas, and at Knossos in particular, the hillside to the west of the town has produced many burials.

The smaller towns of Minoan Crete are of considerable interest because more is known of their total plan and organization. The best example by far is the town of Gournia, built on a small hill close to the sea in the Gulf of Mirabello. Although there are probably some unexcavated buildings beyond the main occupation area, by far the larger part of the town has been completely excavated. It covers an area of about 15,000 square meters, and may have had a population of about 700 persons. It has a small palace to which is attached a large courtyard on the southern side. Access to this court appears to have been open to any of the inhabitants of Gournia.

It was approached on either side by neatly cobbled streets, which are part of a ringroad which runs around the central area of the town. To cope with the slope of the hillside, the road is carefully stepped in places, and from it run a series of narrow lanes which give access to all of the houses within the settlement. Apart from the palace the only "public" building is a small shrine, approached by a lane of its own, in which a collection of votives and cult statuettes were found. Otherwise all the buildings are private houses, many of which were two-story buildings of comfortable size. The basement areas which survive were mainly storerooms and in some cases workshops. At the north end of the town there were at least two bronze smiths and a carpenter, the former

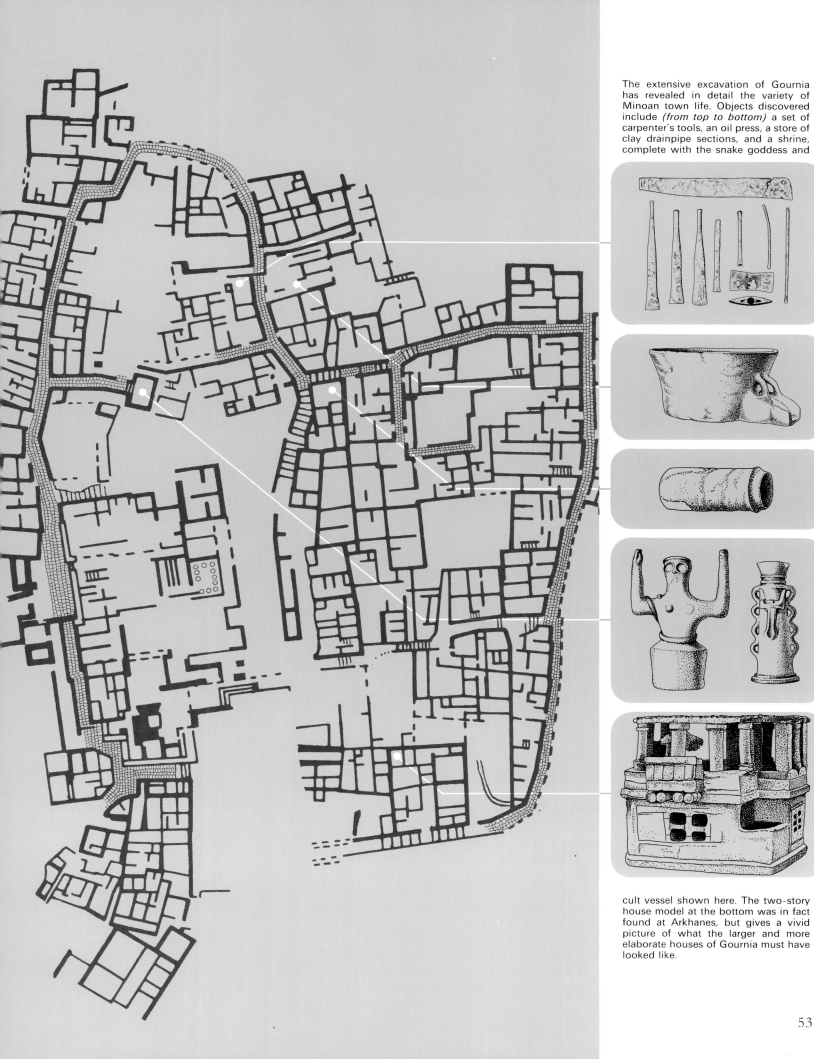

The extensive excavation of Gournia has revealed in detail the variety of Minoan town life. Objects discovered include *(from top to bottom)* a set of carpenter's tools, an oil press, a store of clay drainpipe sections, and a shrine, complete with the snake goddess and

cult vessel shown here. The two-story house model at the bottom was in fact found at Arkhanes, but gives a vivid picture of what the larger and more elaborate houses of Gournia must have looked like.

Almost all of the town of Gournia, Crete, has been excavated. Here we see ruins of several closely clustered houses and an ascending path, in the northwest part of the city.

In the West House at Thera an elaborate fresco was discovered, now known as the fresco of the Naval Campaign, which provides several detailed scenes of Minoan life, which are especially informative concerning ships and cities. In this detail *(opposite)*, a boat is seen arriving in the port before a town which shows close-built houses of stone or block construction. In the hills beyond the town, a lion is pursuing deer (top left of picture).

identified by their stone molds for casting tools, and the latter by a set of eight tools including a double axe, chisels, and saw. In the town of Palaikastro on Crete's east coast, it is possible to identify a weaver's house from the two hoards of loom weights discovered there, and in another building not far away a dye works with a stone vat and a pile of murex shells, from which a purple dye would have been extracted. At none of these workshops is there any suggestion of a shop or showroom, and intending buyers presumably came to the craftsman's house. But one street at Palaikastro contained several buildings which consisted of nothing more than one front room, with a wide doorway onto the street, and one or two tiny storerooms behind. In one building a storeroom contained a mass of pottery, while in another, the front room held a stone platform on which two querns for grinding grain were set. In the classical world, these buildings would at once be identified as shops, and this is what they may have been in Minoan Palaikastro. We must remember, however, that the Minoans had no monetary system and if shops did exist in the Minoan world, then their method of trading would have been quite different to that of shops today.

Trade of some sort, however, was a vital ingredient in the life of towns such as Gournia and Palaikastro, because both of them lay close to the sea and were probably harbor towns. Other harbor towns are known, and partially excavated at Zakro, Mochlos, Pseira, Amnisos, and Komo. Some, such as Mochlos and Pseira, were on promontories which provided anchorage on either side according to the winds, while others such as Zakro and Komo are most notable for the sandy shores which were essential for the beaching of Bronze Age shipping. For this reason the Minoan harbor towns had no need of elaborate harbor works with moles and quays, and there is little to point to the important part they played in the Minoan economy except their coastal position. At present, none of these towns has produced evidence of warehouses or even records offices, suggesting that both incoming goods and the records of them were quickly moved on to other, probably palatial, centers. But at Komo, Palaikastro, and Zakro, occasional discoveries of imported goods provide brief glimpses of the exotic articles passing through these ports.

THE EMPIRE OF MINOS

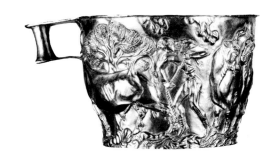

The tradition of a Minoan empire in the Aegean was already ancient when Thucydides wrote in the fifth century B.C. that Minos "ruled over the Cyclades and was the first to plant colonies in most of them."

The discovery of Minoan pottery, stone vases, and other artifacts, on many of the islands of the Aegean, as well as on the Greek mainland and on the coast of Asia Minor, has long seemed to confirm this. Yet evidence is still lacking for the manner in which the Minoans were able to first assert, and then maintain, their control over so many islands and settlements. It is possible that Minoan domination of the Aegean in the period between about 1600 and 1450 B.C. was commercial rather than political or military. The widespread appearance of lead

Most of the Minoan goods arriving on the mainland of Greece were pottery and stone vases, and perhaps perishables such as woolens. These were all probably objects of freelance commerce, but items such as the gold cup found in a tomb at Vapheio near Sparta *(right)* may have been gifts from one king to another. Dating to the sixteenth century B.C., the cup depicts bull-hunting.

Minoan trade with Egypt began in the years around 2000 B.C., and was at first sporadic. Apart from raw materials like gold and perhaps ivory, trinkets like the scarab above found at Knossos were common imports. In the sixteenth and fifteenth centuries the appearance of Cretans carrying gifts to the Egyptians in Egyptian tomb paintings *(right)* and of inscribed stone vessels carrying the pharaoh's name at Knossos *(below right)* suggest political as well as commercial contact.

weights belonging to the Minoan system of weights and measures, and the discovery of tablets and other items inscribed in Minoan Linear A, suggest that trade in many parts of the Aegean was conducted and recorded in accordance with Minoan practice.

Whatever the truth of a Minoan colonial empire in the Aegean, the rulers of palatial Crete certainly appear to have won recognition from the contemporary kings of Egypt. Typical Cretan products are seen being brought as gifts to the Egyptian court by "Keftiu," and among Egyptian imports arriving in Crete is a small number which carry the royal cartouche of one or other of the pharaohs. Almost certainly we are looking here at evidence for the traditional exchange of gifts between great kings of the mid-second millennium B.C.

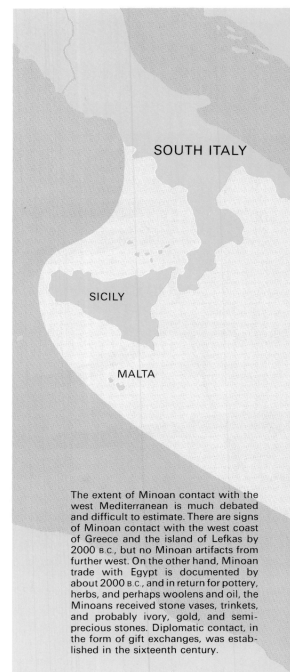

SOUTH ITALY

SICILY

MALTA

The extent of Minoan contact with the west Mediterranean is much debated and difficult to estimate. There are signs of Minoan contact with the west coast of Greece and the island of Lefkas by 2000 B.C., but no Minoan artifacts from further west. On the other hand, Minoan trade with Egypt is documented by about 2000 B.C., and in return for pottery, herbs, and perhaps woolens and oil, the Minoans received stone vases, trinkets, and probably ivory, gold, and semi-precious stones. Diplomatic contact, in the form of gift exchanges, was established in the sixteenth century.

Initially, Minoan trade with the east Mediterranean may have focused on Cyprus and the coast of Syria and Lebanon, rather than on Egypt. Small quantities of Middle Minoan pottery reached these areas, and contemporary Syrian and Mesopotamian daggers and cylinder seals *(right)* are found in Crete. It was probably as a result of these early contacts with the east Mediterranean that lions and mythical creatures such as the sphinx appear on Minoan sealstones of this period *(far right)*.

There are many settlements in the Aegean where Minoan pottery and other artifacts are found, but those with the best evidence for Minoan settlers are on Kythera, Keos, Melos, Thera, and Rhodes. Most of these reveal strong Minoan connections in the period 1600–1450 B.C., but Kythera saw Minoan settlers around 2400 B.C.

The initial impetus for the Minoans to open up trade links with the east Mediterranean may have been to find new sources of copper, ivory, and possibly tin. Cyprus could certainly supply Crete's needs for copper, and Cypriot ox-hide ingots have been found at several Minoan settlements. Syrian ivory may have been exported to Crete, along with small numbers of tanged bronze daggers around 2000 B.C., in return for Minoan pottery and probably other products long since perished. Such trade would have been channeled through the great ports of Ugarit and Byblos.

MACEDONIA

THESSALY

SKOPELOS

EUBOEA

Minoa · ATTICA

ACHAEA

Ayia Irini

KEOS

MESSENIA

SIPHNOS

Phylakopi

Minoa

MELOS

KYTHERA

THERA Akrotiri

Kastri

ASIA MINOR

SAMOS

Miletus

DELOS

Iasos

NAXOS

AMORGOS

COS

LYCIA

Trianda

RHODES

KARPATHOS

CYPRUS

Kition

Ugarit

Orontes

SYRIA

Byblos

Sidon

Tyros

Knossos Mallia

CRETE

Zakro

Phaistos

M E D I T E R R A N E A N   S E A

· Cyrene

CYRENAICA

Buto

Tanis

Sais

EGYPT

Memphis

Nile

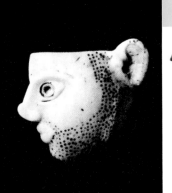

Minoan trade with Egypt is attested by Middle Minoan pottery from several sites in Egyptian, most notably by the fine spouted bowl *(third left)* found in a tomb at Abydos. The Minoans imported many Egyptian stones vases, and occasionally altered them to their own liking, as here *(left)* by the addition of a spout to an Egyptian vase found at Zakro. The bearded head from near Phaistos *(center left)* is probably carved from a shell brought from the Red Sea. *Right:* Egyptian bowl found in Crete.

57

THERA: A MINOAN POMPEII

Minoan trade with the rest of the Aegean had begun during the pre-palatial period, but it reached new heights in the first half of the second millennium B.C., and Minoan shipping began to carry Minoan painted vases, stone bowls, bronze weapons, and probably other perishable commodities such as woven goods and herbs to the east Mediterranean. Here they are still found by excavators in Cyprus, Syria, and Egypt. Returning ships brought cargoes of Syrian ivory, Cypriote copper, Egyptian stone vases, and various trinkets and amulets. Trade within the Aegean developed to such an extent that the Minoans appear to have established themselves, sometimes in considerable numbers, in settlements on several of the Aegean islands, and even on the west coast of Turkey. To the northwest the first Minoan "colony" of all was established on Kythera before 2200 B.C., and from here Minoan trade goods reached western Greece and islands such as Corcyra (Corfu) and Levkas. To the northeast, colonies were founded on Karpathos and Rhodes, and farther north on the Turkish mainland at Miletus. Between these two groups of colonies to east and west, were the Minoan establishments in the Cyclades at places such as Phylakopi on Melos and Ayia Irini on Keos. The stepping stone to these Cycladic colonies was the island of Thera.

At the beginning of the second millennium B.C., Thera was a small, almost circular island, about 16 kilometers (10 miles) from north to south. It lay on the southern edge of the Cyclades, about 100 kilometers (60 miles) north of Crete. There can be little wonder that it attracted the attention of the Minoans, for it was the closest of all the islands of the Cyclades and it appears to have supported a farming economy based on the growing of barley and grapes, and possibly lentils and peas too. As a base from which to exploit the seafood of the southern Aegean it was clearly excellent.

At least three settlements grew up on the island, and no doubt there were others. All three towns or villages were using pottery of Minoan type, and it is possible that in all three there were some settlers from Crete. Only at Akrotiri, however, on the south side of the island can we be virtually certain that this was so. Here an extensive town was built with narrow cobbled streets which zigzagged between blocks of houses and occasionally opened out into small court-

Although many Minoan vases were found in the ruins of Akrotiri, the Cycladic traditions persisted too, as is evidenced by a selection of jugs which are typical products of the Cyclades both in shape and decoration *(above and right above)*. Swallows, seen on a small jug above right, appear to have been particular favorites of the Theran artists.

yards or places. The blocks of houses were very irregular in outline and so too were the individual houses which made them up. There were small magazines or stores, halls with rows or piers in either one or two of their walls, an occasional "pillar crypt," many small box-rooms, and stairwells where flights of stairs led to more spacious first-floor rooms. The houses were, in fact, remarkably similar in design and layout to houses at Minoan towns such as Palaikastro and Knossos.

Even more strikingly reminiscent of Minoan houses was the interior decoration which consisted of superb frescoes, preserved in much better condition than those at Knossos and elsewhere in Crete. Some of the wall paintings had identical themes to those seen in Crete. On one wall, one house owner had decided to have a picture of African apes picking flowers in a rocky landscape, recalling the monkey picking crocuses at Knossos. In a nearby house, three walls of a room were decorated with a brightly colored landscape dominated by up-standing rocks. Flowers were in bloom, swallows flitted through the air, and the whole scene has the unmistakable air of spring about it. Again, the landscape scene has close parallels with frescoes found at Knossos.

Other wall paintings, however, portray themes new to Minoan frescoes, though they are in the Minoan style and find parallels, for example, in some of the contemporary scenes on Minoan sealstones. The house with the ape fresco had another room in which one wall carried a picture of two antelope, full of grace and beauty but conveying an impression of great strength. On the other side of the door into this room were two boxers, but these were not the helmeted pugilists we see on the Boxer Vase from Ayia Triadha, but two young lads with but a single glove each. Of all the Thera

frescoes, however, the most unusual and interesting is a remarkable frieze only 0.4 meters (16 inches) high but 7 meters (24 feet) long. This single scene shows landscapes with plants and deer, Minoan towns and perhaps villas or small palaces, shrines, and ports, and a seascape with schools of dolphins and a quite staggering variety of Minoan shipping. Several of the boats shown appear to be of a ceremonial nature, with up to about forty oarsmen propelling them, and important personages seated on a raised deck, protected from the sun by awnings. But other vessels range from two-man fishing boats, through ships which may have been used mainly to carry

Many of the houses at Akrotiri had well-preserved frescoes, one of the most notable being the frieze of antelope above, from a wall in House Beta. In another house, a fresco found in a room perhaps serving as a household shrine is interesting for the light it throws on female fashions in Minoan Crete *(left)*. Apart from the flounced dress and short-sleeved, tight-fitting blouse, note also this woman's golden earrings and rouged cheeks.

Right: The destructive effects of the earthquakes and eruption of the Thera volcano are demonstrated graphically by this fine masonry staircase which has been cracked from top to bottom, and subsequently covered by a massive deposit of debris and ash.

This view of an excavated house at Thera *(below)* shows both the preservation of the buildings to the upper story and the small, low doors and windows which characterize the houses in the Akrotiri settlement.

troops, to cargo ships propelled by sail with the goods stored on deck. This one fresco has revolutionized our knowledge of Minoan shipping by revealing how isolated islands such as Thera maintained contacts with both Crete and other parts of the Aegean.

Apart from architecture and frescoes the settlement at Akrotiri on Thera also betrays its close links with Crete by the various artifacts that are found inside its houses. Although Minoan stone vases and bronze daggers and swords are occasionally found there, by far the most numerous imported objects are clay vases. Bowls, jugs, cups, and a wide variety of storage jars and pithoi of Minoan type appear in the houses, some of them local copies but others undoubtedly brought from Crete itself. Pottery of Cycladic style, particularly that in use on the island of Melos at this time, was also used. Most significant of all, Minoan lead weights, and objects inscribed with linear A signs, suggest Minoan domination of commerce on Thera.

It is the pottery which allows us to date the frescoes, and indeed the whole settlement at Akrotiri, to the years around 1550–1500 B.C. Nothing of later date comes from any of the houses, and it is clear that nothing later will ever be found there. The reason for our certainty on this point is that the occupation levels of this period are immediately overlain by huge deposits of volcanic ash and debris. It is clear that life in Minoan Akrotiri came abruptly to an end shortly after 1500 B.C. as the result of a massive volcanic eruption. There had probably been some warning of the forthcoming catastrophe, in the form of earth tremors and perhaps some activity from the mouth of the volcano; in any event most Therans managed to escape, on present evidence, before the whole volcano erupted and blew up. The settlements around the fringe of the island were covered in great depths of ash, while those at its center were either blown apart or sank into the great 200-meter-deep hollow formed at the center of the island, into which the sea now rushed.

The size and ferocity of the Thera eruption appears to have been at least on a par with that of Krakatoa, between Java and Sumatra in A.D. 1883. In the latter case full historical records document the terrible effects of the tidal waves which were triggered by the explosion. It is difficult to avoid the conclusion that similar waves must have pounded the coasts of the surrounding islands, and building up as they traveled southward, must have had a major impact on the north coast of Crete. Possible evidence for such a destructive wave or waves was found in the Minoan port at Amnisos where heavy building blocks had been forced out of position. The other threat to Crete was from the fallout of volcanic ash and debris. From deposits found on the bed of the Mediterranean we know that the ash was carried south and southeastward, dropping on the eastern half of Crete, and into the sea up to 500 kilometers (300 miles) from Thera. If a large quantity dropped on eastern Crete, the immediate effects on crops and the fertility of the land would have been extremely serious.

Whether or not this happened we cannot say, but within half a century Minoan civilization had come to an end. Many of its settlements had been abandoned and many

*For Minos, the oldest bearer
of the traditional name,
acquired a fleet and dominated most
of what is now the Greek sea.
He ruled over the Cyclades
and was the first to plant colonies
in most of them.*

Thucydides 1, 4

apparently destroyed. Along the north coast, harbor towns such as Amnisos, Mochlos, and Gournia were all destroyed, and so too was the palatial town of Mallia. At Gournia evidence of fire destruction was vivid and the excavator was convinced that it was "attacked, pillaged, and burned by an enemy." Elsewhere the palaces of Phaistos and Zakro suffered destruction, and the same fate befell rural villas like Sklavo-kampos. Knossos appears to have fallen into the hands of people from the mainland, and the palace to have been but a shadow of its former self. It is difficult to believe that the volcano of Thera was not, directly or indirectly, the cause of its downfall.

The Minoan port at Amnisos *(above)* may well have been hit by tidal waves speeding across the Aegean from Thera at the time of its great eruption ca. 1500 B.C., although it was partially protected by an offshore island. Sea level changes since then have partially submerged Minoan buildings on the shore.

61

HEROES AND MEN

The round face, with all its flesh,
    had been wonderfully preserved
        under its ponderous gold mask;
there was no vestige of hair, but both eyes
    were perfectly visible,
also the mouth...which showed
        thirty-two beautiful teeth....
I have gazed on the face
        of Agamemnon.

Heinrich Schliemann

Schliemann was convinced that the no-
ble, bearded face seen on this gold death
mask from a burial within the citadel of
Mycenae was no other than that of
Agamemnon, leader of the Greeks at
Troy. Actual size. Sixteenth century B.C.

Until Heinrich Schliemann's excavations at Mycenae and Tiryns between 1876 and 1884, the Bronze Age civilization of the Greek mainland had been known only from the heroic tales of Homer—the *Iliad* and the *Odyssey*. It is barely surprising, therefore, that Schliemann should identify Agamemnon among the bodies buried at Mycenae. In fact, this and the other burials dug by Schliemann belonged not to the time of Agamemnon and the end of the Mycenaean era, but rather to the beginning of it, in the seventeenth century B.C. The age which they ushered in on the Greek mainland was one of warfare and heroic prowess, in which powerful chieftains ruled small kingdoms from highly fortified citadels.

When the civilization of Minoan Crete faltered during the fifteenth century B.C., the Greeks of the mainland (the "Mycenaeans" as we loosely label them) were able to expand their influence and their commerce, first into the Aegean and then into both the east and west Mediterranean. Crete itself fell under Mycenaean influence.

Between about 1400 and 1200 B.C., Mycenaean Greece was in its heyday. At home the agricultural prosperity of the countryside provided the basis on which the citadels and their bureaucracies were able to exist. From the seat of government, in turn, came the organization which ensured both security and the steady flow of raw materials needed by the rural craftsmen. Abroad, Mycenaean traders sought scarce commodities, and carried Greek textiles, oil, and painted vases to Cyprus, Palestine, Sicily, and southern Italy.

The reason for the sudden collapse of this "golden age" is still unknown, but Greek legends such as that of the Trojan War and its aftermath suggest that rivalries between the Mycenaean kingdoms may have contributed to their downfall.

63

THE FIRST GREEKS

*Just before 1600 B.C.
a few well-organized groups
of professional warriors
invaded Greece.
They possessed a new weapon
which had a tremendous effect
upon the simple agricultural people of Greece:
the chariot and the horse.*

Professor S. Marinatos

The idea that the Greeks swept southward into Greece from a "homeland" somewhere to the north of the Black Sea is no longer accepted; nor is the equation between the appearance of the gray polished Minyan pottery *(left)* and that of the Greeks. Yet movements of peoples from northern and western Greece into Attica and the Argolid may help to explain the emergence of Mycenaean Greece.

One of the earliest portraits we have of a "Greek" is this superb carving, on a small amethyst bead, of a handsome, bearded man who may well have been a chieftain or prince of seventeenth-century Mycenae. He bears more than a passing resemblance to the gold death mask identified (wrongly) by Schliemann as that of Agamemnon, found in grave circle A at Mycenae. This portrait, from grave circle B and dating a century earlier than the gold mask, might lend some support to the speculation that the two circles enclose the remains of successive and related dynasties.

Greek tradition and legend stated quite clearly that the Greeks were not indigenous to Greece but had arrived there as immigrants. The principal dialects of the Greek language—Ionian, Arcadian, and Dorian—appeared to support tradition and have allowed classical scholars to think in terms of successive waves of Greek-speaking invaders establishing themselves in the country over a period of perhaps a thousand years between about 2000 and 1000 B.C.

Similarly, some of the earliest Greek heroes, belonging to the era long before the Trojan War, were accorded explicitly foreign origins in Greek legend. Danaus, for example, whose line of descent led directly to Perseus, the founder of Mycenae itself, came to Greece from Egypt, though legend had it that he was not himself an Egyptian. Cadmus, who founded the Mycenaean city of Thebes, is said to have come from Syria, and Pelops, who founded the dynasty to which Agamemnon belonged, emigrated to Greece from Asia Minor.

As the varied origins of these three heroes alone suggests, Greek tradition concerning Greek origins was confused and sometimes contradictory, but the Greeks nevertheless remained convinced that their ancestors had

		Period of slow development of mainland Greece	(until about 1800 B.C.)	Rise of Mycenaean chiefdom	
2200	2100	2000	1900	1800	1
Widespread destructions in southern Greece	Palace of Knossos built			Destruction of Minoan palaces in earthquake	

THESSALY

Ithaca

Orchomenos
Gla
Thebes
BOEOT

ACHAEA

ARGOLID
Mycenae
Tiryns

MESSENIA

Sparta
Pylos

LACONIA

KINGS AND HEROES OF LEGEND

The memory of the heroes of the Greek Bronze Age was kept alive by the epic poems of Homer, by Greek legend, and by the vase painters of classical Greece who portrayed their exploits in great detail on hundreds of fine vases. In the five illustrations below, we see *(from left to right):* Theseus, Menelaos, Cadmus, Odysseus, and Agamemnon. Two of these legendary figures, Theseus and Cadmus, belong to the first age of heroes, before the Trojan War. Theseus was the Athenian hero who freed the city from its subservience to Crete, and Cadmus the founder of the Boeotian city of Thebes. Menelaos, Odysseus, and Agamemnon, on the other hand, were heroes of the Trojan War and were respectively the kings of Sparta, Ithaca, and Mycenae. Below these heroes we see to the left Heracles and Nestor. Heracles wears the skin of the

Nemean Lion which he slew with his bare hands while performing his famous twelve labors for the king of Argos. Nestor is shown as an old man, for he spanned the two heroic ages, and by the time of the Trojan War was the elder statesman in the Greek camp.

The cities founded or ruled by all of the heroes seen above are shown on this map, as well as other major Mycenaean cities. The lower arrow is symbolic of the strong Minoan influences to be seen in the Argolid in the formative years of Mycenaean civilization.

The changing fortunes of Minoans and Mycenaeans are symbolized by the throne room at Knossos *(below).* The cultural and economic dominance of Crete in the earlier part of the second millennium B.C. had been replaced by the end of the end of the

fifteenth century by the military domination of the Mycenaean Greeks. It is likely that a Mycenaean rather than a Minoan sat on this famous throne.

	Envoys to Egypt	Mycenaeans expand into Aegean	Mycenaean trade expansion to east and west Mediterranean	Breakdown of Mycenaean civilization
00	1500	1400	1300	1200
	Thera explodes Destructions in Crete Fall of Knossos		Trojan War	

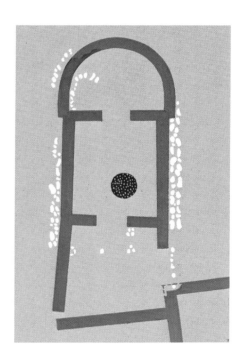

The apsidal house from Eutresis is typical of many houses on the Greek mainland, around 2000 B.C., with its porch, principal living room with central hearth, and apsidal annex. It is a type of building probably introduced to southern Greece from the north, and ultimately perhaps from southeast Europe, where it occurs more than a thousand years earlier. The basic form is elaborated later and forms the basis of the design of Mycenaean palaces at Pylos, Tiryns, and Mycenae.

come to Greece from elsewhere. But if that is so, where did they come from, and when did they arrive in Greece?

We have only one direct clue to help us solve the problem, and that is the language itself. It is of course the use of a common language which allows us to speak of "the Greeks" at all, and the evidence for the first appearance of Greek is therefore of prime importance to the question of Greek origins. Most experts are now agreed that the language of the Linear B tablets found on Mycenaean sites is an early form of Greek. That being so, we can fix the arrival of the Greek-speaking peoples in Greece no later than the beginning of the fourteenth century B.C.—the date of the earliest tablets in Linear B yet found. How much earlier than 1400 B.C. we place their arrival depends entirely on the interpretation of archaeological evidence.

In looking for successful invaders of Greece in the period before 1400, our attention is inevitably drawn to the Mycenaeans themselves. They seem to appear abruptly at Mycenae in the middle of the seventeenth century B.C. and clearly establish themselves as warrior-chieftains capable of amassing great wealth and ruling the rest of the population by force. Their material belongings differ markedly in some respects—such as the use of horse and chariot—from that of the existing population, and their funerary customs are also distinctive. The chieftains and their families are buried in deep shafts marked by gravestones and covered by a low mound. Most important of all, the Mycenaeans are the people who use the Linear B script, and therefore, presumably, speak Greek.

It is now widely accepted that the Mycenaeans were indeed Greeks, but it is not so widely agreed that they were the *first* Greeks. A careful study of the shaft graves at Mycenae reveals a gradual growth in wealth and opulence from relatively moderate beginnings, suggestive of the gradual rise to power and prosperity of a local dynasty, rather than the sudden imposition of one by victorious invaders. Similarly, the custom of burying the bodies of a ruling elite in shaft graves within a circular enclosure and beneath a low mound, can be traced back in central and western Greece, first to the century immediately before the construction of the Mycenae shaft graves, and ultimately to the middle of the third millennium B.C. At the same time, a more sober look at the

contents of the shaft graves reveals that they are overwhelmingly Aegean rather than foreign in character. In particular there are abundant signs of Minoan and Cycladic influence and trade among the more luxurious objects, while the more commonplace grave goods such as plain pottery are of local ancestry.

But if the Mycenaeans are not the first Greeks, then how much farther back into prehistory must we push their arrival? The most favored period is the century around 2200 B.C. At this time, prosperous settlements in southern Greece such as Lerna, Ayios Kosmas, and Zygouries were all destroyed by fire, and where occupation was resumed after the destruction, there are clear signs of change. Two of the most notable are the appearance of polished gray pottery made on the fast wheel and of long, narrow houses with a porch at one end and an apse at the other. There has been much argument about the origins of the gray pottery, called Minyan Ware, and whether or not it represents the arrival of invaders (sometimes labeled as "Minyans") from Turkey or possibly farther north. Similarly the apsidal houses may have ancestors in southeast Europe which are more than a millennium older than those found built over the burnt ruins of Lerna around 2200 B.C.

Such evidence would fit broadly with the idea that the Greek language, along with its close relatives in the so-called Indo-European languages, had its home somewhere north of the Black Sea.

There remains an alternative solution to the problem, however. Apsidal houses are found in northern Greece as early as the fourth millennium B.C., and some archaeologists believe that "Minyan" pottery was developed within Greece itself. If this is so it is difficult to find evidence for any invaders of Greece since the first farmers of about 6000 B.C. The Greeks, to all intents and purposes, become indigenous. But this does not explain either Greek tradition or the formation of the Greek language. On present evidence these are best accounted for by recognizing the arrival in southern Greece ca. 2200 B.C. of migrants from farther north who already spoke an Indo-European language.

Contacts with Crete, and influences from it, are clearly seen in the finds from the shaft graves of Mycenae. Alongside locally produced plain and rather ugly clay vases are found Minoan stone vessels carved from colorful Cretan stones and rock crystal. Personal belongings include Minoan bronze razors and single-edged knives as well as superbly made gold diadems, necklaces, and signet rings closely inspired by Minoan prototypes. Many of the scenes on the signet rings show armed combat in which warriors use long, straightedged swords like those actually found in the shaft graves and based on Cretan weapons first produced about 1800 B.C. Other goldwork includes the temple façades like that illustrated above, which with their combination of sacral horns, sacred columns, and holy birds, are entirely Minoan in inspiration. Whether or not the appearance in shaft grave IV of circle A of an imported Minoan bull's head rhyton (libation vessel) implies the veneration of the bull here as in Crete is uncertain, but it does symbolize in dramatic fashion the cultural dominance of Crete at this time.

THE MYCENAEAN DYNASTIES

Many of the stories in Greek myth and legend which tell of the exploits of the early heroes appear to contain distant memories of warfare between the emerging city-states of Mycenaean Greece, and of dynastic struggles within the kingdoms. For the most part the stories are confused and confusing, but it is sometimes possible to piece together the dynastic history of a Mycenaean kingdom.

In particular this is true of Mycenae itself, for apart from the Greek tradition that it was founded by Perseus, a passage in the *Iliad* refers thus to successive kings of Mycenae: "King Agamemnon arose with the scepter in his hand...and Hermes gave it to Pelops the charioteer, and Pelops again to Atreus, shepherd of men, and Atreus next to Thyestes, wealthy in flocks, left it, and he to

King Agamemnon in turn." Since Aegisthus slew Agamemnon on his return from Troy and usurped his throne, we have here the names—mythical or legendary as they may be—of five successive kings of Mycenae.

Heinrich Schliemann, when he began excavating at Mycenae in the summer of 1876, had Homer committed to memory, and when he found a royal necropolis within the walls of the citadel, it was natural that he should immediately relate it to the Pelopids—the dynasty founded by Pelops. More specifically, Schliemann recalled the words of Pausanias, who said that the graves of Agamemnon and those who fell with him were buried within the walls of Mycenae, alongside the grave of Atreus. Altogether Pausanias mentioned five graves.

Grave circle A, as we now call it, produced a series of burials of quite outstanding wealth, which to judge from the jewelry and the fine weaponry buried with them, were certainly those of heroes and their families. Schliemann discovered just five graves within the circle, and their number, together with the wealth of gold in them, convinced him that he had found the graves of Agamemnon and his family.

Although we now know that the graves in circle A were more than four centuries earlier than the Trojan War, in one respect Schliemann was surely correct. These graves were those of a Mycenaean dynasty—and the six tombs (the sixth was found after

Schliemann had left Mycenae) held nearly twenty bodies. The five gold funerary masks found in two of the graves even provide us with a portrait gallery of these early rulers of Mycenae.

Whether or not this dynasty is the same as that subsequently revealed eighty years later with the discovery of a second grave circle (B) is uncertain, but an electrum mask found in circle B bears a close resemblance to three of those in circle A, and so too does the face seen carved on a small bead from the new grave circle. The burials in grave circle B belong to a slightly earlier period than those of A, so that with circle B we appear to be back at the very beginnings of the royal house of Mycenae. As befits a kingly line, examination of the skeletons from both circles has suggested that the male members of the family were strongly built and, for their time, relatively tall (almost six feet).

The burial places of the later kings of Mycenae are clearly to be recognized in the superb vaulted tholos tombs built outside the citadel dating to the fourteenth and thirteenth centuries B.C. Altogether there are nine such tombs known to us, and although they had all been looted long ago, the size and quality of their construction plainly show them to be the burial places of princes and kings. If Pelops, Atreus, and Thyestes were indeed more than legendary figures, then it is among these great monuments that we should look for their last resting places.

The two masks above are in marked contrast to the others from the grave circles. The faces are much rounder, the eyes are open and staring, and the noses are short and broad.

The only mask found in grave circle B was one of electrum (an alloy of gold and silver), seen above, far left. Although it may be fifty years earlier than that of "Agamemnon," it shows a close resemblance to it which lends support to the notion that the two grave circles are the burial places of successive and related lines of kings.

The side view of the mask of "Agamemnon" from shaft grave V *(center)* shows, better than the usual frontal view, the strong, noble features of the man on whose face it had been laid. The fine, straight nose, the tight, thin lips, the neatly trimmed moustache, and the marked cheekbones suggest we are looking here at a true portrait of a Mycenaean king.

Opposite page: The two gold masks at far left found in grave circle A show strong facial resemblances to each other and to that of the superb mask at left above, which Schliemann thought was that of Agamemnon.

Something of Mycenae's dominating position can be judged from the fine view of the acropolis *(left)*, which shows part of the Argive plain beyond, ringed in the rear by high mountains. Although the immediate environs of Mycenae are rocky and of little use for agriculture, from its position at the rear of the Argive plain the citadel could dominate not only the plain itself, but also the passes behind it which lead through the mountains to the rich and fertile lands around Corinth. Whether or not Mycenae's strategic position originally determined its foundation and

rapid rise to wealth and power is uncertain, but in the *Iliad,* the kingdom of Agamemnon is clearly described as including land not only in the Argive plain but along the southern shore of the Gulf of Corinth as well: "And they that Mycenae's well-built citadel held, rich Corinth and fair Cleonae's bastioned wall, and they of Orneae and lovely Araethyrea and Sicyon, where once Adrastus ruled as a king, and Hyperesia's ridge and steep Gonoessa, and they that round Pellene and Aegion dwelt and all the coastland country and Helice's plain—all these did Atrides, Agamemnon, command in a hundred ships."

HEROIC BURIALS

Grave circle A, found within the walls of Mycenae by Schliemann, was marked out by a broad circular wall faced inside and out with upright stone slabs. Within the enclosure were six deep shaft graves in which a total of eighteen or nineteen bodies had been buried. The bodies were those of both men and women.

The position of the individual shafts had been marked by sculptured gravestones, which unfortunately carried no inscription to record the names of those buried below. Apart from a highly attractive frieze of running spirals, however, several gravestones carried pictures of warriors riding in horse-drawn chariots—the first appearance of the chariot in Greece and indeed anywhere in Europe.

Beneath such gravestones one might expect to find the graves of warriors, and this expectation was fully realized when Schliemann eventually reached the bottom of the shafts. Tall, strongly built men had been buried there together with superb straight-edged swords up to a meter in length, and beautifully decorated daggers which often carried scenes of hunting, combat, or chariotry.

In some graves, however, the bodies of ladies were found, richly bedecked with gold diadems, necklaces, and dress ornaments. Around all the bodies lay a mass of other grave goods representing a formidable display of wealth. Gold and silver drinking vessels were plentiful—shaft grave IV alone had eleven of gold and five of silver—suggesting princely banquets and free-flowing wine. Further vessels were made of bronze, colorful stones, faience, and pottery. Objects made of exotic materials such as amber, ivory, ostrich eggshell, and faience point to the far-flung trade connections of the early kings of Mycenae. In addition gold, silver, and obsidian were obtained within the Aegean, and tin and copper to alloy for bronze were brought perhaps from the west and the east Mediterranean.

The manner in which the rulers of Mycenae came to accumulate such wealth in so short a time remains a mystery. Warfare, piracy, and the control of essential trade routes are all possible explanations, but it may be that Mycenae managed to seize and exploit all of the rich agricultural lands between the Gulf of Corinth and the Gulf of Argos.

The grave circle A as it is seen today *(center)* has lost much of its original grandeur. Some idea of its original appearance may be gained from the reconstruction of it below, where the orthostat-faced enclosure wall is completed by covering slabs, the monumental entrance is in place, and the gravestones have been restored to their original positions. The faced enclosure wall was built some three centuries after the graves had been dug, at the same time as the citadel defenses which can be seen to curve around the cemetery area.

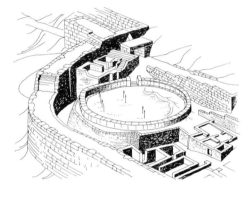

The mass of goldwork in the shaft graves of circle A seemed to Schliemann fully to justify Homer's epithet for the city—"rich in gold." Apart from sheet goldwork with superb repoussé decoration of running spirals like that below, gold and silver drinking cups *(right)* of wide variety and fine workmanship were plentiful. The second cup from the left, with a bird on the top of each handle, is often known as "Nestor's cup" because of its similarity to that described by Homer as belonging to the King of Pylos.

72

The level of craftsmanship displayed in the goldwork of grave circle A is remarkable. Libation vessels like that above in the form of a lion's head have been embossed from a single sheet of gold by a master craftsman, probably of Minoan origin.

Although the longswords are the most fearsome weapons in the shaft graves, the short daggers are the most eye-catching. Set into the blades of these weapons are delicately inlaid designs *(above left)* which are sometimes intricate patterns but more often miniature scenes. Scenes of combat and of fowling and lion hunting all conjure up the impression of a heroic society where prowess in the chase and in warfare was important to a man's prestige. The daggers themselves, with but a solitary rivet to hold them firm in their haft, were probably status symbols rather than effective weapons.

AGAMEMNON'S MYCENAE

Although the burials in the shaft graves at Mycenae proved to belong to an earlier era than Agamemnon, most of the buildings and defenses excavated by Schliemann and later searchers did indeed belong to the century leading up to the Trojan War—that is, to the thirteenth century B.C. Agamemnon's Mycenae consisted of a highly fortified citadel of about fifteen acres, within which were crammed a mass of buildings. The defenses of Mycenae were built of the so-called Cyclopean masonry—great blocks of rough-hewn stone, crudely dressed only on the facing surface. They enclosed a natural acropolis and were strengthened by bastions and towers, particularly at the two principal gates, both of which had deeply inset entrances.

Inside the main ceremonial gateway, the Lion Gate, a paved and stepped roadway led past grave circle A and up the hill through crowded buildings on either side, to the palace in the center of the citadel. The focus

The majesty and power of Agamemnon's Mycenae is symbolized by the finely sculptured lions which surmount the monumental west gate of the citadel and recall the *Iliad* (Book 10) where Agamemnon dons "the tawny hide of a fiery lion."

Center: An aerial view of Mycenae reveals how the walls enclose a natural hill, with an additional detour to include grave circle A within their circuit. Immediately above the grave circle can be seen the principal roadway and staircase which leads up the hillside to the palace. The palace (now partially restored) utilizes the slope of the hill to give its occupants a fine view to the south and east from their terrace on which stands the main reception hall and its forecourt. The mass of other buildings crowded within the citadel are clearly visible, and these appear to represent the homes of nobles and retainers, store places, workshops, and shrines.

of the palace was the great reception hall, fronted by an antechamber and porch and approached through an open courtyard. In the center of the hall was a great circular ceremonial hearth, flanked by four columns set square which supported the roof. To one side, set against one of the frescoed walls, would have been the throne on which Agamemnon and his predecessors sat. From the palace, the king of Mycenae could look out across the flat roofs of the houses both within and without the citadel, to the Argive plain beyond.

Mycenae's water supply in time of siege was ensured by a secret, underground passageway that led down to a spring beyond the walls *(below)*. The walls and corbeled roof were originally covered with plaster. The dark depths of the water tunnel and the Cyclopean masonry of its walls contrast markedly with the sunny position enjoyed by the megaron of the palace, and with the much finer construction of its walls *(center below)*. In the foreground can be seen the bases for the four columns which supported the roof of the hall, and to the rear are the antechamber and courtyard beyond.

A broad paved roadway and ramp, linked by a flight of stairs, ran from immediately inside the Lion Gate past the venerated burial place of the ancestral kings (grave circle A) toward the palace near the summit of the hill.

THE KINGDOM OF NESTOR

And the knight, Gerenian Nestor going before, to his goodly dwelling his sons and son-in-laws led. And, when to the splendid hall of the prince they were come, there sat they them down in order on benches and chairs; and straightway the old man, Nestor, mixed them a bowl of honey-sweet wine, a vintage mellowed in

According to Greek legend, Nestor was the only surviving son of King Neleus, who was slain along with his eleven other sons by Heracles. Neleus had established his capital at Pylos in Messenia, and it was to this Pylian kingdom that Nestor succeeded.

Excavations have revealed that there was a settlement at Pylos long before the first palace complex was built there in the years around 1300 B.C. At that time the existing settlement was partially cleared and the ground leveled in order to prepare a suitable terrace for the new palace. In terms of the legendary history of this Pylos, this activity and the first palace building should be the work of Neleus.

By the mid-thirteenth century the somewhat cramped and ill-planned building of the palace of Neleus had been relegated to a minor role by the construction of an impres-

store eleven full years when the house dame opened the seal.... Nestor, leading his guest, the son of godlike Odysseus, lodged him within, and a jointed bed in the echoing portico set.

Homer, Odyssey, Book 3

Here Nestor, by now an old man, received Telemachus, the son of Odysseus *(picture above)*. He was led to the palace at Pylos, accommodated for the night, and then provided with a chariot and one of Nestor's sons as an escort for his onward journey.

The clay bathtub *(right)* still in place at Pylos recalls Telemachus' bathing, performed by Polykaste, the eldest daughter of Nestor.

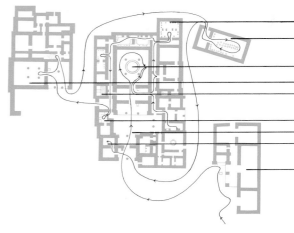

sive and well-designed palace just to the east. This is the palace of Nestor.

Nestor's palace was entered through a columned porch on its south side, to one side of which was a small guardroom, and to the other the office and archives where clay tablets carrying accounts were stored. Beyond the porch lay a small courtyard which fronted a second, more impressive porch with two columns, overlooked by a balcony. This was the entrance to the main hall and throne room, which was approached through an anteroom. The throne room was a splendid sight. Its walls were brightly painted with scenes showing wild animals, and both floor and ceiling were also richly decorated with painted patterns. At the center of the hall was the great circular hearth, about five meters in diameter,

flanked by the four columns, set square, which supported the balcony overlooking the throne room.

To the right of the hearth, against the east wall of the hall, stood the throne itself, flanked by protective griffins like those seen in the throne room at Knossos.

Olive oil stores

Wine store

Throne room

Banqueting hall (or old palace)

Stairs to upper story

Waiting room

Courtyard

Archives room

Armory

The line retraces Telemachus' path through the palace as narrated in the *Odyssey*.

The ceremonial heart of the palace—the porch, courtyard, antechamber, and throne room—were surrounded on three sides of the ground floor by suites of rooms for a variety of functions. The southeast corner of the palace was occupied by domestic quarters including a bathroom. To the east

of the throne room and antechamber was a group of stores and a staircase to the upper floor on this side of the palace. At the northeast corner of the building, and immediately to the north of the throne room, were three rooms filled with oil jars, some standing on the floor, others set into benches around the walls. Clay tablets found in these rooms refer to olive oil by name.

The north end of the west wing was occupied by storerooms or pantries in which were stored thousands of bowls and drinking cups, no doubt conveniently situated to be carried in, as required, to either the throne room or to the banqueting hall of the old palace building.

The rest of the west wing contained the archives and office, a waiting room for visitors, and another staircase to the upper story. The details of the upper floor of the palace are little known, but it was almost certainly here that the main bedrooms were located, and finds of toilet implements and ivory-backed mirrors (fallen from this floor when the palace was destroyed) support this view. Further accommodation, possibly for visitors and guests, may have been found on the upper floor of the old palace block, where the original throne room now served perhaps as a banqueting hall, and where the original palace kitchens and food stores still functioned.

East of the new palace building were two more buildings, the northern of which was the main wine store, with rows of large terracotta jars, each with a clay label identifying the contents. The second building, to the south, was larger, and to judge from tablets found within it referring to hides, harness, and reins, may have been the armory and chariot workshop.

Whether or not Nestor relied on the strength of his infantry and chariotry to defend both his palace and his kingdom is uncertain, but certainly neither the palace complex, nor the town which lay around it, was defended by built defenses such as can be seen so massively constructed at Mycenae, Athens, Tiryns, and Gla. It may be that Nestor felt secure in the heart of his kingdom, shut off by mountains from the rest of southern Greece, except by sea. In the *Iliad* Nestor is accorded ninety ships, almost as many as Agamemnon, "Lord of Men," and the Pylian navy was undoubtedly of great importance to the security of Nestor's kingdom and to that of Pylos itself.

Left: Wealthy chieftains may have established themselves in the vicinity of Pylos as early as about 1600 B.C. The tholos tomb at Koryphasion at the north end of the Bay of Navarino is one of the earliest on the Greek mainland and may reflect contacts between Crete and Messenia which would have been facilitated by the Minoan colony on Kythera.

This large clay storage jar *(below),* or *pithos,* found in the palace of Pylos, was used to hold oil. The lid served further to protect and insulate the contents.

In the pantries of the palace of Pylos more than six thousand plain clay goblets, bowls, and jugs were stored on shelves, ready for use in the frequent feasting and drinking.

> *When tender Dawn had brushed the sky...*
> *Gerenian Nestor got up from his bed, went*
> *out, and seated himself on a smooth bench*
> *of white marble, which stood, gleaming*
> *with polish, in front of his lofty doors.*
>
> Homer, *Odyssey, Book 3*

Pylos lay less than ten kilometers (six miles) from Navarino Bay, where a large force of ships could find anchorage. Almost certainly Nestor's navy was concentrated here, at the bay's northern end.

To the north and the east the kingdom's defenses were formed by the Tetrazi mountains and by the Taighetos ridge, rising to 2,400 meters (7,800 feet). From the archives found at Pylos we can draw a rough map of Nestor's kingdom and see that it was divided into two provinces. It stretched from Cape Akritas in the south, to the valley

Visitors to Nestor's palace were no doubt suitably impressed by the colorful and monumental porch and portico through which the throne room was approached *(below)*. In this reconstruction, the entrance to the antechamber, and beyond it the main hall, is through the double doors to the left. The throne room itself *(center)* was a blaze of color, the focal points of which were the ceremonial hearth and the throne of the king flanked by painted griffins.

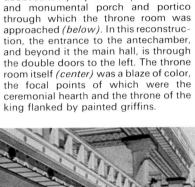

Behind the throne room were two small rooms in which oil jars were set into a low bench *(right)*. Olive oil and perfumed oil were two of the kingdom's important products, referred to on tablets found in the palace.

of the River Nedha in the north—a distance of about 70 kilometers (45 miles). At its broadest it was about 55 kilometers (38 miles) east to west. But the location of its chief towns such as *Piswa* and *Metapa* elude us, although Pylos can be recognized as *Puro*.

Scrolls and rosettes, as seen above, were typical decorative motives of Mycenaean palace ceilings. This detail comes from a limestone burial chamber at Orchomenos, dated about 1300 B.C.

The wall paintings at Pylos, in addition to abstract patterned designs, depicted animals and human beings. Here we see a gracefully shaped griffon and lion in a modern artist's watercolor copy of a fresco from the Queen's Hall.

The floor of the throne room (below) was brightly painted, perhaps in imitation of the fine paving seen in Minoan palaces at Knossos and Phaistos, while the rim of the great hearth carried a frieze of running spirals.

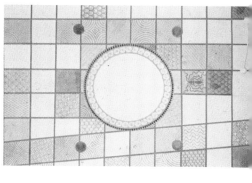

MYCENAEAN BUREAUCRATS: LINEAR B

Tablets written in the script known as Linear B were found by Sir Arthur Evans at Knossos in Crete within a week of his excavations beginning in March 1900. The discovery of earlier writing systems at Knossos, and elsewhere in Crete, allowed Evans to identify three phases in the development of writing in the Aegean, of which Linear B was the latest. At this time there was no reason to suppose that the script and the language written in it were not Minoan. Evans thought that Linear B was perhaps a "royal" script which was used exclusively at Knossos.

Evans' good fortune at Knossos in 1900 was

During the last few weeks, I have come to the conclusion that the Knossos and Pylos tablets must, after all, be written in Greek—a difficult and archaic Greek, seeing that it is five hundred years older than Homer and written in a rather abbreviated form, but Greek nevertheless.... Although many of the tablets remain as incomprehensible as before, many others are suddenly beginning to make sense.

Michael Ventris announces the decipherment of Linear B, June 1952

The Linear B script used widely in Mycenaean Greece included syllabic signs, as well as ideograms such as the unmistakable symbol for an amphora *(above)*.

Tablets containing Linear B inscriptions were intended for short-term accounting and were not usually fired. Occasionally Linear B signs have been found painted in vases, as in the example from Knossos seen below.

surpassed by that of Carl Blegen at Pylos on 4 April 1939. On the very first day of his excavations he discovered the archive room of Nestor's palace, with its store of Linear B tablets. Subsequently Linear B tablets were found at Mycenae, Thebes, and Tiryns too, so that the script was clearly more widely employed in Mycenaean Greece than Minoan Crete. In fact, the tablets found at Knossos now appear to belong to a Mycenaean occupation of Minos' capital. The language in which the tablets were written remained unknown, however, and their decipherment unaccomplished. Many and varied were the solutions offered— some scholars believed the tablets were written in Greek, but others suggested Etruscan, Basque, Cypriot, or a Semitic language. Careful research by the Americans Kober and Bennett in the 1940s paved the way for Michael Ventris' brilliant decipherment which he announced in 1952—Linear B was written in an archaic form of Greek after all. Inevitably his decipherment was not universally accepted, but there are few today who do not accept the language of Linear B as Greek.

The Linear B script consists of about ninety signs, each of which represents a syllable, and an unknown number of other signs (in excess of 150) which represent things, or in some cases units of measurement (ideograms). These signs were incised onto clay tablets, sometimes shaped like the page of a book, but often more like a palmleaf. Linear B was also written on clay labels and painted onto the side of pottery vessels, and it is likely that it was written with pen and ink on papyrus or skin, although no documents of this sort have survived.

When the tablets were written they were immediately stored in baskets or boxes without being fired. For this reason the only tablets that have been found are those which have been accidentally fired, usually in the conflagrations that destroyed the palaces where the archives existed.

The boxes and baskets in which the completed tablets were stored were in fact files, in which a single group of tablets all dealing with the same matter were kept. The box or basket was usually sealed with a small clay label on which was written a word to indicate the subject matter of the contents. At Pylos, for example, a group of tablets concerned with body armor was labeled "corselets."

It appears from a study of the tablets that the "files" were emptied annually so that the archives were only kept on clay for about a year. Thereafter, the most important information may have been recorded on papyrus or skin, but most of it was simply destroyed. The Knossos archives, of about 3,000 tablets, and the 1,200 tablets from Pylos therefore represent a single year's records in each of these palaces.

From a careful examination of the writing on the tablets it is possible to recognize the hand of individual clerks. Then, as now, people formed their letters or signs in different ways, and left telltale signs of their identity. It is thought that the Knossos tablets were written by about seventy differ-

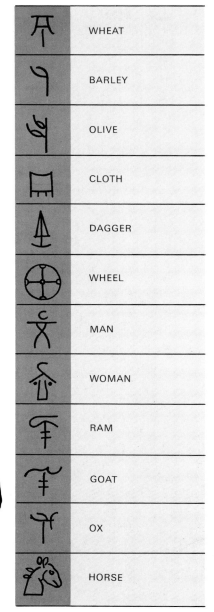

	WHEAT
	BARLEY
	OLIVE
	CLOTH
	DAGGER
	WHEEL
	MAN
	WOMAN
	RAM
	GOAT
	OX
	HORSE

different files or a large group of tablets can be ascribed to a single writer, then it is sometimes possible to see what the responsibilities of this particular official were. At Knossos one of the men was clearly involved in overseeing textile production, for his handwriting is found on tablets which deal with cloth, wool, and the women who worked these materials. One of the officials in Nestor's administration at Pylos was concerned solely with the manufacture, repair, and storage of chariot wheels, which perhaps says something for the size of the chariot forces under Nestor's command.

Basically, then, the Linear B tablets are concerned with bureaucracy and bookkeeping. Nowhere in the tablets do we find history, let alone literature or poetry, and the Linear B script was not designed for writing such things. In this respect the tablets are disappointing, and it is unlikely that new discoveries will change the situation. But from the bare facts and figures of the Mycenaean accounts of Pylos and Knos-

ent persons, and those at Pylos by forty different clerks.

The appearance of so many different hands among the Knossos and Pylos tablets almost certainly means that there were no full-time "scribes" at either palace. It is altogether more likely that the tablets were written by various officials whose responsibilities included recording the information which they collected during their work. How each official learned to write is unknown; the civilizations of the east Mediterranean certainly had schools in which future scribes were taught their craft, but there is no evidence at present to suggest the existence of schools in Mycenae, Pylos, or Thebes.

Where it has been possible to identify and collect together all the tablets from a single basket or file, they have usually been found to be written in a single hand. When several

sos it is possible to glean a great deal of information which archaeology alone could never supply. Many of the tablets deal with supplies of raw materials, with manufactured goods, and with the craftsmen who made them. Others are concerned with land tenure, farming, and agricultural production. From others we gain information about the organization of the state and its administration, while further tablets provide information about the army and its command structure. In addition, many of the tablets give precise details of the current contents of the king's armory.

Finally, we learn something about the deities of the Mycenaean pantheon. From no other source do we get such invaluable insights into the social, economic, and religious affairs of the Mycenaean kingdoms.

The ideograms of Linear B (words that represent a thing itself) are sometimes instantly recognizable (as, for example, dagger and horse, above) and sometimes conventionalized (as ram, goat, and ox). Some of the ideograms also have a syllabic value; the sign for ox, for example, also represents the sound "mu."

The two tablets here (above left) are the most common forms found.

THE COMING OF THE GODS

Nowhere is Minoan influence on Mycenaean civilization apparently more pervading than in Mycenaean religion. The archaeological evidence of monuments and artifacts is not as rich on the mainland as it is in Crete, but it nevertheless includes models of snakes and bulls, depictions of sacred trees and columns, and horns of consecration, which immediately recall the main elements of Minoan religion. Furthermore, the mass of figurines found on Mycenaean sites represent females, and accord with the predominance of female deities in Minoan Crete. There are reasons for supposing, however, that the Minoan influence on Mycenaean religion was superficial and more apparent than real. If we are correct in believing that the Minoans were not Greeks whereas the Mycenaeans were, then the widely differing geographical backgrounds and cultural traditions they experienced make it unlikely they would have shared a common religion. Furthermore, recently excavated Mycenaean shrines and their cult furniture at Mycenae, Tiryns, and Phylakopi all reveal marked differences to the nature and the furnishings of Minoan shrines.

Embossed metal plaques showing ladies with bared breasts and flounced dresses *(right, and below, second from left)* confirm a Minoan influence in Mycenaean religion, though this influence is only superficial in nature.

A wall painting from a shrine at Mycenae shows a goddess with an elaborate headdress holding a spray of wheat in each hand *(below)*. Such sprays are normally interpreted as evidence of a fertility cult.

addition it contained lamps, offering tables, and terracotta snakes. There were also several pots in which jewelry was stored, possibly to be worn during ceremonies either by a priestess or by an idol. The west shrine was notable not only for a goddess wearing a long robe and jewelry standing in the inner shrine, but for the frescoes found

The commonest votive figurines used in Mycenaean settlements were stylized figures of women painted with red stripes *(far right)*. Their significance is uncertain. They are sometimes interpreted as divine nurses (note that the nearer figure cradles a child), but they are more likely to represent the women on whose behalf they were offered.

Both the Mycenae and the Phylakopi shrines were double shrines, with an east and a west cult room, and one or two small storerooms attached. The east shrine at Mycenae contained tall, tubular idols which appear to represent both male and female deities. In

in the cult room showing two goddesses, one of whom is holding two sprays of wheat. This would suggest that the cult was involved with fertility rites.

At Phylakopi the small east shrine contained mainly bull figurines, but in the west shrine

The richly painted earthen figurine of a goddess or suppliant *(far left)* was discovered at Phylakopi in 1977. The smoothly molded forms (the arms are missing) are accentuated by the painting of the face and the elaborate clothing, in a style considered unusually ornate for the time (ca. 1200 B.C., end of the Mycenaean period).

Left: Horned god, possibly Apollo Keraiates, from a sanctuary at Enkomi, Cyprus; twelfth century B.C. The first settlers of Cyprus brought the cult of Apollo Keraiates with them from mainland Greece. From evidence in Mycenaean tablets we know that several of the classical Greek gods (Athena, Hera, Artemis, Poseidon, Zeus among them) were worshipped in this earlier period.

This ivory triad of figures, found along with several altars in a store at Mycenae, is commonly interpreted as a religious group. The bared breasts and flounced dress of the figure on the right certainly recall the dress of the Minoan Snake Goddess.

83

were found a group of five male figurines, all associated with an altar in the northwest corner of the room. From the small storeroom behind came four more large bull figurines and a superb tubular figure of a goddess in an elaborately painted dress.

None of the cult figures, except perhaps the bulls, are closely comparable to Minoan idols, and there seems little reason to doubt that they represent different deities and a different religion. Some of the objects found in these shrines hint at the sort of rituals practiced here. Libations were poured, offerings made, and votive figurines placed be-

The similarity in the basic design of the Mycenaean palatial megaron and that of the classical Greek temple is at once apparent when the plans of each are placed side by side. Possible examples of classical temples overlying the remains of Mycenaean megarons at Eleusis, and perhaps on the Athenian Acropolis itself, lend support to the belief that there is an ancestral link between the two.

fore the deities. Elsewhere, other finds amplify the picture and attest to the sacrifice of animals, sacred dancing, and ritual processions.

It is from the tablets, however, that we get more specific details of the sort of offerings that were made during these ceremonies. At Knossos olive oil, honey, grain, and wool are frequent gifts, while at Pylos one tablet alone records the offering of thirteen gold vessels to different gods. The same tablet includes in the list of offerings several women, and it is possible, even probable, that these are sacrificial victims. Some of the rituals recorded archaeologically or in the tablets occur also in the Homeric epics, and one of the most surprising discoveries when the tablets were first deciphered and translated was the appearance of many gods and goddesses from the classical Greek pantheon. Among the better known are Athena, Potnia, Eileithyia, Hera, Artemis, Poseidon, Zeus, Hermes, and Dionysus.

The appearance of such names in a list of Mycenaean deities fully justifies the work of the Swedish scholar Martin Nilsson, who as long ago as 1932 argued that Greek mythology was rooted in the Mycenaean era. A continuity between the Mycenaean and the later Greek religions has been stressed by several scholars, particularly in

Artemis, mistress of animals and sister of Apollo, was a popular figure in the classical pantheon, but mention of her name among the deities listed on the Linear B tablets from Pylos was nevertheless a surprise.

recent years, on the basis of Linear B inscriptions and such additional evidence as cult objects found at Ignatos, Gortyn, or in the Hermes Sanctuary newly discovered at Kato Syme in Crete. This does not mean,

As in Crete, gold signet rings are one of the most prolific sources of visual information about the rituals and deities of Mycenaean religion. The superbly detailed scene above was found on a signet ring from Tiryns. At the left, a goddess sits on a folding chair, her feet on a footstool, and holds before her a large conical drinking cup. Behind her chair is a bird, perhaps a falcon. Four demons or genii approach the goddess from the right, each carrying a jug, presumably to fill her cup. The signet on the opposite page, from Mycenae, appears to show two priestesses standing, hands raised in adoration, before a pillared shrine.

Pray now…to Poseidon our Lord, for his is the feast day whereon your arrival has chanced; and when thou hast made libation and prayed as is meet, then give to thy comrade this cup of honey-sweet wine to pour out his offering also.

The son of Nestor to Telemachus, Odyssey, Book 3

however, that the beliefs, rituals, and status associated with these various deities in classical Greece, or even in the Homeric epics, can be automatically accorded to their Mycenaean counterparts. It becomes clear from a careful reading of the tablets that many of these gods and goddesses were at that time of only local importance and that their cults were still in the process of formation. It may be significant nevertheless that Mycenaean sanctuaries at Delos and Eleusis were overlain by Greek temples.

MYCENAEAN SOCIETY

The evidence of the Linear B tablets, of Greek tradition and epic poetry, and of archaeological discoveries all suggests that the Mycenaeans lived in a ranked society ruled by a number of local or regional kings. In the *Iliad*, Agamemnon exercises a general overlordship of the Greeks, and there is an impression that the kings were themselves ranked according to their wealth and power, but neither the tablets nor archaeology has anything to say about a political organization larger than the kingdom or city-state. Beneath the king, who was accorded the title of *Wanax*, there were what might loosely be described as an aristocracy or nobility. This is suggested partly by wealthy burials other than those which appear to belong to kings and princes, but mainly by the tablets referring to high officials. These included

Apart from warriors in armor, portraits of Mycenaean men are relatively rare. Most of those seen wear neatly trimmed beards *(below)* and appear to have wavy hair. Ladies' hair styles are much more elaborate, as seen in the enlarged detail of the lady from a fresco at Tiryns *(bottom, center)*. The full-length figure shows her court attire, with short-sleeved jacket and flounced dress, both richly embroidered. *Bottom right:* Two women on a veranda, from a fifteenth-century fresco.

or headmen, called by the term *basileus*, which in later Greek is, significantly perhaps, the term used for a king. But the tablets also refer to many craftsmen, farmers, laborers, domestic servants, and to soldiers and sailors.

The majority of these people lived in farmsteads, villages, and small towns spread throughout the kingdom. Their homes varied from simple two- and three-roomed

administrators, provincial and district governors, army commanders, and perhaps priests and priestesses. Many of these men appear to have held substantial amounts of land, though none held as much as the king. Below this group of people came the mass of the population, among whom the most important may have been the local chieftains

houses with few home comforts to buildings with seven or eight rooms, simply painted wall plaster in the main living rooms, and sometimes a simple system of drainage. Local chieftains, on the other hand, seem to have built imitations of the king's palace to judge from the two megarons found at Mouriatada and Nikhoria near Pylos.

The contents of the houses in these small towns and villages usually clearly reflect the agricultural basis of their daily life, but they also include evidence for many of the crafts mentioned in the tablets. Carpenters' tools, potters' kilns (and of course their products), and the spinning and weaving equipment of wool workers are all found in excavation. Other craftsmen such as bakers, garment makers, perfume boilers, and shipwrights are known only from the evidence of the archives, and some of these crafts may have only been practiced in the palaces or the towns which surrounded them.

It is mainly in the palatial towns that we get an insight into life of the upper echelons of Mycenaean society. The houses found outside the citadel at Mycenae, for example, are well-built two-storied homes with fresco-

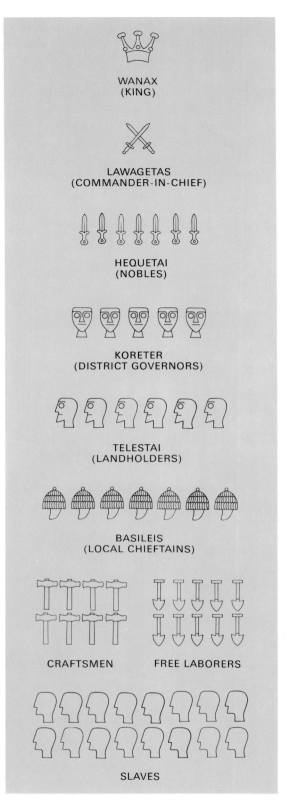

WANAX
(KING)

LAWAGETAS
(COMMANDER-IN-CHIEF)

HEQUETAI
(NOBLES)

KORETER
(DISTRICT GOVERNORS)

TELESTAI
(LANDHOLDERS)

BASILEIS
(LOCAL CHIEFTAINS)

CRAFTSMEN   FREE LABORERS

SLAVES

The near life-size limestone head from Mycenae *(opposite page)* may be that of a sphinx, but it suggests the use of face make-up and careful hair styling for Mycenaean women. The frontal details of the popular bodice and flounced dress are to be seen in an ivory statuette from Prosymna *(below left)*.

The Minoans had already developed an intricate and varied manufacturing system producing a wealth of handicrafted products in clay, faience, metal, stone, and ivory. The Mycenaeans followed in this tradition, becoming especially skilled in the carving of ivory.
This thirteenth century ivory head was taken from a statuette found near a shrine at Mycenae.

This chart of the Mycenaean social hierarchy is a tentative one based on the evidence of the Linear B tablets. The position and status of the *hequetai* (or followers) and the *telestai* are particularly difficult to pin down. Some officials have been omitted from the chart for the sake of clarity.

decorated living rooms upstairs, and stores and workshops downstairs. They were furnished with wooden tables and chairs inlaid with finely carved ivories. In such surroundings moved the elegantly dressed ladies that we see in contemporary frescoes and statuettes, and the officials and commanders that we read of in the Linear B tablets.

COUNTRY LIFE

In some respects country life in Mycenaean Greece was little different to that a thousand years earlier in the Early Bronze Age. Wheat and barley were still the main grain crops, and vines, olives, and figs were grown wherever the right conditions for them could be found. The hills and mountains were still used mainly for raising large flocks of sheep and goats, and pigs and cattle were reared in much smaller numbers for their skins as well as for their meat. The annual round of plowing, sowing, and reaping still determined the basic pattern of life in the Greek countryside.

Yet further, without the courtyard…was an orchard of four plowgates, enclosed by a fence, wherein all manner of tall trees blossomed and bore; pears and pomegranates, apple trees gleaming with fruit, fig trees also and blooming olives…a fruitful vineyard was planted thereby, and here, on the one side, raisins full-mellowed were spread to dry in the sun.

Homer, Odyssey, Book 7

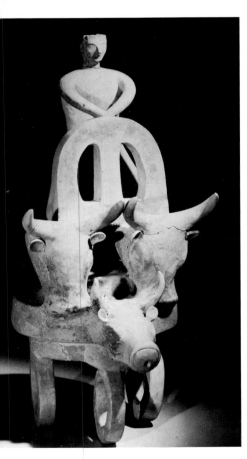

Evidence of wheeled vehicles other than chariots is slight in Mycenaean Greece, but it is unlikely that they were not used for transporting farm produce, particularly since the Minoans had such wagons by 2000 B.C. This clay model of a wagon dates to 1200–1000 B.C.

The Linear B tablets, however, reveal that beneath this picture of rural continuity there were fundamental changes in the countryside. By far the most important and far-reaching of these was probably the organization of estates and the division of landholdings. Among the archives discovered at Pylos are a set of tablets which appear to be a land register for the district based on Pylos itself. From these we learn that the largest estate in the kingdom is that of the king, probably about 9,000 acres of land. Other large estates belong to the *lawagetas* and the *telestai,* each of whom holds about 3,000 acres. The rest of the land is held for the gods ("temple" land) and by private tenants and sub-tenants. The smallest holding recorded is only half an acre in size, but it may be that this man held other plots elsewhere. Although the details and the tenurial relationships recorded on these tablets are by no means clear or fully understood, these archives leave the firm impression that life in the countryside was highly organized. Furthermore, the dominant role of the king and the aristocracy is clearly revealed. Other tablets from Pylos provide further illustrations of the way in which the life of the peasant farmers was now highly organized. Farm workers are listed according to the principal task they undertake. Thus we read of reapers and millers, shepherds, goatherds and oxherds, fire-burners (charcoal makers?) and woodcutters. Although their day-to-day routine was no doubt largely of their own devising, the overall pattern of farming in the kingdom was clearly dictated from above.

Similarly the remarkably detailed figures which were kept of rams and ewes, meat-producing and wool-producing sheep, and boars and sows suggest that the days of the happy-go-lucky farmer were past. Farmers were now expected to account for their animals and other products. In the same way, goods manufactured from farm products, such as textiles and leather goods, were subject to stringent control. Textile workers were divided up into carders, spinners, fullers, weavers, garment makers, and flax workers. The raw materials with which they worked were rationed by the administration, and a careful check was kept on production. Similarly, leather workers were issued with hides and skins to be used for making specific items, and both the quantities of leather and the number of finished items were expected to be recorded at the time of issue.

Apart from the main range of foods and products, the countryside was also expected to produce smaller quantities of other items. Spices and herbs are particularized on tablets from Mycenae, and include fennel, sesame, coriander, and mint. Honey also appears frequently in the accounts, and there are also references to fruit, though apart from figs no specific fruits are listed.

Although the Pylos tablets do not provide the same details of agricultural production, in terms of liters of wheat and sizes of herds and flocks, two brief and incomplete references which do occur give some idea of the scale of fruit and vine cultivation. Two estates are recorded, one planted with fig trees, the other possibly with vines, and each boasting well over a thousand plants.

The picture which emerges from the tablets, therefore, is one of great estates and many much smaller tenancies, all of which are subject to government scrutiny and all of which contribute to the inflow of agricultural produce into the system of distribution operated by the state.

It is hard to overestimate the importance of the olive to the Mycenaeans, both as a food crop and for oil. Certainly, olives appear frequently in the lists of products in the Linear B tablets, and storage facilities for oil form a prominent part of the palatial architecture at Pylos.

MYCENAEAN TRAVEL AND TRADE

Greek mythology and legend present a hazy and confusing picture of Mycenaean travel abroad, through tales such as those of Jason and the Argonauts, and the wanderings of Odysseus. Fortunately, the archaeological record is much clearer and more explicit. The first Mycenaean contacts with both the east and west Mediterranean appear to have been made in the sixteenth century B.C., at a time when Minoan trading activity both within and beyond the Aegean was increasing. After the abrupt decline of Minoan Crete around 1450 B.C., the Mycenaeans stepped up their commercial activity to levels never achieved by the Minoans. Thousands of Mycenaean painted pottery vessels reached southern Italy and Sicily in the west and Cyprus, Syria, and Palestine in the east. Some of these vessels almost certainly acted as containers for products such as oils and perhaps perfumes, but others seem likely to have been exported as desirable objects in their own right. In exchange for these products, and no doubt others which can no longer be identified, the Mycenaeans obtained raw materials such as Cypriot copper and Syrian ivory. Some Mycenaean imports, such as amber and perhaps tin, came from central and northern Europe, and it has been suggested that

The wanderings of Jason and the Argonauts and of Odysseus following the fall of Troy are confused and confusing. In some places their travels certainly overlap and probably represent a single story. But they do suggest that the Mycenaeans had some knowledge of, and perhaps contact with, areas such as the Black Sea where archaeological evidence for Mycenaean activity is lacking.

This cylindrical seal stone (detail above) combines Syrian and Mycenaean stylistic elements, a suggestion of the interaction of these two cultures. The piece dates from the fourteenth or thirteenth century B.C., a time when Mycenaean trade contacts through the eastern Mediterranean had reached their greatest extent. The travel and trade of the period are also reflected in legends: The Argive vase at right depicts Odysseus and his companions blinding the giant Polyphemus who had captured them.

CIRCE
Odysseus rescues some of his companions whom Circe had turned into swine. He spends one year with Circe and begets Telegonos with her. Circe sends Odysseus to the Land of the Departed Spirits (Hades) to ask his fate of the blind sage Tiresias.

LAISTRYGONES
Odysseus loses eleven of his twelve ships to the cannibalistic Laistrygones.

AEOLUS
Odysseus receives favorable winds in a leather sack; his companions unleash a chaos by letting loose Aeolus' winds.

POLYPHEMUS THE CYCLOPS
Odysseus blinds Polyphemus the Cyclops, a son of Poseidon, and escapes from his cave by clinging to the belly of a ram.

LOTUS-EATERS
Odysseus rescues only some of his companions from their lotus-induced lethargy.

LAISTRYGONES

CIRCE

Ischia

SIRENS

AEOLUS · Lipari Is.

Milazzo

POLYPHEMUS THE CYCLOPS · CATTLE OF THE SUN

Syracuse

Malta

CALYPSO

LOTUS-EATERS

Mycenaean textiles or bronze weapons may have been exchanged for these. Trade with central Europe was probably sporadic and indirect, but that with the east and west Mediterranean was regular and organized. Settlements such as Scoglio del Tonno (in Apulia) and Syracuse, and Enkomi (Cyprus) and Ugarit (Lebanon), appear to have acted as major ports through which Mycenaean trade was channeled. Mycenaean Greeks may also have resided there.

Alongside raw materials, like copper, tin, and ivory, the Mycenaeans imported luxuries such as the ostrich-egg jar *(third left)* from a shaft grave at Mycenae. Mycenaean exports included the attractive pictorial jars, usually showing chariots like that seen here from Enkomi in Cyprus. Delicate flasks for carrying oils and perfumes are also found in the east Mediterranean, that shown second left coming from Egypt. The ivory carving alongside, from Ugarit, may be a Mycenaean import.

PHAEACIANS
Odysseus is wrecked on Scheria (Corfu), the Island of the Phaeacians. He narrates his adventures to Nausicaä and is provided with a boat to take him home.

ISMAROS
Odysseus destroys the city of Prince Ismaros who had helped the Trojans.

Voyage of the Argonauts who went with Jason to fetch the Golden Fleece in the ship "Argo."

COLCHIS

●Aia

Above: Jason, watched by Athena, is ejected by the sea monster.

Scoglio del Tonno
Torre Castellucia
PHAEACIANS Iolkos
Parga

●Ismaros

●Troy
Mytilene
Pitane
●Sardis
Smyrna

YLLA AND
ARYBDIS

SIRENS
Odysseus sails past the dangerous singing Sirens.

ITHACA

Mycenae

●Miletus

●Trianda

Mersin
Tarsus
Alalakh
Ugarit

SCYLLA AND CHARYBDIS
Odysseus sails between the terrible rocks of Scylla and Charybdis.

Salamis
Enkomi
Paphos
Citium

CALYPSO
Odysseus spends seven years on the island of Calypso.

Byblos

CATTLE OF THE SUN
On the Island of Helios the Cattle of the Sun are plundered by Odysseus' companions, despite warnings. Odysseus alone survives.

Tell Abu Hawam
Megiddo
Jericho

ITHACA
Odysseus' home. He accomplishes Penelope's test of stringing and shooting with his own old bow. Penelope accepts him as her long-lost husband.

Ascalon
Tell El Ajjul
El Arish

Cyrene

Abusir   Heliopolis

Later Greek vase painters frequently used the story of Odysseus' travels as a source for their illustrations. To the far left here we see Odysseus and his crew blinding the one-eyed giant Cyclops, and immediately left, Odysseus tied to the mast of his ship to enable him to pass the wicked sirens in safety. The vase to the right depicts Odysseus' wife, Penelope, and behind her the unfinished weaving.

HEROES AT WAR

The stability and prosperity of the Mycenaean states depended as much on the successful exploitation of the land as it did on overseas trade, economic organization, or military might. Indeed, the armies of Mycenaean Greece were probably intended to prevent the invasion and annexation of good farming land as much as to protect the inhabitants and the wealth of the citadels.

Pictures of soldiers, arms, and armor are common in Mycenaean art, and many of the excavated and deciphered tablets are also concerned with these things, so that it might be thought that we now know a great deal about Mycenaean warfare. In fact, neither source of information tells us anything about military history and wars, nor do they

So closely their helmets and high-bossed shields were arrayed, shield and helmet and warrior pressing each other, and the horse-hair crests on the gleaming ridges of bronze touched as they nodded, so closely they stood in the ranks. But in front of them all, two heroes, in spirit as one: Patroclus and brave Automedon.

Homer, Iliad, *Book 16*

Right: One of the finest of all representations of a boar's tusk helmet is found on this carved ivory from Mycenae, dating to about 1400 B.C.

Although the crude carving of the chariot on the shaft grave stela *(far right)* contrasts markedly with the delicate carving of the sardonyx sealstone from Vapheio *(above),* both pictures show the same light Mycenaean chariot carrying a single warrior. The Vapheio warrior is about to hurl his spear, while the Mycenaean tightly grips his dagger.

signed to military duty, but it is quite possible that these men spent most of the year as farmers and craftsmen. The quantities of weapons recorded in store, particularly at Pylos, are not large enough to suggest they are the contents of a regimental

tell us very much at all about tactics and organization.

We do not even know for certain whether the Mycenaean kingdoms had armies in the sense of regular troops whose full-time job it was to defend their territorial integrity. The tablets certainly contain lists of men as-

armory. It must also be remembered that the tablets refer to events which take place immediately before the destruction of the palaces in which they were found and the quantity of arms and armor, and the references to units of troops, may have been greatly inflated at such a time. On the other

This frieze of bearded soldiers is found on a painted vase of about 1200 B.C. discovered by Schliemann at Mycenae, and usually known as the Warrior Vase. The details of the troops' equipment are easily visible. They wear horned helmets with plumes and covered perhaps with skin or fur. On their bodies they wear short corselets, and on their legs leather greaves. They are armed with a single long spear and sub-circular shields.

One of the most remarkable finds in Greece since World War II was this complete suit of bronze armor and boar's tusk helmet, found on the body of a warrior of about 1400 B.C. at Dendra. Such an outfit must have been worn by either a prince or a military commander.

hand, the number of chariots recorded at Knossos, for example, is sufficient to envisage several chariot squadrons, and the Warrior Vase from Mycenae shows a line of uniformly equipped troops who have all the appearance of regulars rather than a peasant militia.

Whether the units recorded on the tablets were regulars or not, it is clear that in times of war the kingdom of Pylos could muster considerable numbers of men and deploy them in a highly organized manner. One series of tablets from Pylos refer to the coastal watching stations which are responsible for covering the 150 kilometers (90 miles) of Pylos' coastline. The coast has been divided into ten sections, and military units are assigned to each of these. The chain of command is not clear from the tablets, but assuming that the king is commander in chief, his chief of staff appears to be the *lawagetas*. Individual units may be under the command of the *hequetai* (followers), who in

the Pylos tablets are clearly men of important rank and the owners or users of chariots.

Chariots are recorded in detail on the Knossos tablets and these suggest there was a force of perhaps two hundred commanded by the Mycenaeans there around 1400 B.C. Their use on the mainland by 1600 B.C. is attested by their appearance on the grave stelae from the shaft graves, and there are later pictures of them too. At Pylos, however, their presence can only be inferred by references to pairs of wheels, which we know from Knossos were usually stored separately from the bodywork. The Mycenaean chariots were light vehicles with a wicker or leather body over a wooden frame, two four-spoked wheels, two horses, and leather reins and harness. The tablets and contemporary wall paintings agree that they were commonly painted crimson. They rarely carry more than two warriors, and the impression of both paintings and tablets is

And Ajax approached him, bearing his shield like a tower, sevenfold oxhide that Tychius wrought by his craft—who wrought him his gleaming shield of sevenfold hide of full-grown bulls and overlaid the seven with bronze.

Homer, Iliad, *Book 7*

The scene on a gold signet from shaft grave IV at Mycenae *(above)* is typical "heroic" warfare, with hand-to-hand combat between individuals. Note the plumed helmets, swords, spear, and shield.

that they were used primarily as transports for the officers. This, of course, is precisely the role they play in Homer's *Iliad*.

The Mycenaean officers and aristocracy (Homer's "heroes") wore defensive armor in the form of a corselet of bronze plates, bronze greaves, and a leather or bronze helmet. A leather helmet would be protected by bronze embellishments or by "boar's

tusks" stitched in horizontal rows, which alternately curved to left and right. Apart from the remains of the helmets themselves, there are many pictures and miniature carvings of these helmets in Mycenaean art, and they bear an uncanny resemblance to the helmet which Odysseus dons in Book 10 of the *Iliad:* "and boar's teeth without it were thickly arrayed gleaming white, that broi-

The bull's-hide-covered shields described by Homer seem to be represented on the wall paintings at Mycenae *(far left)* and in gold beads *(left)*, as well as seen in depictions of heroic combat on sealstones *(two pictures right)*. The actual shields have never been found, although some burials in grave circle B may have had them, to judge from skeletal positions. They are assumed to be made on a wooden frame covered with ox or bull hide and trimmed with bronze. The small bumps seen on the gold model and in the sealstone may represent bronze studs.

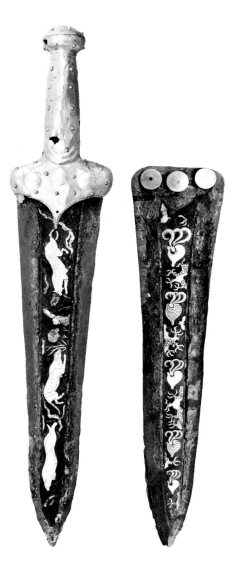

dered it this way and that." The plumed helmet of Agamemnon, on the other hand, may have been more like the bronze helmet with plume knob found at Knossos in a Mycenaean grave.

The most complete picture we have of a Mycenaean officer's battle dress comes from the discoveries in a tomb at Dendra. The man buried here was equipped with a pair of greaves and a boar's tusk helmet, but the most surprising item in the burial was the bronze cuirass he wore. The torso was made of two pieces, fastened with leather thongs at the side. The hips, thighs, and buttocks were protected by three flexible bronze bands front and back, while the shoulders and neck were covered by shoulder guards and a deep bronze collar. This discovery throws light on early Mycenaean body armor on which the tablets have little to say. The Dendra warrior may have been buried with a leather covered shield of which no certain traces remained. The art of the shaft graves, however, shows both figure eight and tall semicylindrical shields, both covered with hide, in use in the early sixteenth century. They continued in use later, but by the late twelfth century had been replaced by smaller circular, or sub-circular shields.

The classic weapons which this armor and defensive equipment was intended to combat were the dagger and the sword, at least in "heroic" combat as seen on the daggers and engraved rings of the shaft graves. The long straightedged swords of Cretan origin were improved and refined through the Late Bronze Age and joined by short swords too. In addition the spear, which is also seen already in shaft grave art, becomes increasingly important and appears to be the principal weapon of the Warrior Vase troops. Although the bow was in use in Mycenaean Greece, it seems to have been only of minor importance. Mycenaean warfare seems to have been essentially a hand-to-hand affair.

Many of the shaft grave weapons are very elaborately decorated and were primarily objects for display rather than warfare. But Mycenaean burials of the later period have produced daggers, swords, and spearheads, which were plainly the weapons of warriors rather than status symbols.

The scene on a dagger from the shaft graves below recalls Homer's description of Hector's shield as beating "against his neck and his ankles."

TROY: THE FACTS

The need for a long siege to reduce the city of Troy is certainly suggested by the strength of the walls which surrounded the sixth and seventh cities excavated at Hissarlik. Neatly, but massively built, with a slight batter and with shallow offsets, these walls were reused after the earthquake which destroyed Troy VI to defend the inhabitants of the seventh city—eventually, we believe, against the Greeks.

It has never been seriously doubted that the Homeric account of the Trojan War was based on events which actually happened, although where and when they occurred has aroused bitter controversy. We still do not know for certain where the Homeric city of Troy stood, but most archaeologists agree that Heinrich Schliemann was right in identifying the mound at Hissarlik, in the northwest corner of Turkey, as the Troy of the *Iliad*.

But excavations by a succession of German and American archaeologists have found seven superimposed cities at Hissarlik, dating between about 2700 and 1100 B.C.

The single object of my excavations from the beginning was to find Troy, whose site has been discussed by a hundred scholars in a hundred books, but which as yet no one has ever sought to bring to light by excavations....I have excavated two-thirds of the entire city; and, as I have brought to light the Great Tower, the Scaean Gate, the city wall of Troy, the royal palace...I have also made an exceedingly copious collection of all the articles of the domestic life and the religion of the Trojans.

Heinrich Schliemann, describing his excavations at Hissarlik in Troy and Its Remains *(1875)*

The death of a hero? We cannot be sure, but the American excavator Carl Blegen thought this might be the body of a Greek who had been brought down as he attacked the walls of Troy, and whose body was never recovered for burial.

Which, if any, of them is likely to be that destroyed by Agamemnon's army?

There are two, complementary, approaches to this difficult problem. The first is to compare the evidence of the *Iliad* itself with the remains discovered at Troy. Homer repeatedly uses the same stock adjectives to describe his Troy. These epithets are believed to be of greater antiquity than Homer himself and to reflect a contemporary idea of what Troy was like. Some of them are very general, like "rock-girt" and "windy", and although they fit the identification of Hissarlik well, they do not help to decide which of the cities at Hissarlik might be that of the Trojan War.

Others are more specific and helpful. For example the terms "bastioned" and "many-gated" well describe the defenses of Troy VI and Troy VIIa. The evidence of artifacts and animal bones suggests that Troy VI was indeed "wealthy" and "horse-rearing." Equally the spacious arrangement of houses

on the terraces of Troy VI recalls the epithet "wide-wayed." On the other hand, the term "populous" is far better applied to the densely occupied city of Troy VIIa. Homer's epithets, then, apply best to Troy VI, but do not totally exclude Troy VIIa.

The second approach to the problem is to look at the chronological and historical context of Homer's and Schliemann's Troys. Although the Greeks had a variety of dates for the start of the Trojan War, it was generally agreed in classical antiquity that it fell in the period around 1200 B.C. Troy VI came to an end in the years around 1300. The date for the destruction of Troy VIIa is still vigorously debated but probably to be put somewhere between 1230 and 1200. From elsewhere in the Aegean, and in the east Mediterranean, there is abundant evi-

"Steep," "Rock-girt," and "Windy" are terms Homer repeatedly uses to describe Troy in the *Iliad,* and all of them can be applied to the site at Hissarlik where the tangled remains of seven superimposed cities are found. Schliemann, who first excavated here, was convinced from the start that this was Homeric Troy: "Ever since my first visit, I never doubted that I should find the Pergamus of Priam in the depths of this hill."

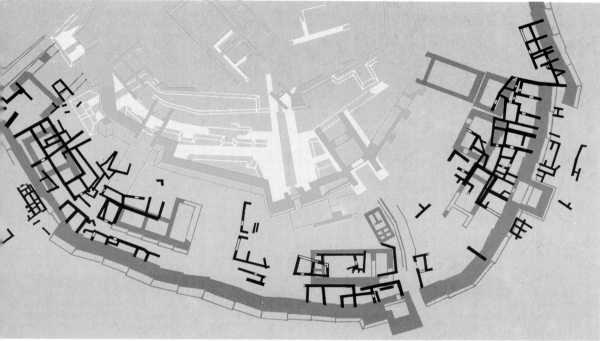

Because of the leveling of the top of the mound at Hissarlik in classical times, the center of the site is now occupied by remains of the first and second cities, dating to the third millennium B.C. The outer rings of walls, with offsets, gateways, and bastions, belong to Troy VI and VII. Inside, the spaciously arranged large buildings of Troy VI can be seen, contrasting with the smaller and much more densely packed houses of Troy VIIa.

dence that the end of the thirteenth century B.C. was a time of disruption and widespread hostilities, providing a context in which the Trojan War might be seen as a historical reality. Historically, then, Troy VIIa seems most likely to be the Troy of Homer, and the final pieces of evidence support this conclusion. Troy VIIa was destroyed by fire, which left its traces everywhere and in which at least some of the inhabitants lost their lives. This can plausibly be equated with the sack of Troy, as depicted in Homer, whereas the earthquake destruction of Troy VI cannot. The evidence of Homer and of the archaeological exploration at Hissarlik, then, best coincides if we identify Troy VIIa as that attacked by the Greeks. Homer's epithets no doubt portray the city as it was in its heyday in Troy VI, which was most likely the way it

was remembered by subsequent generations. The Trojan War itself was an episode in a more widespread picture of political and economic collapse in the late thirteenth century B.C.

The dense cluster of houses in Troy VIIa is thought perhaps to reflect the onset of troubled times, if not the actual siege of the city in the later thirteenth century. The increased provision of storage facilities, with big jars set into the floors of the houses of Troy VIIa, confirms this.

THE TROJAN WAR

For the Greeks, the Trojan War was not legend but ancient history—an event which took place around 1200 B.C. Although there is little direct archaeological evidence for the siege and fall of Troy, most archaeologists accept that these were historical events. In particular Homer's *Iliad* contains many details of weapons, armor, and other artifacts which do match archaeological remains of the Late Bronze Age. In contrast to these, the vase painters of classical Greece have left us their picture history of the war as they envisaged it.

Hephaestus, a son of Zeus, was god of fire and plays an important part in the war by manufacturing a special set of armor to be worn by Achilles.

Athena, a daughter of Zeus, was slighted by the Trojan prince Paris, and therefore supported the Greeks. It was she who lured Hector to his death at the hands of Achilles.

Poseidon, a brother of Zeus and god of the sea, supported the Greek cause and himself fought with Apollo outside the walls of Troy.

Hera, the wife of Zeus, h[…] also been slighted by Pa[…] and had thus taken t[…] Greek side. With Athe[…] she frequently interven[…] to help the Greek heroes[…]

1

2

The seeds of the Trojan War were sown when Hera, Athena, and Aphrodite all laid claim to a golden apple inscribed "for the fairest." Zeus sent them to the shepherd Paris (who was in fact the second son of Priam, king of Troy), for him to judge who was fairest. (Picture number 1, above.) Paris judged in favor of Aphrodite, which earned him and the Trojans the hatred of Athena and Hera, but also brought him as his reward from Aphrodite the fairest woman in the world for his wife. Aphrodite chose Helen, wife of King Menelaus of Sparta, for Paris, and helped him to abduct her. Since the other kings of Greece had already agreed to defend Helen's choice of husband, when she was carried off by Paris they rallied to the king of Sparta. Under the command of Agamemnon,

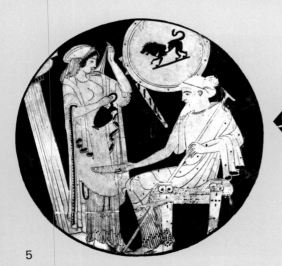

5

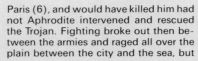

6

7

on the open battlefield watched by Priam and Helen (5), but Paris challenged the Greeks to produce a hero for single combat with him. Fittingly, Menelaus stepped forward to do battle with Paris (6), and would have killed him had not Aphrodite intervened and rescued the Trojan. Fighting broke out then between the armies and raged all over the plain between the city and the sea, but neither side could seize the decisive advantage. In order to swing the battle in their favor the Greeks sought to entice Achilles back into the fray; the cunning Odysseus was sent to persuade him to take up arms again (7), but he refused. Soon after, Odysseus and Diomedes managed to capture a Trojan spy, Dolon (8), and learned from him of the arrival of the Thracian prince Rhesus and his

Zeus, the supreme god of the Greek pantheon, tried, often unsuccessfully, to keep the gods intervening in the course of the war.

Apollo, the god of light, and his sister Artemis took the Trojan side. Apollo was responsible for the deaths of both Patroclus and Achilles, as well as sending a plague on the Greek army.

Aphrodite provoked the war by selecting Helen as the wife for Paris, and thereafter aided the Trojans, and Paris in particular.

Ares, another son of Zeus and a savage warrior, was the secret lover of Aphrodite, and like the goddess took the Trojan side in the war.

3

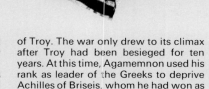

4

king of Mycenae, a force of 100,000 men and over 1,000 ships were assembled and sailed for Troy. For years the Greeks and the Trojans fought each other (2), with neither side winning. After one

such encounter, Achilles, the greatest Greek warrior, had to attend to the minor wounds of his closest friend and companion Patroclus (3), whose death was subsequently to play a key role in the fall

of Troy. The war only drew to its climax after Troy had been besieged for ten years. At this time, Agamemnon used his rank as leader of the Greeks to deprive Achilles of Briseis, whom he had won as

a prize of war (4). Achilles withdrew from the battle, determined to take no further part until Briseis was returned to him. Meanwhile the gods had intervened to lure both armies into meeting

8

9

cavalry. After executing the spy, they found the sleeping Thracians, slew them, and made off with their horses. When battle was renewed the advantage gradually swung to the Trojans, as

many of the Greek heroes were wounded and withdrew from the field. The Trojans managed to penetrate the enclosure the Greeks had built to protect their ships, and the situation was only

saved by Patroclus' donning the armor of his friend Achilles and almost single-handedly driving the Trojans back to Troy. With the assistance of Apollo, the Trojan hero Hector killed Patroclus be-

neath the walls of the city, and a battle for Patroclus' spoils began. Menelaus slew the Trojan warrior Euphorbus, and withdrew when Hector intervened (9). Having killed Patroclus, Hector in cele-

10

11

12

bration donned the armor of Achilles (10) which he took from Patroclus' corpse. On hearing of his friend Patroclus' death, Achilles resolved to return to the battle and was presented with new

armor made by the god Hephaistus. He sought out Hector, and having chased him around the walls of Troy, eventually slew him; Athena supported Achilles in this battle, while Hector was backed by

Apollo (11). Achilles dragged Hector's body back to the Greek camp behind his chariot. Then he made the preparations for Patroclus' funeral and built a great pyre on which the dead hero was laid

(12). At first the body of Patroclus refused to catch fire. But then Achilles made offerings to the north and west winds, that the pyre might start to burn. Hurtling down the sky, they blew it into

15

16

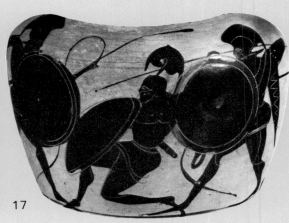

17

18

resumed, with the Trojans now receiving assistance from the Amazons led by their queen Penthesilea and from Memnon, king of the Ethiopians. Achilles, however, killed the queen in battle (15).

Only after the combat, seeing her dead body before him, Achilles became infatuated with it and carried it off the battlefield (16). King Memnon he also came upon in battle and killed (17), for

all that he was the son of Eos, the goddess of dawn. At this point he might well have led the Greeks to victory, but for the intervention of Apollo and the treachery of Paris. Legend has it that

Paris found Achilles unarmed in the temple of Apollo and slew him with an arrow guided by the god himself to Achilles' vulnerable spot—his heel. His body was recovered by Ajax (18) and

21

22

23

24

camp. When he realized what he had done, he was overcome with shame and fell on his sword (21). With the loss of another great hero the Greeks now sent for Achilles' son Neoptolemus, who,

dressed in his father's armor (22), performed great feats on behalf of the Greeks. Eventually, however, the Greeks had to resort to cunning to enter the besieged city, and it was then they built

their famous horse. While the best of the Greek warriors hid inside the wooden figure, the rest of the Greeks pretended to sail away, back across the Aegean. The Trojans were led to believe that if

they took possession of the horse they would rise to great power, and so the horse was pulled into the city (23). At night the Greek warriors clambered from the horse, and helped by the soldiers of

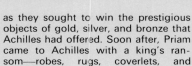

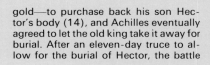

13

14

flame. With him were burnt four horses and two of Patroclus' dogs, and twelve Trojan prisoners whom Achilles himself slew with the sword. After the bones had been collected and stored in a

golden urn, Achilles brought forth prizes to be won in the funeral games in honor of his friend. Chariot racing (13), boxing, wrestling, and sprinting were all fiercely contested by the Greek heroes

as they sought to win the prestigious objects of gold, silver, and bronze that Achilles had offered. Soon after, Priam came to Achilles with a king's ransom—robes, rugs, coverlets, and

gold—to purchase back his son Hector's body (14), and Achilles eventually agreed to let the old king take it away for burial. After an eleven-day truce to allow for the burial of Hector, the battle

19

20

there followed great mourning for the greatest of all the Greek heroes (19). His body lay in state on a bier, surrounded by his armor. Thetis, his mother, called on her sister nymphs to gather round the

bier in lamentation, together with the Muses. The hero's funeral followed. He was cremated and his ashes placed in the urn with those of Patroclus, and eventually the urn itself was buried be-

neath a great burial mound on the promontory of Sigeum, near Troy. Lots were drawn for the wonderful armor of Achilles (20), and in a dispute which arose over the result, Ajax and Odysseus

asked some Trojan captives to arbitrate between them. When the captives decided in favor of Odysseus, Ajax was driven to madness by the insult and slaughtered the flocks in the Greek

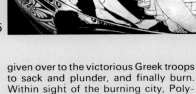

25

26

the returning fleet, were able to capture the city and slaughter its people. Neoptolemus himself slew the aging Priam (24), while Hector's son Astyanax was thrown from the walls. The city was

given over to the victorious Greek troops to sack and plunder, and finally burn. Within sight of the burning city, Polyxena, Priam's youngest child, was killed at Achilles' tomb. Paris' sister, Cassan-

dra, was torn from the altar in the temple of Athena (25) and carried away together with her mother, Hecuba, and Hector's wife, Andromache, by the Greeks. As for Helen, she was found and

taken away to Greece by her husband, Menelaus (26). The only member of the Trojan royal family to escape was Aeneas, who eventually founded the city which conquered Greece, Rome.

THE COLLAPSE OF MYCENAEAN CIVILIZATION

Scattered traces of destruction by fire at some Mycenaean settlements in the middle of the thirteenth century B.C. are followed by evidence of repairs and improvements to existing fortifications at important centers such as Mycenae, Tiryns, and Athens. The work undertaken includes not only the strengthening of the defenses but also new measures to ensure the water supply of the citadels even in time of siege. At the same time the Linear B tablets from Pylos record the disposition of Pylian troops, especially along the coast, and distribution of bronze to smiths throughout the kingdom, possibly in an attempt to produce new weapons and armor as quickly as possible.

Whatever the background to these events, they were certainly followed in the closing years of the century by widespread and violent destruction of many settlements, including most but not all of the centers of

cal evidence from Hissarlik—identified as Homer's Troy—does not support such an early date. Additionally, there is little evidence in the decades after the destructions around 1200 for the settlement of new peoples in Greece.

A variety of other reasons for the sudden collapse of Mycenaean civilization can be put forward. The economy could have been destroyed by deforestation and exhaustion of the arable soils, or by the onset of prolonged drought. Plague or epidemic may have resulted in an abrupt decline in population which destroyed the carefully organized running of the Mycenaean states. The mass of the population may have risen against the excessive control and taxation imposed on them from the palaces and citadels. Economic disaster may have been brought on by the collapse of Mycenaean trading systems in the east Mediterranean, where there were

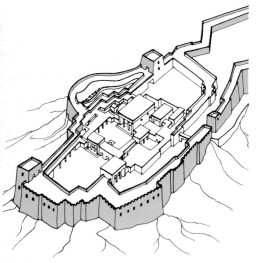

The defenses of Tiryns by the time it was attacked in the late thirteenth century B.C. were perhaps the most impressive in the whole of Greece. The palace and the surrounding citadel area *(below)* were enclosed by bastioned walls, strengthened with towers, and approached through a narrow gateway flanked by bastions. These were built in the heavy "Cyclopean" masonry seen to the right, which is actually part of the citadel gateway at Tiryns.

The masonry is not attractive to look at, but it is extremely strong, and in a civilization in which siege weapons were almost unknown, must have provided a daunting obstacle to would-be attackers. Some impression of the immense strength of these defenses is perhaps to be gained from the view along the gallery built into the thickness of the south defense wall at Tiryns *(opposite page)*. The corbeled roof was necessary to carry the great weight of the wall above.

power. Tiryns, Mycenae, Pylos, Gla, and Thebes were all victims, and many smaller settlements were either destroyed or abandoned.

Traditionally the blame for these events has been laid at the door of the Dorians—whose arrival Greek tradition placed about seventy or eighty years after the Trojan War. Since the Trojan War must clearly have taken place some while before the destruction of Agamemnon's Mycenae or Nestor's Pylos, this would put the Trojan War back into the earlier thirteenth century. The archaeologi-

certainly serious disruptions at this time. None of these explanations is entirely convincing, and none has much supporting evidence. Perhaps a more likely cause is interstate rivalry and warfare, such as was common in classical Greece, and is hinted at in Greek tradition and in Homer. Economic and social problems may have exacerbated such situations—the collapse of Mycenaean civilization was probably the result of the interplay of several different processes.

The palace of Pylos had no built defenses like those of Mycenae and Tiryns, and in this sense lay exposed to attack. From the tablets found in the archives here, however, we get a vivid impression of mobilized troops and coastal observation stations, as well as naval dispositions, which were presumably all part of the kingdom's defenses. Before 1200 B.C., however, the palace of Pylos succumbed to attack and was burnt down.

Everywhere, the excavators found smashed pottery and other debris (above), undisturbed since the spring day over three thousand years ago when the palace was destroyed. The same fire which razed the palace to the ground was responsible for baking, and therefore preserving, the palace archives on clay tablets, which now form such a valuable source of information about the kingdom of Pylos in its last months of existence.

INVASION: SEA PEOPLES AND DORIANS

The twelfth century B.C. seems to have been a time of disruption and chaos throughout much of the Mediterranean basin. Both the Homeric epics and the archaeological evidence suggest that Greece was in turmoil in this period, and in the east Mediterranean the collapse of empires and destruction of great cities is recorded both by the written documents and by the excavated remains of destroyed settlements.

In the Near East, we not only know the names of the peoples who wrought much of this destruction, but we have portraits of them, preserved on Egyptian reliefs. These are the Peoples of the Sea, or Sea Peoples, who were already harassing Egypt by about 1220 B.C. Repulsed by the Egyptians at this time, they returned again in force around 1190 B.C. Having swept southward from successful raids along the coast of Turkey and destroyed and looted many of the great cities of Syria and Palestine, they fought a

Apart from the ships shown in great detail in Ramses III's relief in the temple at Medinet Habu, we know little of the vessels by which the sea-borne raiders were able to sweep through the east Mediterranean. The somewhat confused drawing of a ship found at Enkomi in Cyprus *(right)* may show a similar vessel, with a high stern and in this case possibly a ram on the prow.

can only say that these Sea Peoples settled in the west Mediterranean *after* the raids on Egypt—we do not know where they came from originally. The same is true of the Pulsati—almost certainly the Philistines—who are settled in southern Palestine by the later twelfth century, but whose origins are obscure.

For us, the most intriguing of the Sea Peoples must be the Aquaiwash, for many scholars have suggested that these are the Achaeans. Whether or not this is so we shall

Although there has been some disagreement about the extent to which the passage of the Sea Peoples can be identified in Cyprus by the destruction of existing settlements, Egyptian records clearly state that among the victims of the raiders in the early twelfth century was Alasia. It is widely agreed that Alasia was situated in Cyprus, and some believe that it may be identified with Enkomi. Excavations here show occupation at this time, and from a burial vault of the period came a sealstone *(above)* decorated with this frieze of strange people, whom some would identify as Sea Peoples.

great land and sea battle against Ramses III, who defeated them decisively.

In the Egyptian records, these raiders are listed by name—the Lukka, the Danuna, the Sherden, the Sheklesh, the Tursha, the Aquaiwash, the Pulsati, the Washash, and others. Despite their outlandish names, we can perhaps identify at least some of these peoples. The Lukka also appear in Hittite documents, and apparently came from Lycia in Asia Minor, while the Danuna may be placed in Cilicia, according to earlier Egyptian records. Less certainly identified are the Sherden (Sardinians?), the Sheklesh (Sicilians?), and the Tursha (Etruscans?). Even if these three identifications are correct, we

probably never know with certainty, but there are some indications that peoples from the Aegean may have been involved in the Sea Peoples' raids. The Egyptian records associate the Sea Peoples with little known islands to the north, and since Cyprus was well known to the Egyptians, the islands of the Aegean seem to be the most likely haven of the raiders. Furthermore, Greek tradition itself, in the form of Homer's *Odyssey*, connects the events following the Trojan War with widespread raiding, and records Greek ships under the leadership of Menelaus, king of Sparta, wandering the seas around Cyprus, Phoenicia, and Egypt. At one point in the epic, Odysseus himself makes up a story about his own wanderings, in which he describes how his men raided and plundered in Egypt. It is at least possible that Homer is here recording distant memories of Greek participation in the raids of the Sea Peoples.

Be that as it may, by the time of Odysseus' return, Greece had sunk into decline and a period of local, interstate warfare. It is in this context that we must view the Greek tradition of the return of the sons of Heracles, and the "historical" accounts of the arrival of the Dorians. In the return of the Heraclids, we get a garbled account of an early war in which Athens and Mycenae are the protagonists. Although the Mycenaean army is defeated, the sons of Heracles, supported by Athens, fail in an attempt to conquer the Peloponnese. All this happens before the Trojan War, but after the fall of Troy, further attempts to conquer the Peloponnese take place and eventually, according to the historian Thucydides, the Heraclids, together with the Dorians, took the Peloponnese eighty years after the fall of Troy. This would place the arrival of the Dorians in the period around 1150–1120 B.C.

If the story, as told by Thucydides and others, is confused, so is the evidence of archaeology and linguistics. The story of the Dorian invasion neatly explains how the West Greek (or Doric) dialect was spoken in the Peloponnese and elsewhere in later times, and for this reason and others the historical reality of the arrival of the Dorians was never questioned either by the ancient Greeks or by modern Greek scholars. Recently, however, it has been suggested that the Dorian dialect was already in use in southern Greece in the Mycenaean era, and can be identified on some of the Linear B tablets. This "proto-Doric," it is suggested, may have been the language of the lower classes. Its later emergence as the principal language in former Mycenaean kingdoms would then be seen not as evidence of foreign invasion but rather of the survival of the basic Mycenaean population when the society and civilization of the palaces collapsed in the early twelfth century. Such a reconstruction of events would allow for the possibility of civil war between upper and lower classes in Mycenaean society, and also

Below: The story of the coming of the Dorians and of the return of the sons of Heracles is far from clear. Both may contain some historical truth, but whether they originally referred to a single event or two quite separate ones is uncertain. As the story eventually emerged, the Dorian "invaders" were linked to the restoration of Heracles' descendants to the Peloponnese, and thus to the great Greek hero himself— seen here fighting the three-headed Geryon.

explain the notable absence of any clear signs of new peoples with an alien culture settling in Greece in the mid-twelfth century. Such views are still controversial, however. Others believe that the appearance of new types of bronze brooches, rings and pins, dark handmade pottery, and burials in cist graves in the later twelfth century does point to the arrival of "Dorians" from the northwest, and that the Greek tradition of a Dorian invasion is too strong to reject its main thrust so completely.

Outside of Egyptian reliefs, portraits of Sea Peoples are rare and controversial. This recently discovered sherd *(left)* from Tiryns almost certainly shows Greek warriors of the twelfth century B.C. Such men may have joined in the Sea Peoples' raids on Egypt, if we believe references to such raids mentioned in Homer, and if we identify the Aquaiwash of the Sea Peoples with the Achaeans. Certainly their armament, a round shield and spears, is similar to that of the raiders seen on Egyptian reliefs.

THE SURVIVORS

The collapse of Mycenaean civilization did not, of course, lead to the abandonment of all the Mycenaean towns and villages of Greece. Although harder times may have inevitably led to a decline in population, in the twelfth century settlements such as Lefkandi, Mycenae, and Tiryns continued in occupation. Athens, indeed, survived throughout the so-called Dark Ages and saw the gradual transformation of a Mycenaean city into a flourishing Iron Age settlement. There was, however, a progressive breakdown of the larger political units, and by the eleventh century such power as remained was probably concentrated in the hands of local petty chieftains. The process of decline was certainly stimulated by emigrations from the Greek mainland to the east Aegean, Turkey, Crete, and Cyprus, and it was in these areas that settlements of

Mycenaean pottery had found a receptive market in Cyprus, and it is hardly surprising that one result of the influx of Mycenaean refugees to Cyprus in the twelfth century was the eventual appearance of a hybrid style, like that seen on the jug to the right—a late successor perhaps to the Mycenaean chariot vases of the thirteenth century.

Ivory carving was a skill practiced in both Mycenaean Greece and the Levant, but this side panel from a gaming box of the twelfth century from Enkomi was probably the work of a purely east Mediterranean workshop. Its theme of the hunt, however, would have found favor with Mycenaean residents at Enkomi, for it was a popular motif in Mycenaean art.

"refugees" clung most tenaciously to Mycenaean culture. In Crete the settlements at Karphi and Vrokastro typify the villages of these survivors of Bronze Age civilization. Perched on steep-sided hilltops where they could easily defend themselves, these villages were poor shadows of earlier Minoan townships like Gournia and Palaikastro. The little houses still cluster together, separated into blocks by cobbled streets, but they are smaller than their Bronze Age ancestors and their floors are of beaten clay, their walls unplastered. At Karphi, however, the old religion lived on, and the most notable building in the settlement was the

three-roomed shrine built on the edge of a precipice. The cult figures immediately recall the goddesses found in the town shrine of Gournia with their cylindrical dresses and raised hands. Similar goddesses have been found in other twelfth-century shrines at Gazi and Prinias, and there is a general impression that the people of Crete held on to both their religion and the agricultural basis of their way of life. In time, they once more began to open contacts with the Greek mainland, Cyprus, and the east Mediterranean.

In Cyprus itself the strong trading links which the Mycenaeans had established in the

In the village shrine of the "refuge" settlement at Karphi, the cult figures included three ladies with raised arms, like that seen here. The largest of the figures wore a crown surmounted by birds, while the middle-sized idol can be seen to wear a diadem from which project the horns of consecration. Both the type of cult figures, and the specific attributes they carry, are therefore firmly rooted in Minoan religion.

fourteenth and thirteenth centuries were now reinforced by successive arrivals of Mycenaean Greeks. They seem to have settled particularly in the coastal settlements of southern Cyprus, such as Kition (Larnaca) and Enkomi. Here their arts and crafts were stimulated by and intermingled with those of the native population to produce new art styles and fine works of craftsmanship in which echoes of the Mycenaean world survived. As in Crete, the old religions appear to have persisted, and from a large shrine at Enkomi were recovered two painted clay centaurs comparable to others found at Lefkandi in Greece. The form of the shrine and its major deity, the ingot-god, on the other hand, emphasize the Levantine origins of this particular cult to which the new residents of Enkomi had added their own embellishments. The strength and resilience of Mycenaean religious cults is one of the most notable features of the so-called Dark Ages, and all the old gods and goddesses of the Linear B tablets reemerge to take their places in the Greek pantheon. Similarly, the myths and legends of the Bronze Age are passed down, verbally we must assume, to the peoples of classical Greece, and most importantly of all, the Greek language survived and was gradually transformed from Mycenaean Greek to that of Homer and his contemporaries.

Symbols of secular and spiritual power in twelfth-century Cyprus are to be seen in the scepter (above) and the bronze figurine (left). The two hawks which surmount the gold scepter inlaid with white and blue paste probably represent kingly power. The wealth of Cypriot kings may still have depended very largely on the copper sources of Cyprus, and it is significant that the great twelfth-century shrine at Enkomi was dedicated to the ingot-god seen here, brandishing spear and shield, and standing on an ox-hide ingot.

THE SEA PEOPLES

The Sea Peoples' raids, in which peoples of the Aegean may have participated, are best recorded in Egypt. The great land and sea battles of the eighth year of the reign of Ramses III (ca. 1190 B.C.) were shown in great detail on the walls of the temple at Medinet Habu. This reconstructed drawing of one of the reliefs shows part of the sea battle in progress. The battle is taking place either on the coast or in the Nile delta, for out of the picture to the right, regiments of Egyptian infantry armed with high-powered bows are discharging volleys into the Sea Peoples' fleet. The effects of this action can be clearly seen, with the great long arrows projecting from the bodies of the dead and dying attackers

on the right-hand side of the scene. Five ships of the Sea Peoples are shown, each with a high prow and stern, and furled sails. The Egyptian ships, used to working in coastal waters and along the Nile, are sleeker vessels, as seen bottom right, with oarsmen to power them as well as sails. Since both fleets have their sails furled, the ships are presumably becalmed, giving the Egyptians, with their oarsmen, a crucial advantage in maneuverability. One of the Sea Peoples' ships has already capsized and the others hold many dead and dying. Among the Sea Peoples shown here are the Pulsati (Philistines?) with crested or plumed headdresses, and a second group with horned helmets, who might perhaps be the Sheklesh (Sicilians?). Both peoples are armed with a bossed round shield, and either a long, straight-edged sword or a spear. In a situation such as this, where they could not close with the enemy, they were therefore outranged by the Egyptian bowmen on ship and shore, and this may do much to explain Ramses' victory.

THE COMING
OF IRON

By the Protogeometric period, tools, weapons, and jewelry were all often made of iron rather than bronze. The distinctive long dress pins and arched fibulae on opposite page above, found in the late tenth-century graves in Athens, are typical grave-goods of this period.

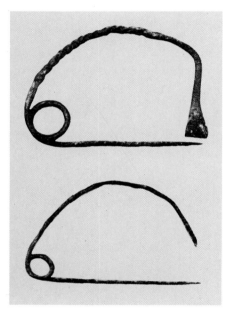

The change from bronze to iron is well documented in the Kerameikos cemetery at Athens, where the earliest graves contain sub-Mycenaean bronze fibulae (brooches) like those seen above, and the later ones produce similar brooches in iron.

The cist grave *(right)* was found in the area that was later occupied by the Agora of classical Athens. It is a typical protogeometric grave of about 1000 B.C., as indicated by the pottery with its characteristic concentric semicircles. This young girl was buried with bangles on her arms, and two long pins holding her dress at the shoulders.

The period between about 1100 and 750 B.C. is traditionally known as the Greek Dark Age, because we have no direct written sources for the period, few surviving traditions about it, and even a scarcity of archaeological evidence, especially for the earlier part of it.

By the end of the twelfth century, while Minoan and Mycenaean religion and other customs and crafts survived in Crete and in Cyprus, the Greek mainland had seen the evolution of a sub-Mycenaean culture. Although the occasional appearance of gold, ivory, and faience points to continued contacts with Cyprus and the east, the initiative for these must have come from the east rather than from Greece. By now, the organized systems of government which had enabled the Mycenaean city-states to thrive and to trade abroad had collapsed. In place of the palaces and citadels, and their adjacent towns, there were now villages, largely made up of small, sometimes single-roomed houses. Many such settlements were on, or close to, the site of a Mycenaean settlement, and there was no doubt a large element of continuity in the population of Greece from the Mycenaean to the sub-Mycenaean period. At Athens, where several cemeteries of this period suggest the survival of a relatively large settlement, the finds made in the biggest of these cemeteries, known as the Kerameikos, provide a good picture of the material culture of the inheritors of Mycenaean Greece, in this one area at least. The burials were made in either earth-cut graves or cists, a custom which had not been popular since the Middle Bronze Age, around 2000–1600 B.C. Pottery deposited with the dead was generally poorly made and decorated with uninspired combinations of horizontal bands and cross-hatched triangles in dark paint. Both the shapes and decoration of the pottery, however, show derivation from the pottery of the late Mycenaean era. In contrast, personal jewelry, apart from a few hair-rings of gold, is quite different to that of the Mycenaeans. Spiral rings, long pins with bulbous swellings, and various forms of bow brooches suggest influences and perhaps new settlers from the north; they also suggest changing fashions in clothing. Many of these items of jewelry are made of bronze, but significant numbers in both the Kerameikos cemetery and elsewhere are made of iron.

Iron was used sporadically in Anatolia from the third millennium B.C. onward, and was widely known though still used only in small quantities by the thirteenth century B.C. Its adoption in the Aegean during the course of the twelfth century is usually attributed to influences from Cyprus, but it is still difficult to understand why the new material grew so rapidly in popularity at this time, at the expense of bronze. One obvious possibility is that with the general collapse of civilizations in the east Mediterranean and Aegean at the end of the thirteenth

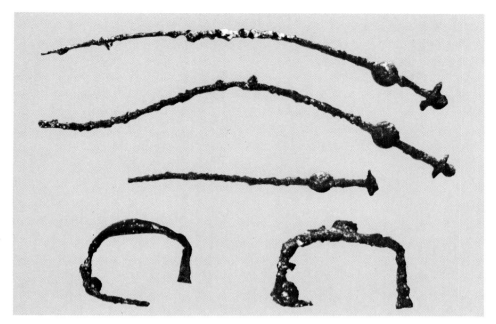

The attractive horse on wheels above, with long mane and tail, was found in a child's grave of the Protogeometric period (later tenth century) in Athens, and was clearly a toy.

Protogeometric pottery was better made than the sub-Mycenaean pottery which preceded it, as can be seen from the neatness of this amphora (below left), and its wavy lines painted with a triple brush.

In the Geometric period, the ninth and eighth centuries B.C., people from the island of Euboea, off the east coast of central Greece, sailed to both the east and west Mediterranean. Earlier contacts with the east are perhaps hinted at by this remarkable clay centaur, from Lefkandi, which belongs to the tenth century, and is paralleled in Cyprus.

century, it was no longer possible to maintain the long-distance trade which brought tin to the Mediterranean. Without tin, copper was no match for iron in terms of hardness and durability. Furthermore, iron ores were far more quickly found than copper ones so that the acquisition of iron was easier for many of the small communities of this period than was copper, let alone tin. Once the more complex techniques for smelting and working iron had been introduced from the Levant or Anatolia, then there were perhaps good reasons why the new metal should be widely adopted. The eleventh and tenth centuries saw iron being used for the manufacture of most of the products which had previously been made of bronze. Apart from pins, rings, and brooches, weapons such as swords, daggers, and spearheads were increasingly made of iron. Similarly tools such as double axes, flat axes, and knives were produced in the harder metal, and by the end of the tenth century more elaborate items such as pairs of fire dogs and horse bits were being made in iron.

The period in which iron emerged as the principal metal in Greece, between about 1050 and 900 B.C., is usually known as the Protogeometric period, on the basis of its distinctive pottery decorated with concentric circles and semicircles, painted with dividers and multiple brushes attached to them. These were invented by Athenian potters, and Athens and Argos emerged as important settlements at this time. Contacts with the rest of the Aegean, Asia Minor, and the eastern Mediterranean were once again forged. Athenian pottery was imported in quantity into Crete for example, and in one grave at Knossos a collection of Athenian vases was accompanied by a bronze bowl carrying a Phoenician inscription. Such contacts blossomed in the ninth and eighth centuries, the Geometric period, as traders and subsequently colonists went to Asia Minor and westwards to Italy, Spain and Africa. Contact with Etruscans and Phoenicians stimulated the Greeks anew. A revival of old skills in pottery making, bronzes and ivories, a newfound literacy, a growing population, and emerging city-states announced the rebirth of Greek civilization.

111

THE AGE

This is the Race of Iron.
    Dark is their plight.
Toil and sorrow by day are theirs,
    and by night
The anguish of death;
    and the gods afflict them and kill
Though there's yet a trifle of good
    amid manifold ill.

HESIOD

Statues of Harmodius and the bearded
Aristogiton, "the Tyrannicides," stood in
the Agora at Athens. They were popularly revered as the liberators of Athens
from the Pisistratid tyranny, opening the
way to further political developments.
The truth, according to Thucydides, was
neither so simple, nor so heroic. The
mainspring of the plot was Aristogiton's
jealousy of Harmodius, to whom advances were made by Hipparchus,
younger brother of the tyrant Hippias.
The plot misfired: Hipparchus was
killed, but Hippias survived to rule with
increased harshness for another four
years. Harmodius was killed in the attempt, Aristogiton was captured, and
subsequently died under torture.

From the eighth century B.C. onward, Greeks came increasingly into contact with the civilizations of the eastern Mediterranean, especially Phoenicia and Egypt. As a result, striking changes occurred in every area of Greek life. New fighting methods were adopted, a development which led to political changes, notably the movement, at times sudden and violent, toward greater political freedom for the ordinary citizen. Luxury goods such as textiles, ivories, and elaborate metalwork were imported, and while they inspired local artists to emulate and often to surpass them, the need to pay for such expensive items forced the sons of impoverished aristocratic families to seek

OF IRON

their fortunes elsewhere and this, together with other factors such as periodic famine and relative overpopulation, led to the creation of colonies elsewhere in the Mediterranean, especially in Sicily, southern Italy, Gaul, or even Spain in the west, and in Cyrenaica in North Africa. The alphabet was another important acquisition from the Near East, but its effects were less drastic in the short term. Literature continued to be a largely oral affair down to the fifth century. Although Greeks were increasingly far-flung throughout the Mediterranean, they preserved a considerable cultural unity thanks to the pan-Hellenic festivals which were held at regular intervals at Olympia, Delphi, and elsewhere. The Delphic oracle, indeed, exercised a considerable moral authority throughout the Greek world. Despite this cultural and religious conformity, however, there was intense political rivalry at a local level, a weakness which was to be exploited by the Greeks' powerful eastern neighbors, the Persians. Their vast empire engulfed all the Greeks of Asia Minor by the end of the sixth century B.C. In 490 the Persians made the first of their incursions into mainland Greece. Their failure at Marathon incited them to come again with much greater forces in 480–479 but again they were repulsed. On both occasions, Athens was at the forefront of Greek resistance to the barbarian.

THE IDEA OF GREEKNESS

In the late eighth and seventh centuries B.C. the pace of social change in Greece increased dramatically: cities—*poleis*—arose in place of aristocratic fiefdoms; economic pressures led to colonies' being founded abroad; and major centers became richer as a consequence of overseas trade. There was a

The isle of Delos in the Cyclades was one of Apollo's shrines. He and his sister Artemis are said to have been born there. At first controlled by the Naxians (who erected these archaic lions) it later became the center of the Delian League, an alliance of Greek states led by Athens.

danger that in so volatile a period, with substantial numbers of Greeks moving about the Mediterranean in search of new lands in which to settle, the traditions of the Greek homeland would be forgotten. In fact the opposite occurred, and a strong Panhellenic spirit emerged, fostered if not actually encouraged by the existence of several reli-

gious centers that were revered by every Greek. Colonies might pay lip service to their links with their mother-city, but they were far more attracted by the Panhellenic festivals that began to be established in the archaic period. Indeed, it has been argued that the preeminence of the Olympic games is attributable to the fact that Olympia was of relatively easy access from Greek settlements in the west. Delphi, too, was in a favorable position in this respect, and the treasuries there belonging to states outside mainland Greece, those for example of Syracuse, Massilia, and Cyrene, bear witness to the influence that Apollo's oracle had in the archaic period and the honor in which it was held in the Greek world.

The priests who conducted the oracle had an important moral role in the spread of Greek colonization. Herodotus, for instance, tells us how the inhabitants of Thera who were suffering from a shortage of food in the early 630s B.C. consulted the oracle and were instructed to go and found a city in Libya, which they did, eventually, at Cyrene, but only after further encouragement from Delphi.

Games were held periodically at several Panhellenic centers. Greeks from the earliest times seem to have been addicted to athletic contests. Homer describes in great detail in the *Iliad* the funeral games of Patroclus, and he refers there to other funeral games, those of Amarynces which were held by the River Alpheus in Elis, the very place at which the Olympic games were established in honor of Zeus in the year we call 776 B.C. Every four

The long jump *(right)* and the foot race *(far right)* were two of the events in the pentathlon (the others being the javelin, discus, and wrestling). Jumpers would hold weights in their hands *(halteres, seen above)* to give momentum.

years, for more than a thousand years, athletes would assemble from all over the Greek world to compete for the olive crown which would bring honor and glory both to themselves and to their cities. Participants had to be free-born Greeks, and male. Women (apart from the priestess of Demeter) were excluded from the sanctuary and from watching the contests. A solemn oath would be sworn over the body of a boar that the rules of the competition would be observed (violators could be heavily fined and excluded from the games for life). Spectators would gather too, and for several days all the Greek dialects could be heard within the sacred enclosure. Participation in the solemnity of the religious sacrifices and the excitement of the athletic competitions could only foster the basic unity of Hellenism.

Panhellenic games were held in other centers besides Olympia. The Pythian games in honor of Apollo were founded at Delphi in 582. There was an emphasis on music here as well as athletics, fitting since Apollo was the god of the arts. The victor's crown at Delphi was made of laurel leaves, cut from trees in

The mountainous island of Samothrace in the northeastern Aegean was the home of the sanctuary of the Great Gods, whose nocturnal rites were open to men and women, both slave and free. The initiates hoped to gain protection at sea, moral improvement, and quite probably immortality. These columns are the remains of the colonnade around the Hieron where the ritual action took place. The cult of the Great Gods was an amalgam of a local pre-Greek deity (the Great Mother), attendant demons (the Cabiri and Dioscuri), and the Greek Hades and Persephone. Thracian was used as the liturgical language until the Roman period.

the vale of Tempe in Thessaly. The Isthmian games, held every two years in honor of Poseidon, were organized by the Corinthians. The prize was a crown of wild celery, the same as that offered at the Panhellenic games at Nemea, likewise biennial, but held in honor of Nemean Zeus. Victors at these festivals would in reality win far more than a

The Burgon Amphora *(above)* is the earliest of a long series of prize vases made for the Panathenaic games held at Athens once every four years.

Left: Javelin and discus throwers and wrestlers (the other events in the pentathlon).

115

garland of leaves, for like many modern Olympic champions, they would gain certain social and financial advantages in their native states. In sixth-century Athens, for example, an Olympic victor would be awarded five hundred drachmas, and food at public expense for the rest of his life.

The fortunes of individuals, however, were of secondary importance compared with the influence of such festivals in fostering common values throughout those parts of the world inhabited by Greeks. No one was more aware of this than the Athenian orator Isocrates, who wrote on the occasion of the hundredth Olympiad (in 350 B.C.) as follows:

"Now the founders of our great festivals are justly praised for handing down to us a custom by which having proclaimed a truce and resolved our pending quarrels, we come together in one place, where, as we make our prayers and sacrifices in common, we are reminded of the kinship which exists among us and are made to feel more kindly towards each other for the future, reviving our old friendships and establishing new ties. And neither to common men nor to those of superior gifts is the time so spent idle and profitless, but in the concourse of the Hellenes the latter have the opportunity to display their prowess, the former to behold those contending against each other in

The Sacred Way up to the Temple of Apollo at Delphi. On the right, the altar of Apollo; on the left, the site of the golden tripod set up to commemorate the Greek victory at Plataea in 479 B.C.

the games; and no one lacks zest for the festival, but all find in it that which flatters their pride, the spectators when they see the athletes exert themselves for their benefit, the athletes when they reflect that all the world is come to gaze upon them."

The interior of an Athenian Attic white-ground cup found at Delphi showing a youthful Apollo seated on a folding stool and pouring a libation of wine (symbolic perhaps of a pilgrim's libation to him). He holds a lyre—a suitable attribute for the god of music—and is attended by a raven.
Top right: The bronze Charioteer from Delphi, fifth century B.C.

Opposite page:

DELPHI, THE NAVEL OF THE UNIVERSE

Delphi, the site of the sanctuary of Pythian Apollo at the foot of Mount Parnassus, is extremely impressive, even today: In left foreground *(and also below)*, the Temple of Apollo, the center of the cult, entered by means of a ramp from the northeast. In front of it, the altar of Apollo, paid for by the inhabitants of Chios in 518 B.C. This is where animals would be sacrificed to the god. At center, the theater, built in the fourth century B.C. and rebuilt in Roman times. It could seat 4,000 spectators. At top, the stadium, the site of the foot races at the Pythian games; chariot races were held on the plain below. There was seating for 7,000 spectators. At far left *(and bottom)*, the treasury of the Athenians. Perhaps erected as a thank-offering after the Battle of Mara-

thon in 490 B.C. Just left of the temple, the portico of the Athenians. It had eight widely spaced Ionic columns of Parian marble and was probably built at the end of the sixth century B.C. Not shown: the Lesche (clubhouse) of the Cnidians. Only the foundations are extant, but the walls were originally decorated with murals by the painter Polygnotus.

ORIGIN OF
THE CITY-STATE

The Greek landscape, with its high mountain ranges and narrow valleys, fostered the location of independent city-states.

Every Greek city had its foundation legend. The Laconian cup *(above)* may depict Cadmus, the mythical founder of Thebes, killing the dragon. Cities had law codes, too. One of the earliest of which we know is that of Gortyn in Crete *(above right)* which was set up in about 500 B.C.

Between ca. 750 and 650 B.C. a great change occurred in the way that most Greek communities were governed. In the earlier eighth century the norm was for a tribal chieftain—a *basileus*—to wield sole, and often arbitrary, power over the inhabitants of a given locality. By the late seventh century the *basileis* had disappeared as leaders of their communities and the new ideal was for a free citizen to exercise his powers within the city-state. The transition from the one form of government was, however, almost completely unrecorded, and we have to arrive indirectly at an idea of what happened.

The tribal chieftains were hereditary leaders who held power for as long as they lived. In Mycenaean times, kingship had been closely based on oriental models, with rulers claiming divine sanction for their actions. The inherent injustices of such a system did not go unnoticed. In the *Odyssey* we are told that Odysseus (who was in favor of monarchy) "wrought no wrong in deed or word to any man... as is the wont of divine kings—one man they hate and another they love," and even in the middle of the period in which the transition from monarchy to city-state occurred we find Hesiod in his Boeotian political backwater complaining of the treatment he had suffered at the hands of the "bribe-swallowing chieftains." The city-state was the antithesis of this type of system: it was an organization in which the interests of society as a whole, and not those of specific individuals or classes, were protected.

The eighth and seventh centuries were a period of great cultural change in Greece. We shall see elsewhere how the visual arts changed rapidly from a localized Geometric style to a branch of what was an international orientalizing style. The political arts underwent a change that was equally profound though different in kind. The way of life in eighth-century Greece, increasingly dependent on oriental imports, may have

been a contributory factor in the downfall of the *basileis*. Since their wealth was derived from their own lands rather than from the community as a whole, they must have found it progressively more difficult to meet the expenses of their civic and religious responsibilities.

Another factor in their decline was a change that occurred on the battlefield. The Homeric hero had traditionally gone into

battle on a chariot, and *basileis* still led their private armies into battles that were won—or lost—by cavalry. Now, though, new kinds of bronze armor from the East—helmet, corslet, greaves, and a shield—and iron weapons, thrusting spears, and a slash-

both of his own importance and the need for solidarity with his fellows.

This solidarity expressed itself in the creation of the city-state, or *polis*. This was the political center of a geographical entity whose character varied from one part of Greece to another. In Attica, Athens became the sole *polis* and other towns which elsewhere in Greece might have become city-states themselves were subordinated to her. Elsewhere, the inhabitants of a valley might come together. The important factor in each case was the civic spirit: "Men are the *polis*," says Thucydides, and elsewhere he indirectly makes the point that architectural distinction was not a prerequisite for a city-state. Sparta, in his day, was still "a struggling village like the ancient towns of Hellas"; and no one would have denied that Sparta was imbued with civic spirit.

The political power in a city-state was vested in officials who were elected annually, usually from among members of the aristocracy. Aristocrats must have played an important part in eliminating the powers of the *basileis,* and they took the lead in manning the new political machinery. It would not be true to speak of an aristocratic takeover of power, however, for they could only count on the support of the rest of the population

An early representation *(left)* of the hoplite panoply: helmet, corslet, greaves, shield, short sword, and spear. The new equipment, introduced from the East, and the new methods of warfare it involved, played a part in the development of the city-state. It was cheap enough to be within the means of the ordinary citizen who, ranked together with his fellow hoplite, could feel a sense of involvement in the fate of his own city.

The site of Argos well illustrates the way in which Greek cities were established near a stronghold—an acropolis—to which the inhabitants could retreat when attacked.

ing sword meant that the infantry had a new importance, and one that quickly made itself felt on a political level. For any person of moderate means could afford this relatively simple and very effective equipment, and even more significantly, the new system of infantry fighting in deeply serried ranks—the hoplite system—is thought to have had psychological effects: the individual was conscious at the same time

so long as they acted in a just and equitable manner. If they did not do so, there was always the danger of a return to monarchial rule in the form of tyranny—a system whereby the ruler's power was not hereditary, but gained by his own resources and sustained with the support of the populace.

Above left:
An Athenian foundation legend concerns Ericthonius, whose birth from the ground is shown on this vase painting. The child is being handed into the safe-keeping of Athena, the city's tutelary deity.

TYRANTS, OLIGARCHS, AND DEMOCRATS

The information we have concerning government and society in archaic Greece comes from later and frequently biased sources. It is therefore difficult to know precisely what occurred, and the details, in some cases even the broad outlines, are still a matter of intense dispute among historians of ancient Greek society. There were eventually to be two principal tendencies: one, to restrict membership of the city-state governing circle to a few (oligarchy), and the other, which only emerged after the Persian Wars, to place political control in the hands of as many free citizens of a city-state as possible (democracy). These forms of government were, however, often preceded by a third —one which was widespread in Greece in the late seventh and sixth centuries B.C., namely "tyranny."

A tyrant was an absolute ruler who gained power and held on to it by unconstitutional means. (It was only later that tyranny came to be equated with oppression, and only then by the aristocracy; the common people were rather less oppressed.) Tyrants were frequently reformist, and though they were usually replaced by oligarchical regimes, the innovations they had introduced would generally survive.

In Argos, according to Aristotle, King Pheidon transformed his regime into a tyranny at some time around 675 B.C. He presumably dispensed with the support of the Argive aristocracy and replaced it with that of the emergent hoplite class. At Sparta, tyranny was avoided altogether, but Corinth and Athens both experienced it, although in different ways.

In 657 B.C. the harsh rule at Corinth of an aristocratic clan, the Bacchidae, was overturned by a revolution led by a certain Cypselus, perhaps with the support of Pheidon of Argos, and certainly with the aid of interested parties at Corinth. Corinth's commercial activities were already highly successful under the Bacchidae: colonies had been founded at Syracuse and Corcyra, and Corinthian pottery was widely exported to both east and west. Cypselus' backers must have included parties who had benefited from all this, but who resented the political restraints of Bacchiad rule. Under Cypselus, more colonies were founded in the northwest, a move which not only protected trade routes with Italy, but opened up markets within the Balkan peninsula. Cypselus, it was said, "ruled Corinth mildly, maintain-

ing no bodyguard and enjoying the good will of the Corinthians." The fact that he had no bodyguard implies that he had the support of the hoplite class.

Most tyrannies did not become dynastic; that of Cypselus was an exception, and he was succeeded in turn by his son Periander and Psammetichus, Periander's nephew. Little is known about the latter other than that he was overthrown, to be replaced by oligarchs, but Periander became a byword for tyranny in the modern sense of the word. Aristotle has him suppressing challengers (another tyrant is said to have advised him to "lop off the tallest ears of corn"), preventing public assemblies, forbidding the flaunting of private wealth, and so on. Even his public building works were intended "to keep the subjects poor and occupied." Periander was undoubtedly brutish (his revenge on Corcyra after a revolt was to send three hundred Corcyrean boys to the king of Lydia to be made eunuchs; mercifully the boys were rescued on the way), but it is difficult to know quite how bad he was, given the nature of our sources.

Sparta differed from most other Greek states in that she did not experience tyranny at all during her early history. This, however, is one of the few indisputable facts about early Sparta; for the rest, scholars are still arguing and, unless major new evidence appears, always will. Laconia was occupied around 1000 by the Dorians, migrant warriors who settled in a group of villages at Sparta. The men lived in common huts and ate their meals together. They were landowners, but the lands were worked by helots—the pre-Dorian population which had been reduced to serfdom.

A document known as the Great Rhetra describes in cryptic terms how the primitive constitution of Sparta worked. A council of elders including two kings held supreme power. The people ("damos") had a kind of nominal authority, but this was clearly limited, for a rider to the Rhetra reads: "If the damos speaks crooked, the elders and kings shall refuse it."

Spartan territory gradually expanded, and more helots were created, especially in Messenia. They were to present a constant threat to the stability of the Spartan state. A Messenian revolt between ca. 650 and 620 revealed weaknesses in Spartan military tactics, and it was probably only then that the Spartans perfected the hoplite system of

The tyrant Cypselus overthrew an oppressive and unpopular regime at Corinth and "ruled Corinth mildly." This gold dish was dedicated by one of his descendants at Olympia between 625 and 550 B.C.

The Pisistratid tyranny at Athens came under attack in 514 when a member of the family was murdered by Harmiodius and Aristogiton, who were subsequently commemorated as tyrannicides and honored with statues in the Agora. The statues were frequently copied; here on a red-figure vase.

Ruins (right) of the Electra Gate, one of the seven gates of Thebes, seat of a successful oligarchy, and supporter of the Pisistratid tyranny in Athens.

A marble bust in Naples which is traditionally called "Solon"; if it was originally meant to represent the Athenian statesman of the early sixth century B.C., it was certainly made several centuries after his death, and so cannot be regarded as being in any way a true likeness.

The Stoa Basileos stood in the Agora at Athens, which became the center not only of commercial activity but also of government and politics, as opposed to the Acropolis, the prehistoric site of the royal palace, which now became the focus of religious and ceremonial activity.

The Stoa itself was used for preliminary hearings in cases of impiety, which was as much a political as a religious offense, as was exemplified by the case of Socrates, who appeared here in 399.

A reminder that not all members of Greek society were free citizens. Slavery was an important institution throughout classical antiquity. Most miners, such as those seen here, were probably slaves.

fighting. There were social and political changes too. The seventh century had for the most part been easy for the wealthy; the poet Alcman gives us a glimpse of a luxurious way of life that most of the damos must have envied: "a rival to the iron is the beautiful playing of the cythera." The old order gave way to an age of austerity. The power of the damos was expressed through five officials called ephors (though the dual kingship survived), and they achieved reforms which gave the Spartan community a structure that has often been attributed to a single legendary lawgiver, Lycurgus. Citizens, now called Spartiates, had theoretically equal allotments of land, and had equal political rights. They were, however, members of a community whose sole aim was to train its citizens to selfless valor in war; as the bellicose poet Tyrtaeus put it: "O young men. . .begin not foul flight nor yet be afraid, but make the heart in your breasts both great and stout, and never shrink when you fight the foe."

Political changes were late in coming to

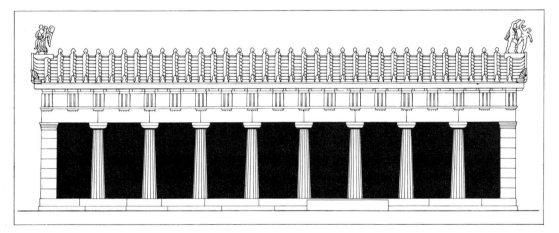

on *tithes* (in fact, "sixths") being sold into slavery. Debtors, too, were liable to a similar fate if they failed to repay their loans on time. Both problems disappeared in 594–593 (or 573–572; the date is disputed) when Solon was archon. He passed a measure known as the *Seisachtheia*, the "shaking off of burdens," by which existing debts were canceled and it was made illegal to transact loans against the security of a person's freedom. Solon described himself

Athens. Control of the governing body —the Council of the Areopagus, made up of ex-magistrates (archons)—was in the hands of the aristocratic clans of Attica who were collectively known as the Eupatridae. An attempt in 630 to establish a tyranny failed, but some ten years later Dracon drew up a law code which in later times was a byword for severity. In the late seventh century, however, it was remarkable that it existed at all.

The need for legislative reform became increasingly apparent in the years around 600. Large numbers of small farmers in Attica were tied to wealthy landowners by means of a system which involved defaulters

as a mediator between rich and poor. A court, the Heliaea, was set up in which every citizen had the right to bring a charge against another, and the Athenian class structure was redefined on a basis of wealth rather than birth. There were now four census classes, but only members of the two richest were eligible for the archonship. But for all the care he took to make these changes, Solon did not go far enough. The old system of tribal allegiances survived, a fact which led to the collapse of the Solonian constitution before very long.

Solon himself had voluntarily gone into exile for ten years in order to give his constitution a chance to work on its own merits rather than his. It was clear on his return that Athens was in imminent danger

tribal system, but by doing it in such a way as to minimize the risk of his newly created tribes' falling under aristocratic control. There was to be a new administrative unit known as the "deme," a unit which became the focus of local loyalty. There were about 170 demes in the whole of Attica, combined into thirty groups called *trittyes,* groups which might contain a single large deme or else a cluster of smaller ones. Ten tribes were then selected by lot, one *trittys* coming from the city, another from around the coast, and the third from inland. In this way each tribe contained a cross section of Attic society and regionalism ceased to be a major problem. Members of landed families continued to occupy the more important posts, but now as elected officials answerable to their con-

The stone inscription of a Solonic text below was set up, probably in a temple or public building, in the early fifth century.

of tyranny: factional struggles conducted on a regional basis were rife. In 561–560, Pisistratus siezed power and held on to it intermittently until his death in 528–527. His was in fact an age of peaceful government. He neutralized the influence of the aristocratic factions, began a program of public works (but what tyrant or dictator does not?), and forcibly put a stop to the drift to the city from the land. His sons Hipparchus and Hippias were less successful; the one was murdered in 514 and the other went into exile in 510.

For two years there was anarchy, resolved in 508 when Cleisthenes reformed the Athenian constitution not merely by revising the

stituents. The day-to-day business of the city was conducted by the Council of the Five Hundred made up of fifty men elected annually from each tribe. Each of these tribal contingents (known as *prytaneis*) would be on duty, resident in the Agora, for one-tenth of the year, and a president was chosen daily by lot. This was to be the framework for Athenian democracy in the fifth century.

Although this was a period of intensive development and innovations in politics, the tenor of daily life was rural rather than urban, and traditional rather than innovative. The herdsman and his dog *(above left)* watching their flocks exemplify the traditional agricultural basis of the societies which at this time were evolving new, complicated, and sophisticated political structures.

123

HERO CULTS

The average Greek in the sixth century B.C. was extremely religious. He saw the actions of the gods in every aspect of life. A clever politician might turn this attitude to his own advantage. Such a one was Pisistratus, intermittently tyrant of Athens between 561 and 527, who calculatedly identified his fortunes with those of Heracles. It was well known that Heracles was under Athena's special protection. Pisistratus tried, with a good deal of success, to persuade the Athenian public that he was in effect a second Heracles. Recent research has shown that the visual arts of the period, both public and private, are not just concerned with Heracles' traditional feats, but that they often show him in new and politically significant ways.

Pisistratus chose to live on the Athenian Acropolis. It was safer there, for one thing, but it was also closer to the gods. Much of the architectural sculpture made for religious buildings on the Acropolis at this time shows scenes from Heracles' career. A limestone pediment shows Heracles fighting the

of the Coast, The Men of the Plain, and The Men of the Hills, during whose struggles Pisistratus had first seized power. A small group showing the introduction of Heracles to Olympus (perhaps to be equated with Pisistratus' rise to greater things) may also belong to this pediment.

It has been observed that the incidence of new and unusual Heracles themes in Attic vase painting at the time of the Pisistratids is such that they can only be explained as propaganda in favor of the regime. The work of an artist known as the Priam Painter is especially full of implicit references to the Heraclean values of Pisistratean rule. On a vase by the Priam Painter in Oxford there is a harnessing scene which includes Heracles and a very large Athena who is about to mount the chariot. The inscription "*Herakleous kore*" (daughter of Heracles) can only make sense if we interpret Athena as Phye, the strapping girl whom Pisistratus dressed up in a procession as Athena, and subsequently married to his son Hipparchus.

There are signs of resistance to Pisistratus

The popularity of hero cults is demonstrated by the frequency with which they are used as decorative motifs, with or without ulterior motives. The amphora below depicts the crucial scene of one of the most popular of all hero legends, the slaying of the Minotaur by Theseus. The Minotaur legend suggests Athenian memories of the Bronze Age power of Crete, but later on other tales continued to gather round the figure of Theseus including a series of labors on the Heraclean model.

The triple-headed monster "Bluebeard" (above right) holding water symbol, grain, and a bird, may perhaps have served as a symbol for the party struggles between the Men of the Coast, the Men of the Plain, and the Men of the Hills during which Pisistratus seized power in Athens.

many-headed hydra, perhaps a reference to Pisistratus' enemies. Another shows the hero wrestling with the sea creature Triton, and this has been connected with Pisistratus' successful amphibious campaign against Megara in 566. Other fragments, which may come from the pediment of a Temple of Athena, whose foundations may still be seen today lying between the Parthenon and the Erechtheum, again show Heracles and Triton, but this time accompanied by the famous triple-bodied monster popularly known as "Bluebeard." This creature holds in its hands a watersymbol, corn, and a bird, and it has been suggested that these attributes symbolize the three parties: The Men

too on vase scenes. The famous vase by Exekias in the Vatican showing Ajax and Achilles playing dice has been connected with the events surrounding Pisistratus' return to power at Athens in 546, an event which was facilitated by the fact that the Athenian army was off guard, "some playing dice," according to Herodotus. The message of Exekias' vase might be a warning that "in the case of tyranny and defeat, survival lies with the alert" (Boardman).

Another story in the Theseus legend, the abduction of Antiope, is represented in this fragment from the west pediment of the Temple of Apollo in Eretria. Aided, according to one version of the story, by Heracles, Theseus carried off the Amazon Antiope, or Hippolyta, to Athens. The Amazons attacked Athens in revenge, and Antiope died fighting at Theseus' side.

The legend of the death of their son Hippolytus was the basis of one of Euripides' tragedies, for the Greek dramatists, as much as the painters and sculptors, also found inspiration in the rich subject matter of the hero legends.

This scene, on a vase by the Priam Painter, appears to provide clear evidence of the manipulation of a popular hero figure to his personal advantage by an astute politician. In the details we see a generously proportioned Athena mounting a chariot, with Heracles also present. The inscription labels the Athena figure as the ''daughter of Heracles.'' The figure of Heracles may represent Pisistratus, and that of Athena, Phye, a girl he is known to have dressed as Athena for a procession, and who married his son Hipparchus.

125

THE ALPHABET

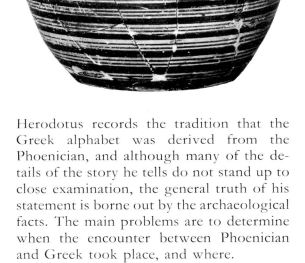

This Attic Late Geometric jug (oino-choe) bears the earliest Greek inscription known from mainland Greece, and can be dated to ca. 740 B.C. The vase was intended as a prize in a dancing competition, and the inscription which is written retrograde (that is from right to left) reads in translation, "He who now of all the dancers dances the most gracefully..."

The derivation of the Greek alphabet from the Phoenician original is depicted in the three simplified alphabets (right). There were, of course, many local and regional variations in letter shapes, and in directions of writing—and hence the way in which the letters faced—but the basic development can be seen clearly.

The fragment of the Salamis decree (right) demonstrates one important use the archaic Greeks put writing to: the recording of political events and decisions. This use of writing in the sphere of government provides us with important, if often fragmentary, contemporary evidence.

Herodotus records the tradition that the Greek alphabet was derived from the Phoenician, and although many of the details of the story he tells do not stand up to close examination, the general truth of his statement is borne out by the archaeological facts. The main problems are to determine when the encounter between Phoenician and Greek took place, and where.

In order to establish the date at which the characters of the North Semitic alphabet were adopted and adapted for the purposes of expressing Greek sounds, we have to examine the earliest extant inscriptions. These occur on pottery made in the eighth century B.C. The earliest of all is on a tiny fragment of locally made pottery found at Pithecusae on the island of Ischia. This was the site of the first Greek colony in the west founded from Euboea in the middle of the eighth century B.C. Only two letters of the inscription survive: pi and alpha. The alpha is remarkable in that it is written on its side, similar to the way the equivalent Phoenician letter is shown in contemporary inscriptions. The inscription must date to around the mid-eighth century, close to the occupation of the site by Greek colonists. Another early inscription comes from Pithecusae, too: the so-called cup of Nestor, which was found with vases that can be dated to 720–710. Here, though, the alpha is upright, although the five-stroke mu which occurs on it is a primitive feature that is close to its Semitic original. The earliest inscription so far found in mainland Greece appears on a late Geometric jug (oinochoe) that must have been made at Athens in about 740. This has the early form of the alpha on its side, as well as unusual forms of the letters iota and lambda.

PHOENICIAN

b	g	d	h	w	z	ḥ	ṭ	j	

ARCHAIC GREEK

a	y	g	d	e	z	ē	th	i	k	l	m

CLASSICAL GREEK

A	B	Γ	Δ	E	I	H	Θ	I	K	Λ	M
a	b	g	d	e	z	ē	th	i	k	l	m

It was probably the case that the earliest Greek alphabets simply took over the twenty-two signs, sounds, and names of the Phoenician alphabet. It was only later that extra letters were added to represent sounds

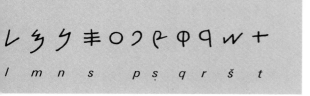

l m n s   p ṣ q r š t

n o p s   q r t u ks ō

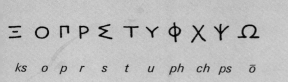

ks   o p r s t u ph ch ps ō

that did not exist in Semitic languages. The letter *chi*, for example, was one of these, and since there is a *chi* employed in the alphabet used in the Attic oinochoe inscription, it would be difficult to accept this as belonging to the very earliest generation of Greek alphabets. The origin of the Greek alphabet cannot have been much earlier than 740, however, and probably occurred between 775 and 750.

The answer to the question of where the adoption by Greeks of the Phoenician alphabet took place is, paradoxically perhaps, supplied by the existence of the two early inscriptions from the Euboean settlement in the far west at Pithecusae. Some of the earliest pottery found on the site of another Greek trading post, Al Mina on the North Syrian coast, has been shown either to come from Euboea or to be closely modeled on Euboean products. Al Mina was probably not the only Greek trading center in the area, although since it was at the mouth of the River Orontes, and thus closely in touch with the hinterland and Mesopotamia, it certainly the most important. It was here, or so one argument goes, that Euboean traders saw the possibilities presented by the Phoenician alphabet and adopted it for use with Greek. This explains the early alphabets in Euboean contexts in the west (sadly, there is nothing of an early date from Euboea itself), but does not explain the awkward fact that of the Greek alphabets, that which is closest of all to Phoenician is the Cretan. There were undoubted commercial links between the Cretans and the Phoenicians in the eighth century, although we do not have evidence to show to what extent Cretans may have taken part in the trading venture at Al Mina. It should not perhaps be forgotten that the Phoenicians were if anything more mobile than the Euboeans, and that in theory at least, all it needed for the alphabet to be transmitted was that a single Phoenician should have passed his alphabet to a single Greek. This, it has been argued, could have occurred in Crete just as easily as at Al Mina. The question remains open, though new evidence may well resolve matters.

The earliest extant inscriptions, which are frequently in verse, have a variety of purposes. They may simply denote ownership, or be used to dedicate a vessel or a statue to a deity; tombstones might be inscribed at an early date, but surviving law codes and decrees tend to be later.

Archaic Greek stonecutters were indifferent to the direction in which an inscription might be read. On this list of names from Thera, carved in a local alphabet in the second half of the seventh century B.C., the first line (Reksanor) goes from right to left, the next two (Arkhagetas and Prokles) go from left to right, and the last line (Kleagoras, Peraieus) goes from right to left and part of the way up the left-hand margin.

Unlike the Bronze Age Greeks, who as far as we currently know used writing for practical and utilitarian purposes only, the archaic Greeks eventually applied their rediscovered skill to everything from epic poetry to epigram.

This drinking cup from Pithecusae on the island of Ischia (720–710 B.C.) bears an invitation to love-making: "The cup of Nestor was pleasing to drink from; but whoever drinks from this cup, desire of Aphrodite of the beautiful crown will immediately seize him."

A detail of a fragmentary chronological table—the Parian Marble—drawn up in the Hellenistic period and which lists important historical events in Greek history. It was taken to England in the early seventeenth century and part of it was built into a fireplace in the English Civil War and is now lost.

ARCHAIC LITERATURE

Greek literature before Herodotus (fifth century B.C.) was for the most part composed in verse rather than prose. The reason for this is not very far to seek. Although the alphabet was introduced to Greece around the middle of the eighth century, it was not apparently used to write down literary works, but was used primarily for recording more mundane matters. The epic sagas of the Trojan Wars that were told and retold by professional singers were composed in verse so that they could be more easily memorized. The works of the poet (or poets) we call Homer, and of Hesiod the Boeotian farmer-poet, were written down at a comparatively early time, but the survival of most archaic literature is a matter of accident. Much of it is in the form of verses that were composed to be sung to the accompaniment of the lyre, usually at symposia. Given the expensive nature of ancient book production, it is highly unlikely that much poetry could have been committed to writing at all. Even the little that was recorded will have been subject to numerous vicissitudes in the Middle Ages: crumbling papyrus, iconoclasts' bonfires, or monkish prudery. Small wonder that we have only fragments of the works of even major archaic poets. From time to time, though, scholars find hitherto unknown verses among papyrus scraps from Egypt, a recent example being the outspokenly sexy poem by Archilochus that was first published in 1974.

The rhapsode *(above)*, the professional singer, had been for hundreds of years the means by which the Greeks had enjoyed and transmitted their literature. His style was responsible for the forms it took, and even after the gradual introduction of written versions of the famous tales and legends, oral performance remained an important art.

The intimate, intense, feminine world of Sappho and her coterie is captured in this detail of a young girl picking fruit, by the Sotades Painter.

Archilochus was born out of wedlock in Paros in about 716. His father was an aristocrat, but his mother was a slave woman. He was disqualified from any inheritance and consequently grew up with a grudge against society. Much of his poetry is written in a meter—the iambic—which was often employed for invective. Paros was an island, and inevitably much of Archilochus' poetry is concerned with the sea: its unpredictability, its cruelty, and the possibilities of escaping the boredom of the watch in drink:

"Along the rowers' benches bring your cup,
And lift the lids of the big wine-jars up
And drain the good red wine; we can't, 'tis clear,
Be sober all the time we're watching here."

He took part in a colonizing venture to the island of Thasos in the northern Aegean—an island which, he complained, "sticks up like a donkey's back." We catch a glimpse in Archilochus' poetry of the frontier-town atmosphere that prevailed in Thasos, troublesome companions (doubtless misfits like himself), and battles with local Thracian tribes with whom treaties were made and broken. It was in Thasos that Archilochus fell in love with Neoboule, the daughter of Lycambes (although the new fragment describes what he would like to do to Neoboule's sister in gushing detail). The promised marriage did not take place, despite the poet's remonstrances. He took his revenge by pouring a torrent of savage abuse on Neoboule's whole family which is said to

compatriot. Like her he was an aristocrat and a homosexual, and like her was forced twice into exile for political reasons. Alcaeus served in the army and disgraced himself by throwing away his shield on the field of battle, or so he said (Archilochus had employed the same conceit). His poetry is full of rancor at the danger his opponents were bringing about in the state of Lesbos; he complains that the traditional rights enjoyed by his ancestors have been usurped by "graceless burgesses." He was one of the first to employ the image of the ship of state in his verses, likening contemporary politics to a "Tumult of winds; the waves come this way and that, and we in the midst are driven onward in our black ship…"

One of the great themes of Hesiod was the theogony—the war between the gods and the giants which resulted in the establishment of the Greek pantheon. In the detail from the north frieze of the Siphnian treasury at Delphi *(left)* one of the lions drawing Cybele's chariot attacks a giant. *Below:* Zeus in combat with the monster Typhon, shown on a sixth-century water jar from Caere.

have been so effective that they hanged themselves.

Lesbos in the late seventh and early sixth centuries B.C. was torn by revolution, but we would know very little of this if we only had the lyric poems of Sappho to rely on. These are intensely personal works which give us an insight into the life of her coterie, her *thiasos* of girls, toward some of whom she expresses her feelings of passionate love and jealousy in a wholly unself-conscious way: "Love, who sets one quivering, shakes me: the bitter-sweet, irresistible monster, O Atthis, you have come to hate the sight of me, and fly to Andromeda!" Not all Lesbian ladies were lesbians, however, and even Sappho was married.

Alcaeus was Sappho's contemporary and

Theognis of Megara writing in the middle decades of the sixth century was another reactionary conservative whose poetry expressed his opposition to democratic tendencies in his native city. He was driven into exile.

The democracy at Megara was eventually toppled, it had gone too far in confiscating and redistributing property, and the returned exiles formed a new government which Theognis encouraged to "Stamp on the witless people, and smite with the oxgoad keen! Fasten them under a yoke…" The poets may tend to give us a political vision of the world that is one-sided; they are, though, the first Europeans known to us as individual characters. Their kind of personal poetry is one that is still with us.

Left: The Homeric tales became an enduring source of inspiration to Greek sculptors and painters. In the later black- and red-figure pottery, specific scenes from the *Iliad* and *Odyssey* are often identifiable. This eighth-century Geometric scene of warriors disembarking and fighting, may well be an early pictorial representation of a scene from some of the greatest Greek literature.

ARCHAIC SCULPTURE

Examples of archaic treatment of the human form *(left to right):* The seventh-century "Dipylon Head", among the oldest known monumental heads, showing entirely stylized features. The top-heavy "New York kouros" (ca. 580) is supposed to have been found in Attica. Also Attic is the kouros from

Anavysos, which is more mature in style. By the end of the century (between 510 and 500) the kouros of Aristodikos is perfectly formed, but still as static as his fellows. The small "Auxerre goddess" of ca. 640–630 has much of the pattern of her dress incised on the surface. She was originally brightly painted, and may have been made in Crete. The seven-foot-tall kore by Antenor was dedicated on the Acropolis at Athens by the potter Nearchos in about 530–520. She gathers her dress in a gesture which displays the form of her limbs beneath.

Opposite page:
The attractive head of Kore no. 674, from the Acropolis. Archaeologists have named her "the Kore with the pensive face," or "the Kore with the almond eyes." Another nickname she well deserves is "La Delicata." With her calm and serene expression she gazes inscrutably at us across the centuries.

There can be little doubt that the Greeks received the idea for large-scale monumental sculpture from the eastern Mediterranean, but as usual scholars disagree as to quite how the idea was transmitted. It can scarcely be coincidental, though, that life-size (or larger) marble statues began to be made in the Aegean during the reign of the Egyptian pharaoh Psammetichus I (664–610), a ruler who employed Greek and Carian mercenaries in his army and encouraged the foundation of a Greek trading post at Naucratis in the Nile delta. The sculptural monuments of Egypt, so impressive today even in their ruined state, must have been far more impressive in the seventh century B.C.

when they were still in pristine condition. Word of large-scale statues made of stone harder than limestone must have got back to Greece, where craftsmen soon began to use locally available materials to achieve similar ends.

The first Greek center to make life-size statues was probably in the Cyclades, where coarse-grained Naxian marble was to be found. Finer-grained marble was quarried on Paros and was widely exported in the archaic period, even to Athens at first, although the local Pentelic marble soon began to be used there instead. Limestone sculpture, often used for the decoration of pediments—the gable ends—of temples, would be covered with stucco to look like

marble, and all archaic sculpture, whether in marble, limestone, or terracotta, was frequently colored in a way that we would probably find garish. The remaining color on some of the *korai* (maidens) found on the Athenian Acropolis is but a shadow of what was formerly there.

Female statues were usually draped, a convention that was observed until the fourth century B.C., while male figures were frequently nude. This reflects the fact that Greek women were, for the most part, expected to keep themselves modestly covered, while men frequently exercised naked among themselves.

There is a tendency for the figures of nude youths—*kouri*—to become progressively anatomically more accurate—at least such is the conventional view. There were, however, other factors at work which account for the slow rate at which true naturalism was achieved; factors such as the tradition which persisted from Geometric times whereby individual parts of a figure—such as hair, ears, muscles—were treated separately, and in the case of archaic sculpture frequently stylized in a prescribed way.

A striking feature of many archaic statues is the mysterious "archaic smile." The reason for its existence is much debated; its origins may have been accidental, but the mannerism was probably retained since it made the facial features appear more alive.

ARCHAIC ART: THE ORIENTAL INFLUENCE

One of the most interesting features of archaic Greek art is the way in which we can observe how the form, and to some extent the content, of the art of the Geometric period changes as a result of an ever-increasing Greek contact with the eastern Mediterranean. Early Iron Age Greece had been more or less cut off from the rather more sophisticated civilizations of Mesopotamia, Syria, and Phoenicia, and even those of the Anatolian hinterland. As a consequence, Greek Geometric art with its regular, linear patterns evolved in relative isolation. Only in Crete is there much evidence for contact with the east in the form of tenth- and ninth-century decorated pottery, and vase stands with Cypriot affinities. There are but occasional eastern imports elsewhere in Greece, and it is only in the eighth century, when the Greek colonizing movement led to renewed contact with the east, that oriental imports (and probably immigrant craftsmen) have any noticeable effect on Greek artists and artisans.

The principal sources of new patterns appear to have been Syria and Phoenicia. These areas had themselves assimilated motifs from Egypt and Mesopotamia, and there were Greek trading posts (such as the one at Al Mina) there too. Luxury goods—metalwork, textiles, ivories, and perfumes—were brought to Greece and they (or their containers) had an immediate effect on Greek artistic products. A popular import, judging by fragments found in sanctuaries and cemeteries all over Greece, was the bronze caldron on a high stand. The rim would be decorated with handles in the form of sirens, creatures whose birds' tails and wings clasp the shoulder of the vessel, while their human heads look in. These were soon copied by local bronzeworkers who seem to have devised a variant of their own with the foreparts of griffins (animals which were themselves derived from the oriental menagerie) mounted on caldron rims. These were at first rather clumsily hammered out of sheet metal, but by the late seventh century were hollow-cast in bronze. The finest were to be numbered among the most elegant Greek artifacts of any period.

This pattern—to take an oriental motif and to adapt and enhance it—can be observed throughout the orientalizing period (as the age in which Greek artists assimilated oriental models is called). The reaction of craftsmen in different parts of Greece to the

A griffin's-head decoration—one of several which would have been mounted on the rim of a large bronze caldron of around 700 B.C. The griffin, which was the legendary guardian of the Central Asiatic gold mines, was one of several mythological beasts that Greek artists copied from eastern models.

A bronze Geometric beetle found in Olympia. Although stylistically it is akin to indigenous Greek products of the Early Iron Age, its form is similar to that of Egyptian scarabs and is probably derived from such a source.

new models varies, however. At Corinth, the oriental fauna—lions, boars, deer, bulls, goats, and hybrid, mythological creatures such as sirens, griffins, chimaeras, and sphinxes—were taken over in a fairly literal manner by the decorators of pottery, who also adopted a technique from metalwork whereby added detail could be given to figures and patternwork by means of incision. Corinthian pottery during the seventh, and the first half of the sixth, centuries B.C. is often decorated with variations on the "animal style." Sometimes the animals are in rows; sometimes they stand singly or in heraldically affronted pairs. Their immediate models were probably animals woven in oriental textiles; at least we can actually see rows of similar animals on the dresses worn by figures painted on Athenian vases in the early sixth century, and while these garments were presumably produced locally by this time, they too must surely have been copied ultimately from eastern prototypes. Athenian artists were slower to give up their Geometric ways, and although figure decoration occurs in Late Geometric vase painting in response to figure decoration on oriental imports, it is some time before there is much that is at all oriental-looking in Attic art. The two rampant sphinxes on the interior of a Geometric cup in the German Archaeological Institute, Athens (shown at right), are very much the exception in the eighth century, and it is only at the turn of the century that any real signs of orientalizing influence can be seen. Linear motifs become curvilinear and the filling ornament becomes more conspicuously vegetal. Fill-

Far left: Contrasting statuettes: one an Egyptian bronze nude in the manner of oriental figurines, and the other an Assyrian clothed votary, both from the shrine of Hera at Samos.

Center: Two details from pots painted by Sophilos; in both cases the women are wearing garments decorated with rows of animals. Such textiles first came to Greece from the Near East in the eighth century B.C. and the motifs on them were used as models by local craftsmen.

Left: A detail from a wine-mixing bowl by the Analatos Painter of the early seventh century B.C. In his work the rigid linear conventions of Geometric art can be seen to give way to a more lifelike treatment of both humans and animals.

ing ornament, a constant feature in both Geometric and orientalizing art, must have had a practical rather than an aesthetic function on the original textile models. In textiles the filling ornament provided an additional anchorage for the weft, which otherwise would have formed large loops on the back that would have been subject to pulling if not breakage.

The way human figures were shown in Attic art changed during the orientalizing period; at least the evidence supplied by the decorated pottery suggests as much. The rela-

tively simple, pin-headed people of Geometric figure decoration are gradually replaced by figures with outline faces, crude at first as in the work of the Analatos Painter, but relatively sophisticated by the early sixth century. By this time, however, figures were silhouetted (in "black-figure" technique) against the orange color of the pot, though women's flesh was done in added white paint. Woman's place in ancient Greece was clearly not just in the home, but out of the sun as well. Women are, moreover, usually shown clothed in archaic Greek art, in contrast with Near Eastern artifacts where they often appear naked.

Another important artistic development was the way Greek artists took over oriental floral motifs such as lotus buds or flowers and palmettes and made them an integral part of the classical decorative repertoire. These motifs were taken up by Greek architects who incorporated them in the Ionic Order—another major artistic invention of the archaic period.

A winged sphinx, one of several oriental animals done in relief on the side of a Cretan *pithos* (storage jar) of the seventh century B.C. Crete was one of the first parts of the Greek world to receive oriental influences.

Left: A bronze bowl decorated with lion-hunting scenes done in repoussé with the details incised on the inside of the vessel. This bowl was probably made in the Near East in the late eighth century B.C. but was found at Olympia.

Far left: Attic Geometric bowl of the later eighth century B.C. which is somewhat unusual for its period in that two oriental sphinxes are included among the figures in the tondo. Even though the presence of figure decoration on Attic Geometric vases was itself a reaction to eastern models, oriental creatures such as these tend not to appear in Athenian art until the seventh century.

Three vases made at Corinth between the mid-seventh and early sixth century B.C. showing the absorption by Greek vase painters of oriental animal motifs—lions, bulls, deer, and a griffin—into their decorative repertoire.

MONEY

The use of coinage is something that everyone today understands, and it is difficult to think of an era when coinage was unknown. Yet such was the situation in mainland Greece until the mid-sixth century B.C. Until then, large monetary transactions were made in bullion, either in the form of jewelry or vessels or made into some convenient shape such as bars or rings. Iron spits might be used for transactions on a smaller scale, and the terminology from this era survived into the age when coinage was used. A *drachma* originally meant a handful of iron spits, and an *obol* a single spit. Later they came to be the names of two coins, a drachma being at one time the price of a sheep, and an obol a day's pay for jury service.

The reason why coinage was introduced is still uncertain. Coins today are used for minor, everyday business, but the earliest examples, the staters of Lydia and Ionia, contained between 13 and 17 grams of electrum, an alloy of gold and silver, and would have been equivalent today to a high

got the idea to do this from Croesus, of Lydia (561–456), or whether he got the idea from them. One tradition gives the primacy to Aegina, while Herodotus tells us that "the Lydians were the first people we know to strike and use coins in gold and silver."

The earliest coins were of electrum, an alloy of gold and silver, and were made in Lydia and Ionia beginning in the second half of the seventh century B.C. *From left to right:*

The oldest known inscribed coin, probably of Ephesus (the stag was one of Artemis' beasts), bears the name of Phanes, who is otherwise unknown; ca. 600 B.C.

An electrum stater with a lion's head which may come from Smyrna; ca. 575.

Issues of Acanthus in Chalcidice regularly have a lion attacking a bull. This example is thought to have been struck in about 530 B.C.

denomination banknote. Such coins were clearly meant for making large, rather than small, payments. Suggestions have included the payment of wages to mercenary soldiers, the payment of architects and sculptors, or the payment of harbor dues and taxes. Trade was certainly facilitated, but because of uncertainty concerning the proportions of gold and silver in electrum, coins began to be struck, probably around 560 B.C., in these metals too, but for the most part in silver. This may have happened first in Aegina, whose distinctive turtle-back coins are the earliest from Greece itself. It is still not certain whether or not the Aeginetans

Coins were always issued by central governments, never by merchants, and their bullion weight was always slightly less than their face value, the difference after the cost of minting being clear profit for the issuing authority. States could assure themselves of such profit by insisting that payments made within their territory be in the local coinage. The earliest electrum coins were simply clumps bearing punch marks on the reverse and striations on the obverse (front) impressed from the surface on which the coin was struck. Soon, however, dies bearing types and legends began to be employed, though the punch marks remained relatively crude. Gradually, though, these too were made neater, appearing as regular "Union Jack" or "windmill" or swastika shapes. In southern Italy in the late sixth century two interlocking dies were used to produce on the reverse an incuse version of the obverse. In most places, however, separate reverse types were developed. At Corinth from about 500 B.C. the obverse bear the winged horse Pegasus, and the reverse a head of Athena wearing a Corinthian helmet. Athena also appears, naturally enough, on coins of Athens, with owls on the reverse (the Greek for "coals to Newcastle" was "owls to Athens"). It is uncertain, though, whether such issues were introduced by the tyrant Hippias in ca. 520 or whether they began in ca. 510–506 after the downfall of the tyrants. The discovery of a hoard of 900 coins found at Asyut on the Nile in 1969

The first silver coins were issued at Aegina, ca. 560 B.C. The obverse of Aeginetan coins always bears a turtle, and the reverse an incuse pattern, as on this stater of ca. 475.
The reverse of an electrum stater from Halicarnassus (ca. 800 B.C.) which shows the primitive incuse punch marks used on early coins.

supported by the anvil on which they rested). Die links can thus be observed, and the relative deterioration of dies recorded. Such factors make for great precision in the classification of ancient coins which in fact

Far left: Heracles kneels stringing a bow, on this coin from Thebes, 446–426 B.C.

The lion was a favorite device of Asiatic mints. This example comes from Cnidus and was struck about 550 B.C.

(which included 163 early "owls") has lent new force to the latter date. Much of the progress that has been made in improving our knowledge of the chronology of Greek coinage in recent years is due to the detailed study of hoards such as this. A phenomenon that aids such analysis is the fact that reverse dies had a rather shorter life than did obverse dies (the reverse took more of the force of the hammer blow, whereas the obverse were somewhat protected by the metal of the intervening flan and were

constitute an unrivaled source of information concerning social and economic history.

The types that occur on coins generally refer to local cults, legends, or local products. It is scarcely surprising to find Zeus and an eagle on coins of Elis, in whose territory Olympia lay. Diomedes sometimes appears on coins of Argos; and Arethusa always on those of Syracuse. The Minotaur appears on issues of Knossos. Larisa in "horse-breeding Thessaly" usually has a horse, and Cyrene in North Africa a representation of the now extinct plant known as silphium, which was its principal export.

The coinage of Greek Sicily included some extraordinarily fine issues. This silver didrachm of Selinus bears a parsley leaf (in Greek *selinon*), a pun on the name of both the city and the river on which it stood.

THE GREEK WORLD

CELTS

The Celts of Gaul were well-disposed toward the earliest Greek colonists. There is a story which tells how a local princess fell in love with the founder of Massilia and married him. This Celtic bronze of the third century B.C. is a Celtic stylization of a classical form.

Adria ●

Spina ●

Agathe ●

Nicaea ●

Massalia ● Antipolis ●

Olbia ●

● Emporiae

Alalia ●

ETRUSCANS

Rome ○

Tartessus in Spain was the biblical Tarshish, whence Ezekiel mentions the Phoenicians' importing "Silver and iron, tin and lead." The Greeks were in competition for these resources, a fact which led to clashes with the Carthaginians. There was an indigenous metal industry too; witness this Hispano-Punic bronze razor.

Cumae ●

Neapolis ●

Pithecusae ●

Poseidonia ● Metapontum ●

Elea ● Callipolis

Ta

Hemeroscopion ●

Sybaris ●

Tartessa ○

Gades ○

Lipara ● ● Cro

Caulonia

Eryx ● Himera ● Zancle ● Locri Epiz

Selinus ● Rhegium ●

Catana ● Naxos/Aetna

Acragas ● Megara ●

Gela ● Syracuse ●

○ Carthage

"We sit around our sea," said Socrates, "like frogs around a frogpond." The fact that in the late fifth century a Greek could regard the Mediterranean in this light shows how thoroughly many parts of its coastline had been Hellenized as a result of Greek colonization between the eighth and fifth centuries B.C. Al Mina in the east and Pithecusae in the west are the earliest colonies of which we know, and the Greek settlers in both places appear to have come from Euboea. Their main interest was probably mercantile; they sought luxury goods in the east and raw materials in the west. Other colonies had agricultural objectives and were created in order to satisfy the demands of land-hungry farmers for estates of their own. The Phocaeans were perhaps the most adventurous of all colonists: They had strong economic ties with Tartessus in Spain and founded Massilia at the mouth of the Rhone in ca. 600 B.C., introducing the vine and the olive to Provence; in the words of a writer of the Roman period: "It seemed as if Gaul had moved to Greece, not Greece to Gaul."

CARTHAGINIANS

Carthage was founded from Phoenicia in 814/813 B.C., somewhat earlier than Greek colonists penetrated the western Mediterranean, and the Greeks may well have been consciously following the Phoenician example when they began to colonize the area. A polychrome glass mask (actual size) found at Carthage was probably imported from the Phoenician motherland.

Greek colonists from Thera reached Cyrenaica in the latter part of the seventh century B.C. The staple product of this part of the Greek world was silphium, a plant which was put to a variety of uses, but which is now extinct. Here, the nymph Cyrene tends a silphium plant on a silver tetradrachm of 525–480 B.C.

Greek artifacts were much in demand on the fringes of the Mediterranean world, and Celtic chieftains would even commission objects specially. Such was the case with the 1.64 meter (5 feet) high crater imported in pieces from the Peloponnese and assembled on arrival at Vix in northern France.

There were several Milesian colonies in the northern Black Sea area, including Nymphaeum, where this stylized Scythian bronze elk's head was found in a fifth-century B.C. cemetery where the grave goods were a mixture of Greek and local objects.

Greek craftsmen traveled west, too. The artist of the Northampton amphora, a black-figure vase of great elegance and charm, probably learnt his trade somewhere in western Asia Minor before setting up shop in Italy.

SCYTHIANS

● Olbia

Panticapaeum ● ● Phanagoria
● Nymphaeum

Chersonesus ●

Istros ●

Odessus ●

Mesembria ●

Apollonia ●

Dioscurias ●
Phasis ●

● Sinope

● Amisus

THRACIANS

Epidamnus
Apollonia
Methone
Abdera ●
● Thasos
Potidaea ●
Corcyra
Mende ●
Ambracia
ucas ●

Perinthus ● Byzantium
● Chalcedon
Astacus ●
Cyzicus ●
Abydos ●
Lampsacus

● Heraclea

PERSIA

By the end of the sixth century, the whole of Asia Minor, including its Greek cities, was under Persian control. Greek craftsmen traveled to Persepolis, where they worked on the stone reliefs there. It is likely that they were compelled to do so rather than that they went voluntarily.

CHALCIS
LOCRIS
ERETRIA
MEGARA
ACHAEA
ATHENS
CORINTH
SPARTA ■
THERA ■

■ PHOCAEA
■ CHIOS
■ SAMOS
■ MILETUS
CNIDUS
RHODES ■

Aspendus
● Side
Phaselis ●
Celenderis ●

Soli ● ● Mallus

● Al Mina

CRETE

Soli ● ● Salamis
Paphus ●

PHOENICIA

○ Byblos

Tauchira ● ● Apollonia
● Cyrene
Euesperides ●

○
Ascalum

Naucratis ●

EGYPT

Greeks traded on a regular basis with Egypt from the reign of Psammetichus I (664–610 B.C.) onward. The town of Naucratis was established in the Nile delta, only ten miles from the royal capital of Sais, whence came this group of Neit and the infant Horus.

137

MENACE FROM THE EAST

The Achaemenid empire at its greatest extent was vast and stretched from western India in the east to Asia Minor and Cyrenaica in the west. The Achaemenid dynasty was founded by Cyrus the Great (559–530 B.C.), who brought together the Medes and Persians, hitherto implacable foes, and made a unified fighting force with which he set about pushing the frontiers of his empire far beyond those of Iran. Cyrus built his residence at Pasargadae, deep inside the Achaemenid empire. Here were a huge fortified citadel which measured in plan some 200 by 300 meters and which was probably intended to house the imperial treasure, a palace, and an audience hall. A trilingual inscription which was visible until the last century proclaimed on a doorway at Pasargadae that "I, Cyrus the king, the Achaemenid [built this]."

Egypt became part of the empire in 525 B.C. By the end of the sixth century the Greeks of Asia Minor were ruled by Persian satraps, and Darius (522–486) had made abortive attempts at conquering the lawless Scythians to the north of the Black Sea. The setbacks in the north seemed of little importance at the time, and the Persian military machine appeared to be invincible.

Persepolis is the place where we can best gain an impression of the power and majesty of the Achaemenid state. Begun by Darius in about 520, Persepolis took about sixty years to complete. It was probably a religious center where the new year's festival was celebrated. This festival was attended by delegations that came from all over the empire. They would have been received in the huge audience hall some twenty meters high, the parapets and stairways of which were decorated with reliefs showing members of the twenty-three different delegations in realistic, though somewhat stylized detail. We see Susians in their elaborate robes, carrying bows and daggers; Lydians in their woolen gowns holding vessels probably of precious metal as tribute; Sogdians with their broad-tailed sheep; Indians with baskets probably filled with gold dust; and Bactrians leading their two-humped camels. Given the enormous wealth and military resources of the Achaemenid empire, it is extraordinary that her armies and fleets should have met with successive defeats at the hands of the quarrelsome, disorganized, and unsophisticated Greeks. Yet such was the case.

Above: King Darius enthroned; a relief carved on a door jamb at Persepolis.
Below: An impression taken from a cylinder-seal showing Darius taking part in a lion hunt. The cuneiform inscriptions in Persian, Elamite, and Babylonian, the three official languages of the Achaemenid empire, all say "Darius, the Great King."

A fluted vase with ibex handles. Vessels like this are carried by some of the figures on the Persepolis reliefs, although this one is perhaps a century later in date.

A gold phiale with the name of Darius inscribed on the rim: a vivid reminder of the immense wealth of the Achaemenid empire.

139

THE BATTLE OF MARATHON

It might have seemed inevitable that the mighty Achaemenid empire would expand westward indefinitely, and yet even early in Darius' reign there were signs that this might not be so. Greek Cyrenaica had been a Persian tributary since Cambyses conquered Egypt in the 520s, and it is there that the first Greek resistance to Persian rule took place. A revolt broke out in about 515, but was put down harshly. A burnt level found in recent excavations at Euesperides (Benghazi) has been associated with this event, and evidence of destruction has been found at Cyrene too. Darius' failure to conquer the Scythians in the north in ca. 513, however, showed that the Persian military machine was not invincible.

By 500 even the Ionian Greeks, many of whom had prospered under Persian rule,

mainland Greek states which had dared to oppose him.

In 492 Darius' son-in-law Mardonius was sent with an army and a fleet to prepare the way for an attack on Greece by securing the Hellespont and Thrace. Despite certain setbacks, including the loss of much of the fleet in a storm off Mount Athos and a serious injury suffered by Mardonius, the invasion was largely successful. More important still, the message to Greece was clear: the Persians meant business. The next year Darius sent envoys to the Greek states to make the traditional demand for earth and water as tokens of submission. Most states submitted, though Athens and Sparta emphasized their rejection by putting the ambassadors to death.

The promised onslaught came in 490. The

Below: The map shows the vast extent of the Persian Empire. At its greatest, it stretched from northern Greece and Libya in the west to Afghanistan in the east. Darker areas correspond to expansion which brought the Persians into violent contact with the Greeks.
Right: A messenger reports a disaster to King Darius, perhaps the Persian defeat at Marathon. Detail of an Apulian volute crater by the Darius Painter, ca. 330.

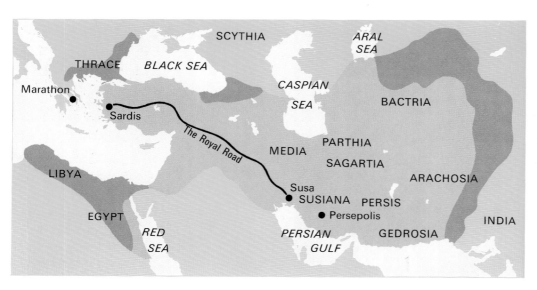

Below: An archaic kouros destroyed when the Persians attacked Cyrene in 515 B.C. in order to put down a revolt.

broke out in revolt. Some mainland Greek states were drawn into the hostilities (Athens and Eretria assisted in the destruction by fire of the local Persian capital, Sardis, in ca. 498) while others remained cautiously neutral, or even professed pro-Persian sympathies. There was no such thing as a unified "Greek" policy. Each state took its own line, usually one which was governed by the outlook of the party that happened to be in control at any given time. Thus Athenian policy with regard to the Ionian revolt seems to have changed with the coming to power of Hipparchus, whose sister had married the Pisistratid tyrant Hippias, now in exile at the Persian court. In Persian eyes, however, the damage had been done, and the first task Darius undertook once the Ionians had been pacified was to punish the

Persians came by sea across the Aegean, proceeding slowly from island to island, punishing those, such as the Naxians, who had taken up arms against Persia in the past, but sparing the shrine of Apollo at Delos. They laid siege to Eretria on Euboea and took it after a few days. The captive population were taken away to be sold into slavery, and the Persians "after waiting for a few days, sailed for the land of Attica."

Rather than sail all the way round Cape Sunium, the Persians decided to land at the Bay of Marathon. They had with them a knowledgeable guide in the person of Hippias, who hoped to regain power in an Athens subject to Persia. A Persian victory over an Athenian army at Marathon would have enabled them to take the city with ease and install a puppet government which would then assist them in the conquest of the rest of Greece. At least, we may legitimately assume that the Persians had something of this in mind.

The Athenians had a general who was familiar with Persian ways. Miltiades had been the ruler of the Thracian Chersonese where his family had estates and had in effect been subject to the Persian king. He returned to Athens in 493, and although attempts were made by Themistocles to keep him out of politics, he gained the support of the Athenian upper classes and was elected to the board of ten generals. His prestige was such that the strategy he proposed was adopted by the others.

The Athenians sent an urgent appeal for reinforcements to Sparta. The message was carried by the professional runner Pheidip-

pides, who covered the 260 kilometers (180 miles) in about 36 hours. The Spartans, however, were celebrating a festival and could not leave until the full moon some days away. The only direct support the Athenians received was from the inhabitants of Plataea in Boeotia who came, so Herodotus tells us, "in full force." The Greek army was decidedly smaller than the Persian, but occupied a favorable position in the mouth of a valley. The two armies faced one another for several days, the Athenians reluctant to advance for fear of the Persian cavalry. But then news was received that the Persian cavalry was being shipped south to attack an undefended Athens. It was clearly time to act, and the Greeks attacked according to Miltiades' plan. Their center was left deliberately weak, and when the Persians pushed through they were caught in a pincer movement by the Greek wings which had already succeeded in putting their opponents to flight. The Persian casualties in the hand-to-hand fighting which ensued were colossal; the Athenians only lost 192. The Persian attack had clearly failed and their forces were withdrawn to Asia.

The Athenian dead were buried in a funeral mound which still rises today above the field of Marathon. Commemorative dedications were made at the shrines of Apollo and Zeus at Delphi and Plataea, and it is quite likely that the Parthenon at Athens (which was not in fact completed until 438 B.C.) was intended to be a memorial to the heroes who had fallen at Marathon. The Persians were, however, to attack again.

Below left: A fight at close quarters between a Greek and a Persian in the tondo of a cup. Persians usually come off worst in such encounters.

A Corinthian helmet found at Olympia and inscribed "Miltiades dedicated [me]," an offering probably made by the victorious general at Marathon.

An oriental helmet from Olympia inscribed "To Zeus, the Athenians who took it from the Medes."

Far left: An iron sword, a lead sling bullet, and bronze arrowheads found on the field of Marathon.

Left: The mound at Marathon where the Athenian dead were buried.

Overleaf: A Greek bronze statuette of a hoplite, late sixth century B.C., and a polychrome brick frieze of warriors from Susa, the capital of the Achaemenid empire, fourth century B.C.

141

These men had invincible courage
in their hearts
When they battled before the gates
against countless foes,
Thwarting the army of the Persians
who planned by might
To burn their far-famed
city by the sea.

Marathon inscription

142

THE PERSIANS DEFEATED

It might be thought that the Athenians' immediate reaction to the events of 490 B.C. would have been to prepare for the next Persian attack, but such was not the case. Miltiades, distracted by a disastrous military adventure, suffered public disgrace. Themistocles was the only person who realized that the Persians would return, and he exploited a war with the neighboring island state of Aegina in order to strengthen the proposals that he was making to enlarge the Athenian navy.

Darius, the Persian king, died in 486 and was succeeded by the energetic Xerxes, who was anxious to avenge the Persians' disgrace at Marathon. He made careful preparations for a massive combined operations assault on Greece by having a double pontoon bridge consisting of 360 ships built over the Hellespont and by planting supply depots along the route he proposed to follow through Thrace and into Greece from the north. It happened that the bridge broke in a gale just as Xerxes was about to cross with a

strangely took a neutral stance, advised the Greeks "to put their trust in wooden walls," widely interpreted as "to take to the sea in ships," although some diehards at Athens chose to barricade themselves in the Acropolis even when most of the population had been evacuated to Salamis.

The site of the battle of Thermopylae, where three hundred Spartans and their allies held out against the Persians for three days in 480—the Spartans dying to the last man.

Right: A Spartan bronze statuette of a hoplite wearing a cloak, made some time before the events of 480, but doubtless similar in appearance to the Greek warriors who fought against the Persians in 480–479.

vast army. He ordered that the sea be beaten—the reaction of a true autocrat.

The Greek response to the Great King's approach was varied. Some city-states chose, for reasons of self-interest, to ally themselves with the Persians, or to "medize," as those other city-states which resolved instead to resist the invasion called such behavior. Those who chose to resist included Athens, Sparta, Corinth, and many others. A meeting they held at the Isthmus of Corinth resolved to attempt to stop the Persian advance in northern Greece if at all possible. The oracle at Delphi, which

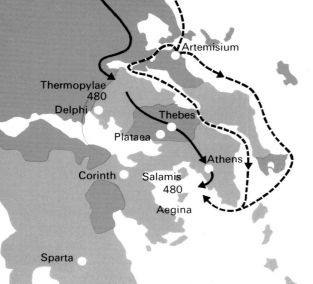

serious losses at sea as much from the elements as at the hands of the Greeks. The Greek land forces had retreated to the Isthmus, which was where they intended to prevent an invasion of the Peloponnese. The fleet assembled in the narrow waters between Salamis and the mainland, ready to prevent the Persian fleet from going farther south. Athens was left undefended and was sacked by the Persian army; one objective of the invasion had been achieved.

It was a month before the Persians could be persuaded to come to a fight at Salamis. The Greeks were determined not to leave the

Xerxes' amphibious invasion force followed the east coast down through Greece as far as Thermopylae where it was checked for a time by a Spartan force. He lost part of his fleet at Artemisium and much of the rest of it at Salamis. The darker areas on the map show those states which either medized or remained neutral in the events of 480–479.

The Greeks' success in the Persian wars was due in large measure to their fleet. Most fighting ships were triremes, propelled by three banks of oarsmen. The usual method of attack was to ram the enemy amidships near the waterline. The "beak" of the ship was effectively designed to rip into a ship's timbers.

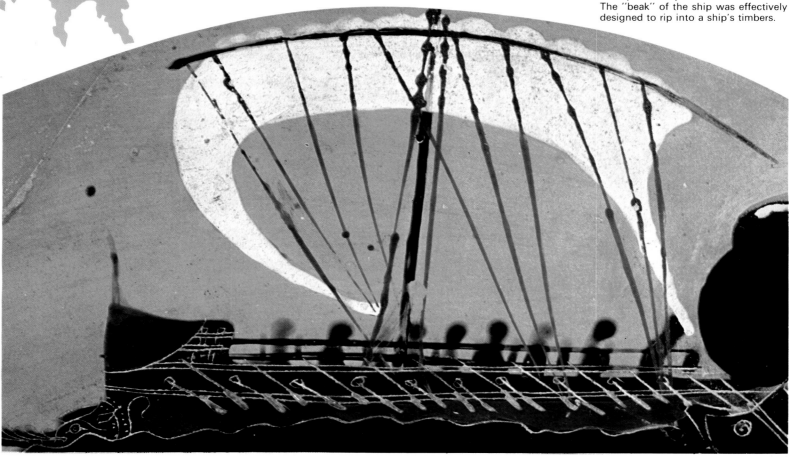

The Greek allies made their first effective stand at Thermopylae, at a point where the road south has to pass through a narrow defile. Here the Persians suffered heavy losses until the Greek position was betrayed and the Persians were shown another way south, enabling them to attack the Greeks from both sides. The brave three-day resistance of Leonidas, his three hundred Spartan warriors, and their allies after they were thus surrounded is legendary. Not one Spartan survived; all had obeyed their law never to surrender on the field of battle. In the meantime, the Persians had suffered

relative safety of the straits and thus give the Persians the opportunity to take advantage of their vessels' superiority in open water. Somehow the Persians were persuaded to enter the narrows and they took up battle formation in sight of Xerxes' throne on the Attic shore. They suffered heavy losses when the tried to avoid the smaller and more maneuverable Greek ships. Xerxes was humiliated by his fleet's poor showing and returned immediately to Asia. His land army suffered a further defeat at Plataea in 479, and as a result the direct Persian threat to Greece was at an end.

A relic of the Persian sack of Athens in 480 in the form of column drums from the earlier Parthenon (begun in 487) which were burnt and hacked about by the Persians and subsequently used by the Athenians as building material for the north wall of the Acropolis.

THEMISTOCLES

Although Themistocles was the architect of Athenian naval supremacy in the fifth century, he was eventually sent into exile by his fellow citizens. His fame, however, lived on, and as late as the second century A.D. this marble portrait of him was made for a client in Ostia near Rome.

An ambiguous prediction from the Pythian priestess at Delphi *(above)*—that the Athenians should put their trust in wooden walls—provided a means of persuasion for Themistocles to his fellow Athenians that naval expansion was not only in their material interest, but also divinely approved.

Far right: The prow of a warship on a coin made by Samian settlers at Zancle in Sicily serves as a reminder of Themistocles' role as the architect of Athenian naval supremacy, and also of his personal commercial interest in the west; two of his daughters were called Sybaris and Italia.

Themistocles might on occasion have been unscrupulous, but he was always farsighted. He was one of the few Greeks after Marathon who saw the need to make new preparations to face another Persian attack. He chose to build up Athens' naval strength, and in so doing brought about certain political changes as well.

Themistocles was an official in charge of Athens' water supply before becoming first archon in 493. His origins were aristocratic, but according to some his mother was a slave, and this may account for the fact that he was something of a loner in politics, acting independently from the aristocratic factions which still largely ran the Athenian government. His first action was to begin to make a safe harbor at Phaleron, a site that was completely undefended. The return of Miltiades put a temporary stop to Themistocles' naval ambitions, and the Athenians faced the Persian threat in 490 on land. Land fighting was traditionally conducted by the more prosperous classes in the community, those who could afford to pay for the upkeep of cavalry horses or for hoplite armor, and the Athenian victory at Marathon (where Themistocles actually served as a general under Miltiades) was regarded by conservatives in later years in nostalgic terms. It was to be the last time that young men from "respectable" families could take the sole credit for victory.

Themistocles was one of the few Athenians who realized that the Persians would come again to avenge the disgrace they had suffered in 490. He also realized that despite the hoplites' success at Marathon, Athens would only be really secure in the future if she had a strong navy. The oarsmen would inevitably be recruited from the non-hoplite classes, who would thus be given a much larger share in the defense of the city.

In order to get his way in the expansion of the navy, Themistocles had to bring about political changes; at least we know that certain changes took place in the Athenian constitution in the years between Marathon and Salamis and they appear to have the mark of Themistocles upon them. The first development was that in 488–487 a provision of the Cleisthenic constitution was reactivated. This provided the means to send into exile anyone who threatened the democracy, and was called ostracism. Hip-

parchus was the first of several aristocratic opponents of Themistocles' policies who was ostracized. In 487–486 an important change took place with regard to the archonship; thenceforward archons were to be appointed by lot. The effect of this was that an ambitious politician would no longer set his eye on the archonship, although the post was still an honorable one. In the long term there were consequences, too, for the Areopagus (the "Upper House" of the Athenian democracy), because its members were drawn from ex-archons; their influence would inevitably be diminished. The post to aim for now was that of *strategos,* or general. The ten *strategoi* were officials elected directly by the people, and there was no limit to the number of times they could be reelected. The ordinary sailor now had a direct say in the conduct of Athenian affairs. The war with Aegina provided an excuse for the construction of a fleet, the money for which came from the surplus accruing to the Athenian state from a particularly rich vein of silver that was struck at Laurium in Attica in 483–482. It was resolved by the assembly that this windfall should be spent on the construction of a fleet at the rate of one hundred triremes a year. Aristides (the "Just" as he was called) argued that the income from the silver mines should be distributed equally among the citizenry, but the naval party won the day and Aristides was ostracized. The ideals of Marathon were still strong in aristocratic circles; indeed, there were to be oblique references to that victory in the decoration of painted vases made commemorating the victories at Salamis and Plataea.

when the Athenians returned to Athens from Salamis they not only rebuilt their houses which had been destroyed by the Persians but set about fortifying the city and the Piraeus as well. The Spartans objected, regarding the Athenians' action as a challenge to their hegemony. Themistocles, however, determined that his city should be adequately defended, went in person to Sparta where he deliberately delayed negotiations until he got word that the walls were more or less completed. Upon hearing this he proclaimed Athens' independence from Sparta, and the Spartans reluctantly accepted the situation.

This is in fact the last time that we hear of Themistocles playing a prominent role in Athenian politics. He tried to promote an anti-Spartan polity, for he realized that the next threat to Athens would come from this quarter, but made little headway. In 476 he

Far left: Part of the wall of Athens built in 479–478 while Themistocles indulged in delaying tactics at Sparta.

The constitutional device for sending a citizen into exile was known as ostracism—so called because names of candidates were scratched on *ostraka* or potsherds. These sherds belong to the period when Themistocles himself was

Themistocles was prominent in the Greek deliberations over how to deploy the allied navy before Salamis. He was against the proposal to withdraw the fleet to the Isthmus, and even threatened that if this happened the Athenians would sail off to Italy and settle there. His brilliant strategy at Salamis, whereby the Persian fleet was lured to its destruction into the narrows between the island and the mainland, vindicated the naval policy for which he had fought so hard. Athens' navy was to be the basis of the city's strength for many decades to come. During the war, Athens had always submitted to Sparta's authority, but once it was over, Athens began to challenge this state of affairs. The moving spirit seems to have been Themistocles. Thucydides tells how

was actually ostracized and went to live in Argos, a city which was traditionally Sparta's enemy. He was hounded from there when Spartan agents suggested that he had been intriguing with Pausanias, a Spartan king who was said to have been in league with the Persians. He was safe nowhere in Greece, and fled eventually to Ionia. In desperation he went as a suppliant to, of all people, the Persian king, who not only received him courteously, but made him governor of Magnesia in Asia Minor. He died, by his own hand it seems, in 460–459, rather than take the field against his fellow Athenians. This must have redeemed his reputation at Athens, for later we learn that his sons were allowed to dedicate a portrait of their father in the Parthenon.

conducting his own successful ostracizing campaign in the late 480s, and seem to indicate an organized attempt to ostracize him instead. They read "Themistocles son of Neocles, let him go," and many are incised by the same hand.

Tribute bearers from Persepolis remind us that Themistocles ended his days as a subject of the Great King, but that he committed suicide rather than fight for the Persians against his fellow countrymen.

THE RULE OF ATHENS

O shining and wreathed in violets,
city of singing,
Stanchion of Hellas, glorious Athens,
citadel full of divinity.

PINDAR

The Greek equivalent for the expression "coals to Newcastle" was "owls to Athens." For Athena's Little Owl was very much the city's trademark. The olive sprig is a reference to Athens' principal agricultural product. The olive oil industry was badly hit in 480–479 when the Persians destroyed most of Attica's olive groves. Silver tetradrachm, 460–450 B.C.

The defeat of the Persians in 479 B.C. left a
power vacuum in the Aegean which was
quickly filled by Athens. The anti-Persian alliance she created gradually became an empire
("allies" become "subjects"), and the annual
tribute which was at first housed on Delos
was moved to Athens "for safekeeping" in
454 and a proportion of it was subsequently
used to adorn the city with fine new temples
and other public buildings. Athens' behavior
antagonized other cities, notably Sparta, and
the second half of the century was marked by
frequent wars between Athens and members
of the Delian League on the one hand and
Sparta and her Peloponnesian allies on the
other. Athens' domestic politics were democratic, a fact which was not to the liking of
most of her landed gentry. Literature and the
arts flourished in fifth- and fourth-century
Greece. Pindar and Bacchylides praised the
victories won at the great games by their
aristocratic patrons. Herodotus and Thucydides, the first great European historians,
were provided with ample material for their
narratives.

Tragic dramatists such as Aeschylus, Sophocles, or Euripides transposed the disturbing problems of the day to the world of
ancient myth, and saw them as universal issues. Aristophanes purged his audience of
their troubles by making them laugh at them.
Athens' imperial revenues financed the construction of temples, porticoes, and theaters
on a lavish scale—buildings which frequently
bore sculptural decoration (which has often
survived) or painted murals (which have not).
Echoes of the latter can be found in vase
paintings, where we can also gain insights
into Greek religious and social life.

Philosophy, at first concerned with the observation and interpretation of physical phenomena, came in the work of Plato, Socrates'
disciple, to deal with moral questions and the
pursuit of "the good."

Athens lost the Peloponnesian War, but Sparta's leadership of Greece was comparatively
short-lived. Thebes, and finally emergent Macedon under Philip II, gained control over
the Greek states. Philip's real aim, however,
was to conquer the Persians, an objective
accomplished in a few short years by the
greatest general the world has ever seen,
Alexander the Great.

THE ATHENIAN EMPIRE

The coin below was minted at Athens in the second quarter of the fifth century. The wreath that Athena wears is in honor of the victory over the Persians. The other coins were issued by states in and around the Aegean during the fifth century, some allied to Athens, others not. The Chalcidian League whose issues bear a lyre was set up when Athenian control over northern Greece was relaxed during the Peloponnesian War. The city of Rhodes, whose coins bear a frontal head of the sun-god Helios, was founded in 407 as the Athenian empire was coming to an end. The unfortunate city of Melos, whose inhabitants were slain or enslaved after an Athenian as-

For a few months after the Persians had been ousted from Greece, the Spartans continued to be in charge of naval operations in the Aegean and Hellespont area, but when their commander Pausanias began to behave in what they thought to be a tyrannical manner, the allies turned to Athens and asked her to lead the anti-Persian alliance. A meeting was held aboard the Athenian Aristides' flagship at Byzantium late in 478 B.C., and the allies agreed to convene at the shrine of Apollo at Delos in the spring of 477. There the Delian League was formed. Thucydides describes its objectives and organization as follows: "The Athenians... assessed the amount of contributions, both for the states which were to furnish money for the war against the Barbarians, and for those which were to furnish ships, the avowed object being to avenge themselves for what they had suffered by ravaging the King's territory. And it was then that the Athenians first established the office of Hellenic treasurers who first received the *phoros*; for so the contribution of money was termed. The amount of the tribute first assessed was four hundred and sixty talents, and the treasury of the allies was Delos,

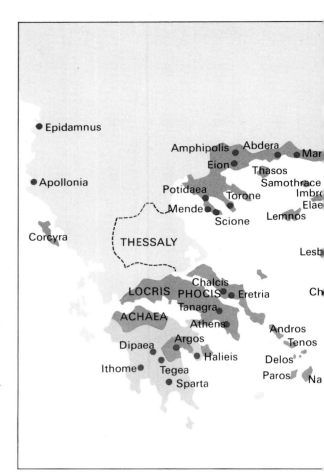

sault in 416, included a ram's head among the types of its last independent issues. Amphipolis in Thrace was an Athenian foundation, but was captured by the Spartans in the Peloponnesian War. It continued to issue coins bearing references to local torch races in honor of Artemis until it was captured by Philip II in 357. Phocaea, on the coast of Asia Minor, issued coins bearing female heads in the second quarter of the fifth century. Samos, one of the founder members of the Delian League, had the forepart of an ox as well as an olive spring on tetradrachms put out in ca. 454.

where the meetings were held in the sanctuary. At first the allies whom they led were autonomous and took counsel at meetings attended by Athens and the allies alike." Perhaps 150 cities from the islands and the eastern shores of the Aegean as well as from the Hellespont and Bosphorus areas constituted the membership of the earliest Delian League, and numbers grew as a result of the activities of Aristides and then Cimon (the son of Miltiades, victor at Marathon) in freeing Greek cities in the northern Aegean, and as far afield as Lycia and Cyprus, from Persian control. The largely sea-based Delian League was thought of at Athens as

being complementary to Sparta's traditional supremacy on land, and it was certainly not devised as an anti-Spartan alliance, although such it eventually became. Cimon, indeed, was the leader of the pro-Spartan element at Athens. The high point of his career was the decisive victory that the League's navy won over the Persians at the River Eurymedon in about 466. The Persians may have been contemplating a sea-borne offensive on the Aegean at this time, but the destruction of their fleet prevented this taking place. Cimon had then to deal with a revolt of Thasos, a prosperous island with mainland dependencies in the northern Aegean,

elymbria
thus
santhe
Byzantium
Chalcedon

Cyzicus
os
dos
eum
os

Cyme
hocaea

Colophon
os

Miletus

Halicarnassus

Rhodes

The Athenian Empire was at first a simple alliance of Greek states whose representatives met on Delos, Apollo's island *(above)*, every year to discuss ways in which the Persians could be forced to make retribution for their misdeeds during their invasions of Greece. The members of the Delian League, as it was called, originally contributed either ships or money to the cause, but in 454 B.C. few states apart from Athens possessed a navy, and the League's treasury was moved to Athens "for safe-keeping." Thenceforth, the League rapidly became in effect an Athenian Empire. There were benefits to be derived from a pirate-free Aegean and the inevitable growth in trade, but the resources of the League were eventually to be used to beautify Athens and to help her survive—not very successfully—a war against the Spartans and their allies.

whose loss would have been a serious blow. It took the best part of two years to reduce Thasos, and in the meantime ten thousand Athenian troops were lost in operations in Thrace. The terms imposed on Thasos were harsh—to set an example for others—and included the surrender of her fleet, the dismantling of her walls, and the payment of an indemnity. In the future she was to contribute money and not ships to the League, and there was in fact a tendency for this to happen even with cities which had not revolted. It was clearly to Athens' advantage to direct the money to the construction of ships of what was rapidly

becoming her own fleet rather than to have to rely on the uncertain loyalty of an ally. There was a radical change in the policy of the League in 461 B.C., when Cimon was ostracized. He had led an Athenian force to aid the Spartans in dealing with a helot revolt. Help was rejected, Cimon was humiliated, and the Athenians broke with Sparta. The leaders of the radical democracy which followed Cimon's downfall now had to face both Greek and Persian enemies. A telling commentary on Athens' activities at this period is provided by a casualty list set up by a single Athenian tribe in 459 B.C. In the previous year 177 members of the

151

Erectheis phyle had fallen in battle on Cyprus, in Egypt, in Phoenicia, at Halieis (in the Peloponnese), on Aegina, and at Megara. An alliance was made with the Sicilian city of Segesta in the 450s, insignificant enough at the time, but an event that boded ill for Athens in the long term. A disaster involving fifty ships in Egypt in 454 and a renewed threat from Persia was used as the pretext for the removal of the Delian League's treasury from Delos to Athens. The subject relationship of League members to Athens which had been increasingly implicit for many years was now underlined. Even the language used in inscriptions changes: earlier reference to the "alliance" becomes "the cities which the Athenians

The island of Samos, off the coast of Asia Minor, played an important part in the final years of Athens' leadership of the Aegean. In 412 Samos was given back her autonomy for having helped avert an oligarchic coup which threatened the democracy at Athens. In 405 Athens even extended her own citizen rights to the Samians as a thank offering for assistance at the Battle of Arginusae in 406. One or the other of these events is alluded to in this relief, which shows personifications of Samos and Athens joining their right hands in friendship. The Peloponnesian War came to an end with the Battle of Aegospotami in 405; Samian democrats were among the first to suffer, for the Spartans immediately installed a puppet aristicratic government of ten on the island.

control," and the transformation from league to, in effect, empire was institutionalized: settlers ("cleruchs") were sent to occupy some of the islands, and political agents and garrisons were installed in potential trouble spots. The Athenians even began to spend some of the income from the League on new buildings in Athens. The Parthenon, the Propylaea, and the Temple of Hephaestus were among those paid for by these means. Pericles was now in undisputed control of Athens' affairs: he was general every year from 443 to 429.

Right: The Temple of Poseidon at Cape Sunium is the first sight to greet the sailor approaching Attica from the Cyclades. The marble temple was built shortly after the middle of the fifth century and was designed by the same architect who built *inter alia* the Temple of Hephaestus in the Athenian Agora. The island of Patroclus in the distance is so called after a Ptolemaic admiral, not the Homeric hero.

ATTICA: THE SETTING

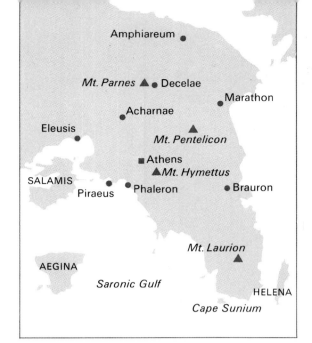

It was customary at Athens for young men of well-to-do families to spend their eighteenth and nineteenth years under military training. Ephebes, for such they were called, would take an oath whose closing words reveal how dependent the propertied classes of Athens were on products of the land. The new recruit would swear to protect the fatherland and then call upon a series of deities as witnesses, ending with an invocation to "wheat, barley, vines, olives, figs." From the point of view of the landowner these commodities were of paramount importance, for his wealth was derived from them, either directly from his own estate or indirectly from rents paid by tenants.

Country matters figure prominently in Greek art. *Above:* A painting shows the transport of wine or oil in a mule cart. A drinking vessel is in the form of a hound's head. *Right:* Countrymen on the way to market with hogs and some kind of produce which one of them carries in panniers over his shoulder.

During the sixth and fifth centuries B.C. we can observe a gradual change taking place in the nature of land use in Attica. The raising of wheat crops had been the predominant element in the subsistence economy of sixth-century Athens, but with the growth of the population that occurred in the prosperous years of the Athenian Empire it became more economical to import grain from elsewhere: the Black Sea region, the Nile delta and Sicily, and the west were all suppliers at one time or another, and it has been argued with some plausibility that the main reason for Athens' apparently reckless adventurism in Sicily in 415–413 was the need to ensure a dependable source of grain supplies.

Attic vineyards would have been sufficient to meet local needs, and their culture would have provided considerable employment, as well as a reasonable income for their owners. The finest wines of ancient Greece, however, were not Attic, but were produced elsewhere, in places such as Rhodes, Chios, or Thasos, and were marketed in their distinctive coarseware amphoras—vessels which varied in shape according to their *pays d'origine* just as do the bottles in which today's Burgundy or Moselle are exported. Vast numbers of foreign wine amphoras have been found in Athens, a fact which does not speak highly of the local grape.

It was the olive that was to be the principal source of income for those Athenians whose wealth was derived from agriculture. Olives

154

A vivid scene of olive-pressing; huge weights have been suspended on each end of a pole in order to crush the olives. An assistant climbs on so as to provide extra weight, and the oil comes pouring out of the bottom of the press.

were part of the staple diet of the average Athenian, but even more importantly, olive oil was Athens' major agricultural export item. The Athenian pottery industry must have been heavily dependent on orders for fine decorated vases—amphoras and lekythoi—in which the oil was exported. It was doubtless with a view to putting a stop to this lucrative trade that the Persians devastated the Athenian olive groves in 480–479. We get occasional hints of the consequences of this in the ancient writers. Plutarch, for example, mentions a conspiracy which occurred at Athens between Salamis and Plataea. The conspirators had all been rich and influential citizens before the Persian invasion, but were now reduced to poverty. Two names are given, those of Agesias of Acharnae and Aeschines of Lamptrae. Acharnae lies immediately to the north of Athens and was thus on Xerxes' direct route in 480; small wonder that it should have suffered. Lamptrae is even more significant for it lies some 45 kilometers (30 miles) southeast of Athens in the direction of Sunium, and the impoverishment of one of its farmers is a symptom of the deliberate and widespread destruction that the Persians wrought. We must envisage cavalry detachments sent out all over the depopulated countryside of Attica sawing down thousands of olive trees.

It is said that the time necessary for the recovery of an olive grove from destruction is about fifteen years, and it can hardly be coincidence that we hear that Callias, one of the richest landowners in Attica, went on a mission to the Persian capital, Susa, in 465

B.C. It may well be that he was seeking an understanding that the Persians would not again attack the source of his livelihood and that of his peers.

As we have noted elsewhere, the Spartans adopted similar tactics to those of the Persians when they invaded and devastated Attica in the early years of the Peloponnesian War. The last invasion was in 425, and it must have been with a certain irony that Sophocles made the chorus of old men of Attica sing in his *Oedipus at Colonus,* produced some seventeen or eighteen years later:

"There is a plant which flourishes mightily in this land—the like of none that I have heard of in Asia or the great Peloponnese—ever bud-

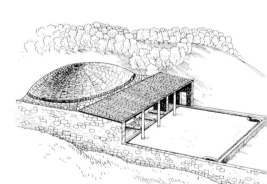

A reconstruction of an ancient silver-mining installation at Agrileza near Laurium investigated in 1977 by members of the British School of Archaeology at Athens. Water was stored in the domed cistern; the ore was washed under the shed and dried in the open area outside. The water was collected again for reuse in a series of sedimentation tanks.

Hunting was a favorite activity of those Athenians who had the leisure and the social standing to enjoy it. This young man (in fact Cephalus, a mythological figure) is shown equipped for hunting with his *chlamys* (cloak), *petasos* (hat), sword, club, and spears.

A sheaf of wheat from a relief at Eleusis, a shrine to Demeter and Persephone situated in the principal grain-producing area of Attica.

ding, immortal, self-renewing, the despair of enemy weapons, the gray-leafed olive, nurse of the young; no one whether old or young will lay hands on it to destroy it; for the eye of Zeus, guardian of the sacred olives, and gray-eyed Athena ever watch over them."

Attica's other principal resources were mineral. The quarries of Mounts Pentelicus and Hymettus, and Eleusis were exploited from the early fifth century onward, so that Xenophon could say a century later: "The land has stone in abundance, from which the finest temples and altars are made, and the most beautiful statues for the gods. It is in great demand among Greeks and foreigners too." He goes on to speak of Athens' main source of wealth which came from "land which produced nothing when sown, but when quarried can provide for many times more than if it grew corn." He was referring of course to the silver mines at Laurium

import necessities that had hitherto had to be produced at home, as well as to withstand the misfortunes that befell the land of Attica as a result of successive invasions. The heavy work in the mines was done by slaves, but the profits were taken by the landowners and the state.

Excavations in recent years have greatly increased our knowledge of the rural industries of Attica. Washeries for extracting silver ore have been explored at Laurium, and farmhouses have been excavated elsewhere. One of them produced interesting evidence for beekeeping: the "hives" were, like so many everyday objects in ancient Greece, made from terracotta.

Atticans were prone to describe their homeland in idyllic terms, as in this passage from *Oedipus at Colonus*:

"Here in our white Colonus, stranger guest,
Of all earth's lovely lands the loveliest,

A sacrifice being offered to a rustic deity. The officiant pours an offering over an altar assisted by a small "altar boy."

Above right: A votive relief from the shrine of Artemis at Brauron in eastern Attica. It shows the goddess with her attribute, a stag, and attended by devotees including small girls who figured prominently in the Brauronian festival which was held every five years in the sanctuary *(opposite)*, whose Doric columns have been reconstructed by the Greek Archaeological Service.

which had been Athens' salvation in 480 when the discovery of a rich new vein enabled her to build the fleet without which the Greek victory at Salamis would have been unimaginable. Aeschylus brings this point out well in his *Persians* of 472, when he makes the Persian Queen Atossa ask in the middle of a series of questions about Athens' military strength: "Have [the Athenians] sufficient domestic wealth?" to receive the answer, "They have a spring of silver, a treasure from the earth." This treasure from the earth was to be Athens' mainstay throughout the fifth century, enabling her to

Fine horses breed, and leaf-enfolded vales
Are thronged with sweetly-singing nightingales,
Screened in deep arbours, ivy, dark as wine,
And tangled bowers of berry-clustered vine . . .
Here, chosen crown of goddesses, the fair
Narcissus blooms, bathing his lustrous hair
In dews of morning; golden crocus gleams
Along Cephisus' slow meandering streams,
Whose fountains never fail; day after day
His limpid waters wander on their way
To fill with ripeness of abundant birth
The swelling bosom of our buxom earth."

PERICLES AND THE REBUILDING OF ATHENS

Pericles was said to have had a "squill-shaped" head of which he was very self-conscious. "For this reason," Plutarch tells us, "artists almost always represented him as wearing a helmet." His Milesian mistress Aspasia was used by Pericles' enemies to attack him indirectly: she was charged with impiety, but was acquitted, having been defended in court by Pericles himself.

Themistocles was responsible for the fortification of the Piraeus and the city of Athens, and Cimon completed his scheme in the early 450s by constructing the two Long Walls (the North Wall and the Phaleric Wall). In 445 Pericles added the Middle Wall.

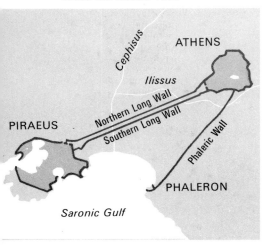

In 472, Themistocles' political fortunes were at a low ebb, and it seems that Aeschylus' *Persians* which presented the Battle of Salamis, Themistocles' finest hour, in a very favorable light was produced in order to assist his return to power. The producer of the play (the *choregus*) was the young Pericles, a fact which perhaps already indicates his political sympathies. Ten years later he was a supporter of the political reformer Ephialtes, a man who paid a harsh penalty for having exploited Cimon's growing unpopularity following a disaster in Thrace and the Spartans' rejection of Athenian help at Ithome. Cimon was ostracized, but Ephialtes was assassinated, probably the victim of an aristocratic plot. Pericles inherited his political mantle and continued to work for democratic ends.

Pericles was elected general for the first time in 454 and commanded a fleet against the Corinthians in 453, in an attempt to assure Athens' sealinks with the West. He counseled caution when an Athenian land force tried to intervene in Boeotia in 447, an intervention which brought to an end Athens' shortlived Land Empire, but one whose outcome had the long-term effect of making the Athenians almost exclusively a maritime power.

It was somewhat paradoxical for Pericles to support the interest of the *demos,* as the nonaristocratic majority of Athenian citizens were called, for he was himself an aristocrat. His father had been an opponent of Miltiades, and his mother was actually an Alcmaeonid. Independently wealthy, Pericles was thus immune from the temptations and accusations of corruption to which his contemporaries and successors were subject. Thucydides, who admired him, commented:

"During the whole period of peacetime when Pericles was at the head of affairs, the state was wisely led and firmly guarded, and it was under him that Athens was at her greatest.... Pericles, because of his position, his intelligence, and his known integrity, could respect the liberty of the people and at the same time hold them in check. It was he who led them, rather than they who led him...."

Pericles was a man of considerable intellectual gifts. His first teacher was Damon, who was to be Socrates' mentor, and he enjoyed the company of artists and intellectuals. These included the philosophers Anaxagoras of Clazomenae, Protagoras of Abdera, the sculptor Phidias, and of course his mistress Aspasia. When Pericles' enemies—traditionally minded landowners for the most part—chose to attack him, as they did toward the end of his life, it was by indirect means; they brought charges of impiety

The first Parthenon was begun as a memorial to Marathon, but was destroyed in the Persian Sack of Athens in 480. Building was resumed to a different design in 447, but the intention was doubtless the same. The Athenian army spent the eve of the Battle of Marathon encamped in a shrine of Heracles, hence his inclusion on the east pediment of the second Parthenon *(left)*.

It was customary in Greek art to represent the Persian Wars in mythological terms: gods fighting with giants, Greeks with Amazons, or here, on the Parthenon, the major Marathon memorial, Greeks and Centaurs, the embodiment of bestiality and barbarism.

against his associates. Through their philosophical speculation they had encouraged a healthy skepticism concerning the role of the gods.

Oratorical skills were among the principal means of acquiring and maintaining political power at Athens. The popular assembly was the arena in which such power was gained, and Pericles was its master. The comic poet Eupolis observed of him:

"In eloquence no man could equal him—
When Pericles arose and took the floor,
By ten good feet our common orators
As by an expert runner were outstripped.
Not only voluble, but with persuasion
Sitting upon his lips. He bound a spell,
And had this power alone of orators,
To prick men's hearts and leave behind the sting."

By means of such gifts and his skill in eliminating potential rivals, Pericles was elected general every year from 445 to his death in 429. Thanks to his vision, foresight, and leadership, Athens enjoyed a period of unparalleled prosperity for most of this period. Her defenses were improved in such a way that Athens and her port, the Piraeus, might become in effect a self-contained island, just like any other Greek island, in an emergency. As it turned out, however, when the emergency did come, in

431 and subsequent years, the policy of harboring the population of Attica between the Long Walls proved an unwise one, for plague found the confined inhabitants of the refugee camp an easy prey and spread more quickly then it might otherwise have done; Pericles himself fell a victim.

He identified the interests of the empire with those of Athens, and diverted a proportion of the tribute to a building program as a result of which Attica was adorned with fine new temples and other public buildings.

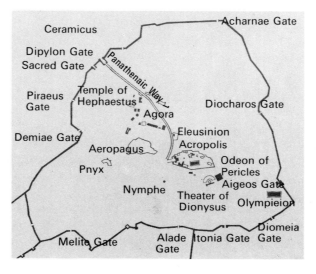

A plan to show some of the principal features of the city of Athens in Pericles' day. The Acropolis, the citadel of Athens, lies near the middle of the walled city, with the Agora, the civic center, a little way to the northwest. The Theater of Dionysus on the southern slope of the Acropolis was given a large covered building with a pyramidal roof during Pericles' generalship.

159

THE ACROPOLIS

The Athenian Acropolis was the city's *raison d'être*. The very existence of this rocky outcrop meant that people chose to live in its vicinity, knowing that it would serve as a citadel and provide refuge in an emergency. In the Bronze Age there was a Mycenaean palace here, and a defensive wall of huge stones was built. The stones were so big that in later centuries it was believed that it was built by the legendary Cyclops. Pisistratus adorned the Acropolis with shrines and temples, and many korai were set up as votive offerings to Ath-

ena. Much of this splendor was destroyed when the Persians attacked Athens on the eve of Salamis in 480 B.C. The Acropolis was to flourish anew, however, later in the fifth century when Pericles (elected *strategos*, i.e. general, annually from 443 to 429 B.C.) diverted some of the funds of the Delian League to what was both a program to beautify Athens and a means of providing labor on a large scale. The Acropolis continued to be "Athena's sacred hill" and a place of pilgrimage until the decline of paganism in the sixth century A.D. In later times it became the seat of the Turkish waywode of Athens, but is now a Greek national monument. A visit to the Acropolis is the high point of any modern traveler's stay in Athens.

PRECINCT OF ZEUS

The shrine of Zeus Polieus was situated somewhere at the east end of the Acropolis. The cult involved one of the most primitive rites of the Athenian religion. Pausanias describes what still happened in the second century A.D.: "Upon the altar of Zeus Polieus they place barley mixed with wheat and leave it unguarded. The ox, which they keep already prepared for sacrifice, goes to the altar and partakes of the grain. One of the priests they call the ox-slayer, who kills the ox and then, casting aside the axe here, according to the ritual runs away, the others bring the axe to trial, as though they know not the man who did the deed." Another Roman author, Varro, provides the reason for this curi-

ous procedure: it was considered a crime in Attica to kill a bull. By resorting to a subterfuge, the priest could perform the sacrifice to Zeus without fear of criminal proceedings. Even though Zeus was the principal god of the Greek pantheon, Athena's cult was the most important at Athens. This fact itself, however, was an implicit compliment to the Thunderer, for Athena was Zeus' favorite daughter, born of his flesh, not Hera's. The "birth" was illustrated in the center of the east pediment of the Parthenon where Athena was shown springing from the head of Zeus.

THE ERECHTHEUM

Erechtheus was a legendary ruler of Athens and foster child of Athena. It is appropriate, therefore, that the building which contained his shrine as well as a multiplicity of others was situated over the site of the Mycenaean palace. There had been a succession of temples and shrines in this part of the Acropolis since the seventh century B.C. if not before, and the Erechtheum was erected between 421 and 409 B.C. in order to

accommodate the traditional cults in a new setting. These included the shrine of Athena Polias where the primitive wooden image (the *xoanon*) of the city's patroness was housed, the place where Poseidon left the marks of this trident on the rock (or where Zeus struck it with a thunderbolt), and the tomb of Erechtheus. In a nearby enclosure stood an olive tree sacred to Athena which symbolized both Attica's principal export commodity and Athens' national spirit. Burnt in the Persian sack of the Acropolis, it is supposed to have grown a sprout 18 inches (45 cm) long overnight. Many details of the building records of the Erechtheum have survived. The architectural decoration is exquisite—the Porch of the Maidens is famous—and measured drawings made of the Erechtheum in the eighteenth century by Messrs Stuart and Revett were to be extremely influential.

ATHENA PROMACHOS

The contract for the Athena Promachos—the first colossal bronze statue in Athens—was given to the young Phidias in about 460 B.C., and the work was completed and set up on the Acropolis by 450. The members of the board created to oversee the work were paid by the state. Payment for public service was one of the innovations made by the radical democracy which was established following the ostracism of the aristocratic leader Cimon in 461. Athens was rapidly expanding her influence at the time, and doubtless hoped to do so with Athena's aid. The original is lost, but statuettes survive which give us an idea of its appearance. She would have held a shield on her left arm and wielded a spear in her right as a warning to Athens' enemies.

THE PARTHENON

The magnificent building we see today was erected over the platform created for a temple intended to commemorate those Athenian hoplites who had fallen at Marathon in 490 B.C. Whatever was in place by the time of the Persian sack in 480 was destroyed and material from it was used to fortify the Acropolis. The site lay fallow until a new temple, probably with the same purpose as its predecessor, was started in 447, very likely at the instigation of Pericles. The architects were Ictinus, Callicrates, and Carpion, and Phidias was the overseer of the sculptural adornment, as well as the sculptor of the colossal gold and ivory cult image of Athena. The Parthenon, which was completed, apart from some of the sculpture, in 438, was used to

house much of the treasure of the Delian League. The building is a byword for careful design and construction, and its proportions and optical subtleties combine to create a harmonious impression. These refinements included a stylobate and entablature which curved upward in the middle, columns which tilted inward, and corner columns thicker than the rest. In the late nineteenth century the Irish scholar J.P. Mahaffy saw a youth with a gun taking pot-shots at the monuments on the Acropolis; it is just as well that thanks to Lord Elgin much of the Parthenon's sculpture is now safely in the British Museum.

SANCTUARY OF ARTEMIS

To the right of the Propylaea there was a precinct dedicated to Brauronian Artemis. There was no temple, but in the fourth century a statue of the goddess by Praxiteles was set up. The name of the deity was derived from the deme of Brauron on the east coast of Attica, where an old wooden cult image was housed. Girls of good family took part in the cult of Brauronian Artemis; they would dress in saffron robes and imitate bears while performing sacrifices in her honor. The chorus leader in Aristophanes' *Lysistrata* mentions how "wearing the saffron robe I was a bear at the Brauronian festival." The practice may be connected with an Arcadian legend in which a companion of Artemis was seduced by Zeus; Hera in her jealousy turned her into a bear, and then incited Artemis to shoot her. Alternatively, it may be that the goddess herself

was thought once to have appeared as a bear, and that her devotees consequently impersonated this animal. Artemis was born on Delos, and next to her on the east frieze of the Parthenon appear her brother Apollo and Poseidon; a conjunction of deities which perhaps recalls the maritime basis of the Delian League.

THE PROPYLAEA

The architect of the Propylaea—the monumental entrance to the Acropolis—was Mnesicles, who had already proved his worth by designing ship sheds in the Piraeus. The artisans who worked on it seem to have been the same as those who built the Parthenon: the styles of workmanship are identical on both buildings, the proportions of the columns are similar, and the one job followed on directly from the other. The Propylaea was begun in 437 B.C., but was left unfinished on the outbreak of war with Sparta. The most obvious signs of unfinished work can be seen in the

southwestern part of the building, where two walls still bear the bosses that were used for levering the masonry blocks into place; bosses which normally would have been smoothed off. Mnesicles successfully overcame the problem of building on steeply rising ground and also managed to create the effect of a symmetrically arranged building, one that appeared to the spectator approaching from below as though it had wings of equal size, even though in fact one was somewhat larger than the other. The southern wing was compressed in order to leave room for the shrine of Nike. The external order was Doric, but slender Ionic columns were used within.

TEMPLE OF ATHENA NIKE

A small shrine of Nike (Victory) existed on the western bastion of the Acropolis from the sixth century, but it was apparently connected with athletic rather than military victories. The emphasis seems to have changed by the second half of the fifth century, for the frieze of the Ionic temple built then (again designed by Callicrates) is concerned with victories in battle, and more specifically with Greek victories over Persians. Building of the temple was authorized shortly after the middle of the century, and there may be a connection here with the Peace of Callias which, some think, brought an end to hostilities with Persia. Construction, however, did not begin until the 420s—perhaps, it has been

suggested, because the best available craftsmen were at work on other buildings on the Acropolis until then. For safety's sake, a balustrade was built around the edge of the bastion. Its decoration, which was designed to be seen from below, consisted of Victories leading bulls to sacrifice.

161

FESTIVALS AND RELIGIOUS LIFE

The greatest Athenian festival was the Panathenaea, which was held once a year and culminated on the supposed birthday of Athena. It was celebrated in a particularly elaborate manner every four years when games were held, the prizes for which were jars of olive oil. The first few days would be occupied with athletic competitions, songs, and festival dances, and then, at dawn on the feast day itself, a procession would set out along the Panathenaic Way, across the Agora, and up onto the Acropolis to bring the new peplos for the primitive image of Athena housed in the Erechtheum.

Dionysus had several festivals dedicated to him in Attica. They ranged from rural celebrations, at which the drinking of wine and general rowdiness seem to have been the main activities, to the major city festivals of the Lenaea, the Anthesteria, and the Greater and Lesser Dionysia. In neither kind of

tragedies had already been performed for decades at the Greater Dionysia.

One of the most interesting festivals was the Anthesteria, held in the spring. They lasted for three days and it was believed that during this time the city was visited by the spirits of the dead. On the first day, the new wine was drunk for the first time and libations poured in honor of Dionysus. Slaves were allowed to participate in the songs and dances that were performed. On the second day, not only the slaves but small boys were included in the festivities and each was given a small amount of wine served in a special jug-like vessel, called a *chous*. On this day too there was a Sacred Marriage, a Hieros Gamos, performed between the Archon Basileus and his wife, who played the parts of Dionysus and Dionysus' bride respectively; it was clearly a rite designed to encourage fertility. There

The priestess of Dionysus and her attendants *(below)* dispense wine for participants at the Lenaea, a winter festival in honor of the god of wine. *Right:* Young boys taking part in the spring festival of Anthesteria. One pulls another along in a go-cart, and both are equipped with *choes*, the special jugs from which they are to drink the new wine.
Opposite page: Dionysus, the wine god, his hair decked with vine leaves, a panther skin over his shoulders, and an

empty wine cup in his hand. In the second painting a drunken Dionysus is helped on his way at the Anthesteria festival by two satyrs, one of whom carries a torch and a *chous*.

festival was the orgiastic side of the cult of Dionysus encouraged, but every two years ecstatic, frenzied rites were held by bands of women from all over Greece (including Athens) on Mount Parnassus above Delphi. This is the kind of event that Euripides describes so vividly in *The Bacchae*. The Dionysiac festivals held at Athens were as a matter of policy somewhat more restrained; indeed some of them became cultural events. By the second half of the fifth century, the main attraction of the Lenaea was the performance of comic plays, and

was also a procession in which the god was taken to his temple in a carriage shaped like a ship (a probable reference to the vessel in which he once arrived in Attica from Asia Minor). The souls of the dead were supposed to rise up on this day, and it was customary to take special precautions against them. On the third day the dead were honored with offerings of cakes containing all kinds of seeds. Finally, all the souls of the dead were ordered to leave the city and the festival was over. Clearly, various features were combined in the Anthesteria: respect

. . . [Dionysus], the son of Semele,
Found out the grape's rich juice, and taught us
mortals
That which beguiles the miserable of mankind
Of sorrow, when they quaff the vine's rich
stream.
Sleep too, and drowsy oblivion of care
He gives, all-healing medicine of our woes. . . .

for the dead, the encouragement of fertility, and the drinking of wine.

The Great Mysteries at Eleusis had their origins in the Mycenaean past, and were concerned with the worship of Demeter, the goddess of agricultural fertility. Candidates for initiation would go in procession from Athens to the shrine at Eleusis and spend several days preparing for the culminating revelation they would receive in the Telesterion. We have no direct information as to what they saw, for initiates were sworn to secrecy, but it is possible that they were under the influence of ergot, a hallucinogenic fungus found on barley and which may have been present in the potion they drank as part of the ritual.

We have an amusing description of a mock Dionysiac procession in Aristophanes' *Acharnians*, where the old countryman Dicaeopolis celebrates his own private

Overleaf: Galloping horsemen from the north frieze of the Parthenon at Athens. It seems likely that they are an idealization of the procession at the Great Panathenaea in 490 B.C., an event which took place six weeks before the Battle of Marathon. The first Parthenon frieze was built as a memorial to the Marathon dead, and the second one (begun in 447) was probably built with the same object in view.

And him shall we behold on Delphi's crags
Leaping, with his pine torches lighting up
The rifts of the twin-headed rock; and
shouting
And shaking all around his Bacchic wand
Great through all Hellas.

From Euripides' The Bacchae

truce with the Spartans during the Peloponnesian War. He has his daughter carry a basket full of offerings and his slaves a phallus on a pole which they are urged to hold erect. The scene may seem a strange one to us, but it can be matched in vase paintings. A black-figure amphora, for example, made in Egypt by an East Greek craftsman in the sixth century B.C., shows a similar procession to Dicaeopolis' with a huge phallus being borne aloft by a multiplicity of devotees. Greek festivals could clearly be quite raunchy affairs.

Above: The main purpose of the Panathenaic procession was to bring up to the Acropolis the *peplos* or robe to dress the *xoanon,* the primitive image of Athena housed in the Erechtheum from the end of the fifth century. The scene here, from the very center of the east end of the Parthenon frieze, shows a woman and a girl in the act of folding the sacred garment.

ATHENA AND HER PEERS

Athena was, it is scarcely necessary to say, the patroness of Athens. Hence, every time the name of the city was mentioned, the goddess was inevitably invoked. The center of her cult at Athens was the Acropolis, the citadel of the city. Here she seems to have been worshipped under two aspects: as an earth goddess and as a virgin warrior. Originally, back in Mycenaean times, these two aspects of Athena may have been represented by two different deities, but by the classical period they had merged into the one great goddess Athena Polias, who both nurtured and protected the city.

The more primitive cult was eventually housed in part of the Erechtheum on the northern side of the Acropolis where a simple seated and unarmed olive-wood figure, draped in a woolen peplos which was replaced once every four years, was to be seen even in Pausanias' day in the second century A.D. Her counterpart on the south side of the Acropolis was Phidias' gold and ivory statue in the Parthenon where Athena was shown in her more martial aspect. She stood, fully armed, with a Victory standing on her outstretched hand.

In Periclean Athens, Athena's cult was enhanced by the construction of the Parthenon, the sculpture of which in part evoked the Athenians' great victories over the Persians in 490–479 B.C., and in part expressed Athena's central position in the city's religious life. In the center of the east pediment, the birth of Athena was shown: fully armed, she sprang from the head of Zeus once Hephaestus had cracked open the latter's skull with an axe. This explicit reference to Athena's paternity was meant to show that Athens was under the protection of Zeus'

favorite daughter. Thus, Aeschylus in the *Eumenides* makes Athena say: "I place my trust in Zeus, what more need be said? I alone of all the gods know where within his house are kept the keys with which his thunderbolts are sealed." The eastern pediment thus expresses Athena's role within the national Greek pantheon.

In the west pediment, however, she is shown as a local deity, victorious in her contest with her uncle Poseidon for the overlordship of Attica. The very allusion to such a contest is a compliment to Attica since it implies that it was a land that even the gods might strive for. There are at the same time references to both the olive tree and the salt spring on the north side of the Acropolis, as well as to the central position of the olive oil industry and seafaring in the life of Periclean Athens.

Athena's importance in the Greek pantheon derives in part from her identity as Zeus' daughter. Her birth, from Zeus' head, is depicted on this red-figure pelike from about 450 B C *(right)*. Hephaestus is seen in center holding the axe with which he split open the head of Zeus who sits on a throne at far right. Athena, according to the myth, is seen at top emerging fully armed from his head. The same theme was the subject of a relief on the east pediment of the Parthenon.

This relief from a temple at Tarentum in southern Italy presents Athena's peers, the Olympian gods and goddesses; from left: Hestia, Hephaestus, Aphrodite, Ares, Demeter, Hermes, Hera, Poseidon.

In the fifth century, Athenians present their goddess in her warlike attribute. The marble statue *(left)* is from the west pediment of the temple at Aphaia, ca. 500–480 B.C.

Above: Two helmeted Athenas. In the fifth-century bronze figurine she is flying her owl, the animal sacred to her. The marble relief shows a mourning goddess: from the Acropolis, ca. 460 B.C.

Below: Three other divinities from the Tarentum relief: Zeus, Artemis (holding a bow,) Apollo. The fully armed Athena painted at the right is from a red-figure hydria by the Meidias Painter, Italy, late fifth century. The decorated aegis, or breastplate, is traditionally associated with Athena.

169

HOW TO BUILD A GREEK TEMPLE

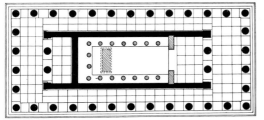

Right: The second Temple of Hera at Poseidonia (Paestum), built around the middle of the fifth century B.C., is one of the best-preserved temples anywhere. The plan of the co-eval Temple of Hephaestus at Athens *(above)* differs in that it has one less column on each side.

Above: The Temple of Hera at Olympia was probably built around 600 B.C. Its proportions, with sixteen columns along the sides, are rather more elongated than those of fifth-century temples. A peculiarity of this building is that the diameters and styles of the columns and Doric capitals vary. The reason may be that the columns were originally of wood and were gradually replaced in limestone as funds became available. Its walls were of mudbrick which rested on a stone footing; compare the modern Arcadian barn below.

A Greek temple was not so much a church as a tabernacle; that is to say, its function was not to provide shelter for a congregation, but rather to house the cult-image of a deity. The ceremonies associated with the cult would be performed outside the temple at an altar situated opposite the main entrance. Here sacrifices would be performed before the open doors of the shrine.

In order to erect a temple, it was necessary first to make a level platform, the *euthynteria*. For obvious reasons, this was especially important on sloping ground; the Temple of Apollo at Delphi is a good example of a temple built on a terrace platform. The foundations would go down to bedrock within the platform, but they would only be built beneath the loadbearing parts of the temple. The intervening spaces would be filled in with earth or rubble.

A series of three or four steps, called collectively the *crepis* or *crepidoma,* would next be built, the upper surface of which is called by architectural historians the stylobate since the columns would rest directly on it. If the temple was to be of marble, then the upper steps could be of marble too. Otherwise they were of rougher stone which, together with the rest of the temple, would be given a coat of stucco to give the appearance of marble. The masonry blocks would be held together, both laterally and vertically, with bronze clamps set in lead. Column drums were held together differently, with wooden dowels (of cypress or cedar).

In a temple of any size, there would be a peristyle, usually a single row (but sometimes more) of columns across the front and back, and along the sides. Surprisingly, perhaps, the columns of Greek temples seem regularly to have been built in advance of the walls of the *cella,* or shrine proper. It is not wholly certain why this should have been the case, but it has been suggested that since temples appear to have been built without detailed drawings prepared in advance, and since a good deal of *ad hoc* planning was involved as the building rose, the proportions of the columns governed those of the rest of the temple.

The lowest course of masonry of the cella of a temple, the orthostate, was taller than the rest, probably a vestige of the time when temple walls had stone footings and courses of mud-brick above them. Even the sixth-century Temple of Hera at Olympia, had mud-brick walls over its orthostate. Indeed, the basic design of the Greek temple—in effect a building with greatly overhanging eaves supported on poles all round—was derived from simple thatched shrines whose

From below up: The *euthynteria* (platform) and the marble *crepidoma* of the Temple of Apollo at Delphi. The Doric columns rest directly on the stylobate. An accurately reconstructed detail of the Temple of the Great Gods at Samothrace showing the use of both vertical and horizontal bronze clamps in the construction of the *crepidoma*. Attempts have been made to rob away the metal from the Temple of Hephaestus at Athens, hence its pock-marked appearance; the curvature of the stylobate can—just about—be seen. Ionic columns had bases, though not often as elaborately decorated as those of the Erechtheum on the Athenian Acropolis. A detail of the Temple of Athena Nike on the Acropolis: a distinctive feature of Ionic capitals is the presence of large scrolls on either side. Finally, the corner of the second Temple of Hera at Poseidonia. The Doric capital consists of a curving echinus surmounted by a square abacus; then comes the architrave and above that the frieze of triglyphs and metopes. The underside of the cornice is adorned with a series of mutules. These decorative features seem to have been devised in the northeastern Peloponnese in the mid-seventh century B.C.

walls had to be protected from the elements and from rising damp, hence the existence of orthostates.

The decision as to which of the classical Orders to employ—Doric or Ionic (Corinthian was not used externally on temples until later times)—will in most cases have been determined on geographico-linguistic grounds. Broadly speaking, Doric was used in Mainland Greece and the West, whereas Ionic tended to be restricted to Asia Minor and the Aegean. Athens is somewhat anomalous in that both Orders are found there. Above the capitals comes the entablature, which comprised (from bottom to top) the architrave, the frieze (in Doric of sculptured metopes and triglyphs, in Ionic of a continuous sculptured frieze or dentils) and the cornice. The pediments (gable ends) of the temple would normally contain sculpture too, and it is important to remember that much of this decoration would be picked out in bright colors. Lions' head spouts along the sides of the temple would carry off rainwater from the tiled roof. A curious feature of these spouts is that only those over the columns would actually function, so that people rushing for shelter would not get drenched.

Above: A severe limitation on Greek architects was the rule that when two-story colonnades were employed the lower diameter of the columns of an upper story had to be the same as, or less than, the upper diameter of the columns beneath. Vanishing point was never very far away.

Below: Bosses used, not for lifting, but for levering masonry blocks into place. Greek masons did not make joining faces of marble blocks completely flush with one another, but just the edges; a labor-saving device known as *anathyrosis*. The bronze clamp and its lead setting have fallen victim to metalrobbers.

THE AGORA: THE CIVIC CENTER OF ATHENS

"The memorials of all your great deeds are set up in the Agora"; so said Aeschines the orator in the fourth century B.C. The Athenian Agora, however, was more than a square full of monuments, it was primarily the focal point of political and administrative life at Athens. Here were the public offices, the law courts, the markets. Artisans' workshops proliferated in the surrounding streets, and it was in the Agora that citizens met informally to discuss the political and social issues of the day.

The Agora only began to be developed as such in the sixth and fifth centuries. The construction of the Great Drain at an uncertain date within a couple of decades or so of 500 B.C. meant that the area was no longer subject to seasonal flooding. The west side, beneath the hill of Kolonos Agoraios, was

The west side of the Agora as excavated. On the hill, the Temple of Hephaestus —a highly suitable patron in view of the presence of bronze workers' shops in the immediate neighborhood. The temple owed its survival to the fact that it became a Christian church in the Middle Ages. Other buildings served simply as quarries, and much of their masonry was robbed for use in new construction. From left to right can be seen: the foundations of the circular Tholos, where duty officials were lodged during their period of office; the Metroon, an archive building erected over the site of the Old Bouleuterion (Council House); the fourth-century Temple of Apollo Patroos; and the Stoa of Zeus Eleutherios with its projecting wings, built in the closing decades of the fifth century B.C.

the first to be built up, but gradually each side of the square was lined with porticoed stoas, fountain houses, and small shrines. In the Roman period temples were even moved from elsewhere in Attica and rebuilt in the Agora whose religious importance was second only to that of the Acropolis.

The Agora has been the subject of detailed study and excavation by the American School of Classical Studies at Athens since 1931, and our knowledge of Athenian life and institutions has been greatly enriched as a result.

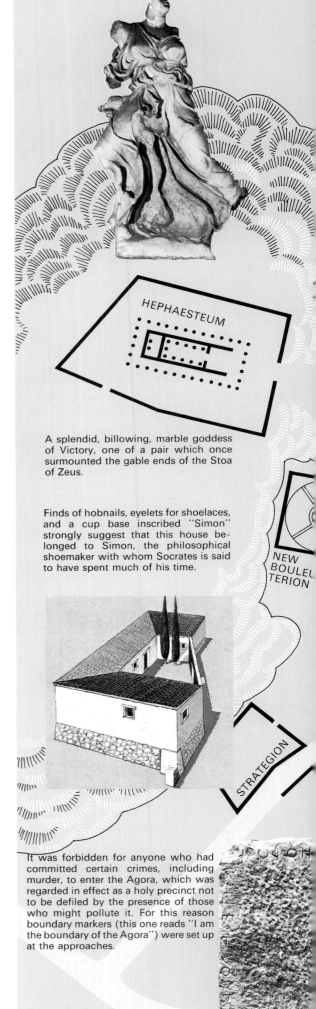

HEPHAESTEUM

A splendid, billowing, marble goddess of Victory, one of a pair which once surmounted the gable ends of the Stoa of Zeus.

Finds of hobnails, eyelets for shoelaces, and a cup base inscribed "Simon" strongly suggest that this house belonged to Simon, the philosophical shoemaker with whom Socrates is said to have spent much of his time.

NEW BOULEUTERION

STRATEGION

It was forbidden for anyone who had committed certain crimes, including murder, to enter the Agora, which was regarded in effect as a holy precinct not to be defiled by the presence of those who might pollute it. For this reason boundary markers (this one reads "I am the boundary of the Agora") were set up at the approaches.

172

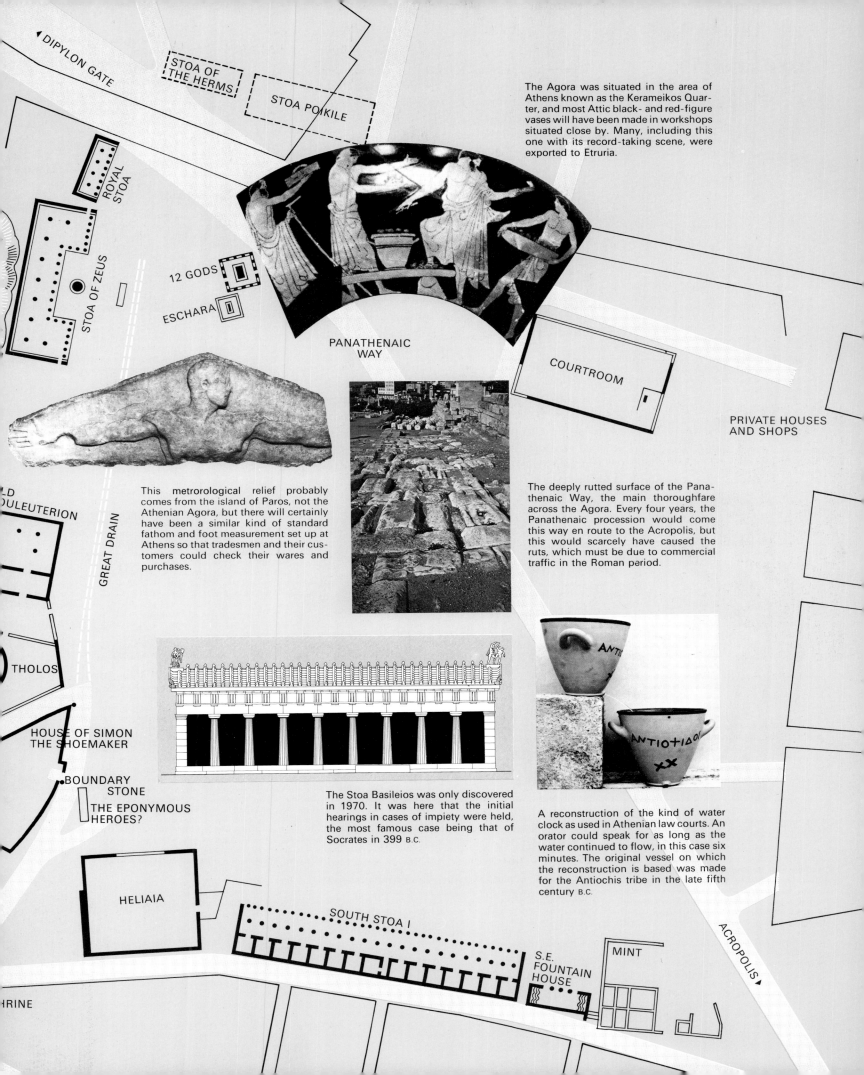

DIPYLON GATE

STOA OF THE HERMS

STOA POIKILE

ROYAL STOA

STOA OF ZEUS

12 GODS

ESCHARA

...LD ...OULEUTERION

GREAT DRAIN

THOLOS

HOUSE OF SIMON THE SHOEMAKER

BOUNDARY STONE

THE EPONYMOUS HEROES?

HELIAIA

...HRINE

PANATHENAIC WAY

COURTROOM

PRIVATE HOUSES AND SHOPS

SOUTH STOA I

S.E. FOUNTAIN HOUSE

MINT

ACROPOLIS ▶

The Agora was situated in the area of Athens known as the Kerameikos Quarter, and most Attic black- and red-figure vases will have been made in workshops situated close by. Many, including this one with its record-taking scene, were exported to Etruria.

This metrorological relief probably comes from the island of Paros, not the Athenian Agora, but there will certainly have been a similar kind of standard fathom and foot measurement set up at Athens so that tradesmen and their customers could check their wares and purchases.

The deeply rutted surface of the Panathenaic Way, the main thoroughfare across the Agora. Every four years, the Panathenaic procession would come this way en route to the Acropolis, but this would scarcely have caused the ruts, which must be due to commercial traffic in the Roman period.

The Stoa Basileios was only discovered in 1970. It was here that the initial hearings in cases of impiety were held, the most famous case being that of Socrates in 399 B.C.

A reconstruction of the kind of water clock as used in Athenian law courts. An orator could speak for as long as the water continued to flow, in this case six minutes. The original vessel on which the reconstruction is based was made for the Antiochis tribe in the late fifth century B.C.

MEN AT WORK

The rate of technological change in classical Greece was in practical terms static and there was, moreover, little motivation for technological advance. The reasons for this were twofold: there was a plentiful supply of cheap labor on the one hand, and on the other snobbery inhibited members of the upper classes from engaging in trade or manufacturing industry, and there was consequently little investment in order to increase productivity. The chief source of labor in antiquity was slaves, and these could be acquired relatively cheaply in the later fifth century (the period from which our best evidence comes). A slave might cost anything between seventy and three hundred times the basic daily wage, depending on his origin and particular skills. Slaves and free workmen might work side by side. The building accounts of the Erechtheum include both kinds of workers, who were paid identical rates for the same job. It is impossible to say what proportion of workers in general were slave or free, or even to distinguish the one kind from the

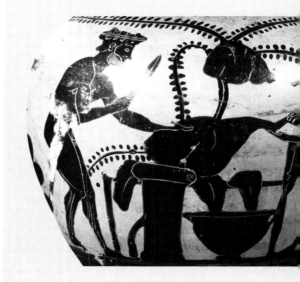

A butcher and his assistant cutting up the leg of an animal on a chopping block. Strips of meat are hung on a low stand, and there is a bowl to catch the blood, or for scraps. The scene takes place out of doors: there is a tree in the background, and one of the pair has placed his rolled-up cloak on it.

A blacksmith's workshop on an Attic black-figure amphora. An assistant holds the red-hot metal in a pair of tongs while the smith swings back his hammer. Various tools are hung on the wall in the background, as well as a waterjar. Are its contents intended to anneal the metal, or to slake the thirst of the workman and their audience? Both, perhaps.

other in the frequent representations of men at work that we see on Greek vases of the sixth to the fourth century. These scenes are usually concerned with trade or manufacturing on a small scale: merchants measuring grain, wool, oil, or wine, butchers or fishmongers cutting up their merchandise, sculptors making statues, potters pots, armorers helmets, shoemakers shoes, and so on. The painters often include rows of tools and instruments.

A carpenter making a wooden chest, work on which is almost complete. He is using a bow-drill to make holes in the lid. Wood naturally played an important role in ancient Greece: it was used for shipbuilding, house construction, charcoal, as well as for furniture, but very little has actually survived from antiquity apart from coffins and bowls found in localities which have a constant environment such as Crimean bogs or the Egyptian desert.

Left: A school room scene: the teacher holds up a text while his pupil stands reading it. It is important to remember that books in Greek antiquity were in the form of continuous scrolls and did not consist of pages bound together as today. Music was an important part of the education of a young man of good family: a lyre and a flute-bag (made from the skin of a small wild cat) hang on the wall behind.

Below: The interior of a potter's workshop. The boy seated on the left is painting the surface of a bell-crater which he balances precariously on his knee. He has a brush in his hand and the "paint" (a solution of clay) is in a small vessel on a low table next to him. A fellow workman carries another pot to the place where vases are left to dry before firing.

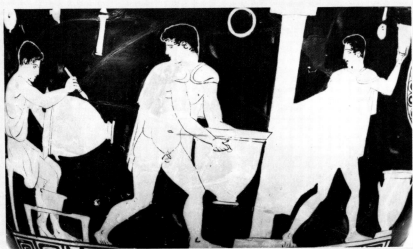

Above: A helmet maker at work, painted in the tondo of an Attic red-figure drinking cup. He sits on a low stool putting the finishing touches with a file to a Corinthian helmet. In front of him is an anvil and behind him an oven. A row of tools—gimlets, awls, and more files—are on the wall behind him.
Below: Merchants carefully weighing some kind of dry goods. A bearded man is pouring the product, probably grain of some kind, into a container while two younger assistants hold the scales steady.
Large amounts of grain were imported to Athens, where the vase bearing this picture was made, some of it from Sicily, where the vase was actually found.

Above: The interior of a shoemaker's workshop. A boy stands on the craftsman's table being fitted for a pair of shoes. The shoemaker is cutting a piece of leather to the shape of his foot. The boy's father, or perhaps his lover, looks on. Again tools of the trade are shown in the background.
Left: A sculptor at work on a herm, a pillar-like object surmounted by a bust and adorned with genitalia on the front. Herms were set up outside houses and at boundaries. They were regarded with great respect; there was a political scandal with far-reaching consequences when Alcibiades was accused of having participated in the mutilation of the herms in the Agora.

175

SCULPTURE IN BRONZE

These two scenes of bronze sculptors in their well-equipped workshop (note the hammers and saw on the walls) come from either side of an Attic drinking cup by the Foundry Painter made shortly after 480 B.C. The first shows two scenes. At left, a craftsman is raking coals in the bottom of a tall furnace. On the right, pieces of a fallen warrior are being put together. It either lies on a bed of clay, or the rock-like object may be part of the finished statue. The arms are being adjusted by another craftsman, and the head has yet to be attached. The scene inside the cup (not shown) of Hephaestus and Achilles' mother Thetis implies that the statue of a heroically nude

The earliest large-scale Greek bronze sculpture we possess is the life-size male figure (often called "Apollo") found in the Piraeus in 1959. It is thought to have been made around 525 B.C. Until then most major sculpture was made of marble, but thenceforth the use of bronze became more common. Being a structurally stable material, bronze offered sculptors the possibility of making figures in more active poses than it was then possible to achieve in marble. It was also a more costly material and thus offered scope for conspicuous consumption. The metal was an alloy of one part tin to about seven or eight parts copper (the proportions varied at different periods). The shining, almost golden surface of bronze was greatly prized, and important statues must have been regularly cleaned to prevent them developing a patina.

Bronze statues were cast in molds, but since it would have been extremely wasteful to

form the mold. Bronze pins (called chaplets) which passed from the mold to the core prevented the displacement of the latter when the mold was baked to melt out the wax prior to the introduction of the molten bronze in its place. The metal was heated to over 1000°C and poured in through funnel-shaped openings. Vent holes (of hollow reeds) enabled the gases created when the liquid metal met the baked clay to escape. A mold for a small male figure of the kouros type was found in the Athenian Agora excavations, together with the pit in which the casting took place. The mold, already baked, was placed in the pit and earth was packed around it so that it would not break under pressure from the molten bronze. The statue made in it was probably intended to be the cult image of the archaic temple of Apollo Patroos which stood close by. This building was destroyed during the Persian sack of Athens and the statue presumably

warrior in the center of the other side of the cup (scene at right) is Achilles. The enormous statue is supported in a wooden frame, to which the finishing touches are being given by the same two craftsmen. If this is Achilles, his fallen adversary will be Hector, the Trojan hero whom Achilles defeated in battle. In fact, the decoration of this cup is of a none-too-subtle erotic nature, but that is another story...

cast large-scale figures solid, these were hollow cast, usually by the lost-wax method. This involved building a clay core over an armature of wood into the approximate shape of the final figure. Then a layer of wax a few millimeters thick was added and its surface carefully worked into the exact form of the intended statue. Successive layers of clay—the first one fine enough to pick up all the details of the model—were added to

taken as booty. Such was the fate of other bronze statues known to have existed in the Agora at the time. The original group of the Tyrannicides Harmodius and Aristogiton by Antenor made in the late sixth century B.C. were removed to Persia (to be replaced in the 470s by Critius and Nesiotes' group). Looting, indeed, is the reason why so few bronze statues have survived from classical antiquity: they were frequently used as

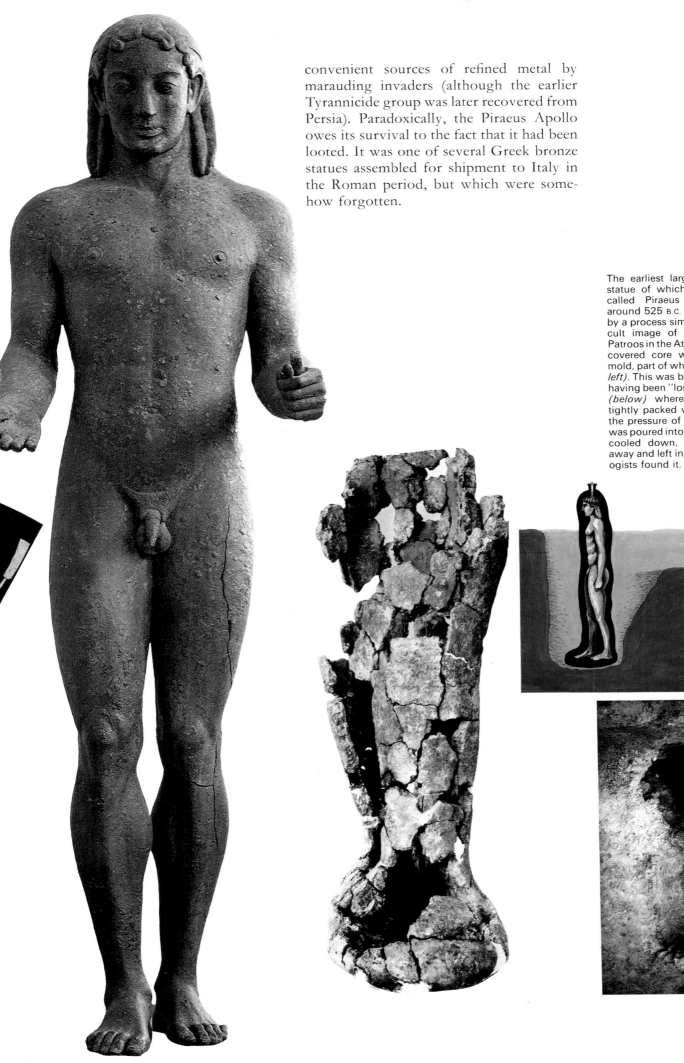

convenient sources of refined metal by marauding invaders (although the earlier Tyrannicide group was later recovered from Persia). Paradoxically, the Piraeus Apollo owes its survival to the fact that it had been looted. It was one of several Greek bronze statues assembled for shipment to Italy in the Roman period, but which were somehow forgotten.

The earliest large-scale Greek bronze statue of which we know is the so-called Piraeus Apollo *(left),* made around 525 B.C. It will have been made by a process similar to that used for the cult image of the Temple of Apollo Patroos in the Athenian Agora. The wax-covered core was encased in a clay mold, part of which still survives *(below left).* This was baked and then, the wax having been "lost," it was placed in a pit *(below)* where it would have been tightly packed with earth to withstand the pressure of the molten bronze that was poured into it. When everything had cooled down, the mold was broken away and left in the pit where archaeologists found it.

PHIDIAS' WORKSHOP

The Athenian sculptor Phidias was commissioned by the Eleans to make the cult statue for the Temple of Zeus at Olympia. He probably carried out the work in the 430s, and had a workshop specially built whose interior resembled in a simplified form the cella of the temple. The site of the workshop has

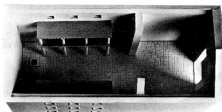

been excavated and it has been possible to reconstruct the building (on paper) along the lines of the model shown here with and without its roof. The numerous windows will have provided daylight to work by, and the two-storied colonnade no doubt approximated to the one in the temple itself.

Members of the German Archaeological Institute have conducted excavations at Olympia for more than one hundred years, and their researches have added a great deal to our knowledge of one of the most important Panhellenic centers, famous above all for the Olympic games which were held there every four years as part of the rites that were performed to honor Zeus, whose shrine Olympia was. Few of the finds made by the German archaeologists have been as fascinating as the discovery in the late 1950s of the workshop of the Athenian sculptor Phidias who was commissioned to make the huge chryselephantine (gold and ivory) cult statue of Zeus for the temple that had been built much earlier in the 460s.

The building that had served as Phidias' workshop owed its partial preservation to the fact that it had been transformed into a Byzantine church in the Middle Ages. Even this was in ruins, however, when excavation began. It would have been difficult to locate the workshop had it not been for a line or two in Pausanias' *Description of Greece* in which he located "a building called the workshop of Phidias, where he worked the statue of Zeus piece by piece" just outside the Altis, as the sacred enclosure at Olympia was called, and near the Leonidaeum, the site of which was well known.

The foundations of the original workshop building were still in place, but the upper parts of the walls had undergone several transformations since Phidias' day. Several fragments of terracotta antefixes and of the cornice of the workshop were found. The lotus and palmette designs on the latter were unlike any others found at Olympia but have

much in common with Athenian patterns; Phidias was after all an Athenian sculptor. The workshop's dimensions, 32.18 by 14.575 meters (some 100 by 48 feet), approximate to those of the cella of the temple where the cult statue was eventually to be situated. The building, moreover, has exactly the same alignment as the temple, presumably so that the effects of light from the door could be gauged in advance. There is evidence for a series of windows in the walls—probably nine on each side—which will have provided the daylight necessary for the sculptor and his assistants to see what they were doing. Several small Doric capitals probably came from two-storied colonnades along each wall. These were presumably meant to correspond to the colonnades in the cella of the temple itself. The roof must have been at least thirteen meters (ca. 43 feet) high.

The statue will have consisted largely of a wooden framework over which the gold drapery and ivory flesh were placed, but in such a way that it could be dismantled for removal to the temple, or even for inventory taking: Phidias had earlier been suspected of embezzlement in connection with this work on the chryselephantine statue of Athena Parthenos at Athens. Some terracotta molds were found which may have been used for casting drapery, and others for casting glass leaves for inlaid palmette motifs. Glass, surprisingly, was an extremely precious commodity in the fifth century. A goldsmith's hammer, bone chisels, and lead patterns and stencils were among the other finds. But the most satisfying discovery of all was a small black mug decorated with

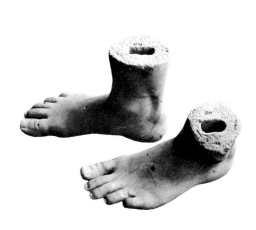

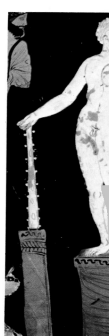

The god sits on a throne, and he is made of gold and ivory. On his head lies a garland which is a copy of olive shoots. In his right hand he carries a Victory which, like the statue, is of ivory and gold; she wears a ribbon and—on her head—a garland. In the left hand of the god is a scepter, ornamented with every kind of metal, and the bird sitting on the scepter is the eagle. The sandals also of the god are of gold, as is likewise his robe. On the robe are worked figures of animals and lily-flowers. The throne is adorned with gold and with jewels, to say nothing of ebony and ivory. Upon it are painted figures and wrought images. . . .

Pausanias, Description of Greece

fluted sides and inscribed underneath with the words *Pheidio eimi*, "I belong to Phidias." This provided the final proof that the workshop was indeed that of Phidias. Let the last word be with Pausanias: even the known statistics "fall far short of the impression made by the sight of the image.

Nay, the god himself according to legend bore witness to the artistic skill of Phidias. For when the image was quite finished Phidias prayed the god to show by a sign whether the work was to his liking. Immediately, runs the legend, a thunderbolt fell on . . . the floor."

Phidias' Zeus is now lost and can only be reconstructed indirectly by means of Pausanias' description, a polychrome head found at Cyrene, and some Roman period coins of Elis. It is a curious fact that the custom of representing Christ as bearded was derived from this pagan statue.

A mug found in Phidias' workshop proclaims itself to belong to the sculptor. The graffito on the underside states "I belong to Phidias" and was presumably scratched on by the artist himself.

Far left: Fragments in marble and bronze of a Greek statue from southern Italy which resembled Phidias' Zeus in that the drapery was made in one material and the flesh in another.

Left: Detail of a south Italian vase of the fourth century B.C. showing a sculptor putting the finishing touches to a statue of Heracles.

Right: Bone chisels of various shapes found in the excavation of Phidias' workshop. They would have been suitable for working the gold from which the drapery of the Zeus was made.

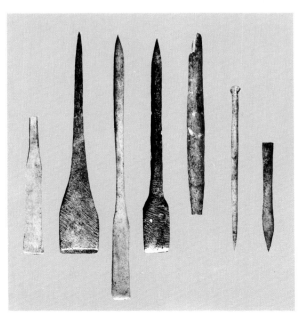

INDIVIDUAL
PAINTING STYLES

Most readers of this book will be able to distinguish the work of, say, Renoir from that of Van Gogh. Research done during the past century or so, most of it by Sir John Beazley (1885–1970), has meant that it is now possible to attribute many painted Greek vases to individual artists. Since we know the real names of but a few painters, new names have had to be created, names such as the Achilles Painter, whose work was characterized by Beazley as follows: "There are no nobler heads in vase painting than the

best of our artist's, and in his minor works we find the same mild and beautiful type." The white-ground lekythos *(right)* was made for funerary use and actually shows a man and a woman at a tomb.

The Pan Painter's name is another invented one. He is so called after a bell-crater in Boston where there is a scene of Pan chasing a shepherd boy. In Beazley's words, the Pan Painter likes "unusual scenes...piquant contrasts,

deliberate and amusing disproportions... round heads with tiny nose and delicate nostril but big chin and bull neck." The similarity between the heads of the dancing boys on this fragment and that of the furniture carrier on the red-figure pelike is clear. The boy is carrying the basic equipment for a symposium: a couch and a three-legged table.

There were major mural paintings done in the fifth century B.C. such as the panels by Micon and Polygnotus in the Stoa Poikile at Athens, or Polygnotus' decoration of the Lesche of the Cnidians at Delphi, which were as famous in antiquity as, say, the Arena or Sistine chapels today. Sadly, these great works of art are lost, and we have but a faint reflection of major painting in the decorated pottery produced at Athens in the fifth century B.C. It is as though Renaissance painting had completely disappeared and all we had to reconstruct it was majolica.

Students of Greek archaeology have gradually come to recognize individual hands among the artists who painted Greek vases. The major work in this area, however, was done by the late Sir John Beazley (d. 1970), who, in a series of magisterial catalogues, attributed thousands of vases, many of them fragmentary, to hundreds of artists. To the uninitiated layman, one Greek vase may look very much like another, but just as the educated man or woman in the street can recognize at a glance the difference between, say, a painting by Auguste Renoir and one by Henri de Toulouse-Lautrec, so too, one could quickly learn the difference between, say, the Pan Painter and the Achilles Painter.

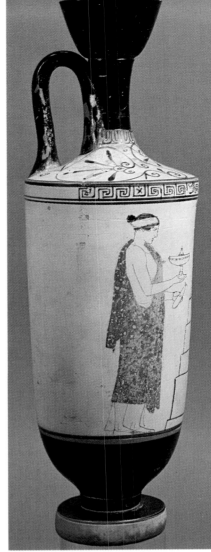

The names now given to Greek vase-painters perhaps require some explanation. Only a few vases are signed by the artists who actually painted them. Such signatures occur in the form "so-and-so *egrapsen* (painted)," and in this way we know the names of such artists as Exekias or Euphronios, to name perhaps the finest painters of black- and red-figure respectively. Another kind of signature reads "so-and-so *epoiesen* (made)"; and it is on most vases plain that this does not necessarily mean the painter and this kind of expression is taken to be either the potter or the owner of the workshop in which the vase was made. Names recorded in this fashion are useful pegs on which to hang the work of otherwise nameless painters who are now called, for example, the Amasis Painter or the Brygos Painter.

Yet other painters whose hands are distinctive but who still remained anonymous were given names which Beazley invented for

The Eretria Painter derives his name from a vase in Athens found at Eretria in Euboea. The scenes on his works are usually concerned with the boudoir, as on this red-figure amphoriskos (the actual vase is not much bigger than these pictures). A seated girl, who is perhaps a

them, based perhaps on the theme of their most characteristic vase (e.g., the Pan Painter called after a horny Pan on a bell crater in Boston), or the city or the museum in which their most distinguished work is now to be seen (e.g., the Berlin Painter, or the Painter of Munich 1686—the latter called after a museum inventory number). Alternatively, an artist's mannerism might become the basis for his given name (e.g., the Affecter Painter or the Elbows Out Painter).

"The process of disengaging the work of an anonymous artist is the same as that of attributing an unsigned vase to a painter whose name is known. It consists of drawing a conclusion from observation of a great many details: it involves comparing one vase with another, with several others, with all the vases the enquirer has seen.... However obscure he may be, the artist cannot escape detection if only sufficiently delicate tests be applied. It was hard at

first, I remember, to distinguish the Syriskos painter from the painter of the Copenhagen amphora, or even the Villa Giulia painter from the painter of the Chicago stamnos. But now it is quite easy."

So Beazley, writing in 1918 on one of the few occasions he described his working methods.

It is sometimes thought that the attribution of vases to individual painters is an end in itself; it is, however, but the necessary preparatory stage to studying the content of the scenes represented within the context of Greek culture and history.

bride, looks at herself in a mirror, while a lady called Theano holds a ribbon in one hand and a box in the other. The delicate palmette and scroll patterns recur on this fragment of a stemless cup also by the Eretria Painter, "a fine artist...exquisite work...one of the most excellent painters of this time" (430s B.C.).

WOMEN IN A MAN'S WORLD

A saying attributed variously to Thales or Socrates cogently expresses the Greek male's view of womankind: "There are three reasons why I am grateful to Fortune: first, that I was born a man and not an animal, second, that I was born a man and not a woman, and third, that I was born a Greek and not a foreigner."

Women in classical Greece were undeniably underprivileged. Their legal rights were limited and political ones non-existent. There was a law, for example, which prevented women from making a contract worth more than a bushel of barley. And much of the humor in Aristophanes' "feminist" plays, the *Lysistrata, Thesmophoriazusae,* and *Ecclesiazusae,* depends on the fact that women are shown in rôles which would have been unthinkable in everyday life.

Woman's place was in the home, and the law and male prejudice conspired to keep her there. Pericles is supposed to have said that a woman was only truly honorable if her name was never mentioned by men for either good or evil. His concern may, however, have been a personal one, for his own

work, and is couched in the form of a Socratic dialogue. A certain Ischomachus describes the different rôles of the sexes: "God made the heart and body of men better able to endure cold and heat and long journeys and campaigns. So he enjoined outdoor activities upon man. But upon woman he apparently enjoined indoor ones because he made her less physically able to stand up to such things. Then, aware of having given woman the task of looking after new-born children, he gave her a larger share than the man of love for new-born infants. Then because he had given her the additional task of guarding the stores, god consciously made woman more apprehensive than man, knowing that it is no bad thing for a guardian to have an apprehensive disposition." Ischomachus then gives a list of his wife's duties: "You will have to stay inside and help in sending out the servants with outdoor tasks; you must supervise the indoor servants, and receive any revenues; from these you must meet any necessary expenses, and look after the surplus providently, so that you don't spend the whole year's budget in a month. When wool is brought to you, you must see that the right clothes are made for those who need them. And you must see that the dried corn remains fit for consumption. There is also one duty that may not appeal to you much—looking after any servant who falls ill. 'Oh, no, that will be a great pleasure' she said."

Attitudes toward marriage, divorce, and adultery were male-oriented. A girl's father would choose a husband for her, and it was he, not the bride, who made the betrothal

Below: An instrument known as an *epinetron,* which was placed on a woman's knee while she prepared wool for spinning on the roughened upper surface. Xenophon's ideal wife is told that "when wool is brought to you, you must see that the right clothes are made for those who need them"; most Greek women would have spent a considerable amount of time carding, spinning, and weaving wool. The scene on this epinetron is a very apposite one: preparations for a marriage. It was painted by the Eretria Painter.

relationship with the Milesian Aspasia was one which gave rise to a great deal of gossip. Men were puzzled how a woman could get the better of an argument with politicians or philosophers, and were diverted by tales that, like Lady Metroland, Aspasia was president "of a business that was neither decent nor respectable—bringing up young girls to be prostitutes." Her place of birth, too, cannot have helped her reputation, for Miletus possessed in Greek the connotations that Paris used to have in the Anglo-Saxon world.

Books of household management were written by men, not Mrs. Beetons, in classical times. Xenophon's *Economicus* was such a

Right: Two women winding wool. A large skein lies in a basket between them. *Far right:* Another women's task was to fetch water from the public fountain. The women on this vase (itself a hydria, or water-jar like those being filled) are decking the ornamental water spouts (in the form of lions' heads and horsemen) with garlands in connection, no doubt, with a festival.

182

Left: A scene from the boudoir: a seated girl, Thalea, is being adorned with jewelry by her entourage. A woman stands in front of her holding out a trinket box, while behind her Glauke is about to put a necklace on her. A hand mirror hangs on the wall behind. This is but one of many such scenes by the Eretria Painter. *Above:* A baby feeder made of black glazed terracotta. The liquid would have been placed in the hole on top and the baby fed by means of a teat of cloth or leather attached to the aperture to the right. It bears the graffito MAMO.

agreement before witnesses. The provision of a dowry was an important element in any marriage settlement, and the prospects of a girl who did not have a dowry were slight. The end of marriage was not sex, but the birth of legitimate heirs. For this reason there were harsh statutory penalties for adultery: death for the man and divorce for the woman, although we rarely hear of the first penalty actually being carried out. Aeschines cites a law of Solon which forbade a wife taken in adultery "to adorn herself or attend any public ceremony, lest by mixing with guiltless wives she should corrupt them; if she does attend or adorn herself, Solon bids anyone witnessing it to tear her garments and strip her of her finery and beat her...thus does Solon seek to disgrace such a wife and make her life unbearable."

The painting directly above shows a baby holding a rattle and sitting in a terracotta high chair-cum-potty of a kind that has actually been found in the excavations in the Athenian Agora. To the right is a simple toy go-cart consisting of a wheel on a stick.

Guests at a Greek dinner party, or symposium, would recline on couches while they ate and drank, leaning on their left elbows. The symposiast shown here, one of the finest extant small bronzes we have from the sixth century B.C., is doing precisely this.

The couches on which symposiasts reclined were placed on a low plinth around the edge of a dining room. Such rooms often had mosaic floors, and a particularly fine example was found recently at Eretria in Euboea by a team of Swiss archaeologists.

The dinner party, or symposium, was an important institution in archaic and classical Greece. Strictly speaking, the word *symposion* should only be applied to the serious drinking that took place after the meal proper or *deipnon* was over, but both eating and drinking took place in the one place —the *andron*—which was specially designed for the purpose, and whose form was derived from the way in which a Greek dinner party was conducted. The host and his guests would recline on their left elbows on couches arranged around the sides of a room. A low table would be placed before each couch, and wine would be brought in and poured into the diners' cups. The first couch to the right of the doorway was the place of honor, and then the couches were arranged in sequence around the walls to the last, where the host lay, to the left of the door. The effect of such an arrangement was that the door of a dining room was inevitably not in the center of the wall, but a little to one side. This simple rule makes it an easy matter to recognize a Greek dining room, and several have been found in religious, civic, and domestic contexts. Sanctuaries, for example, had dining rooms in which important visitors might be entertained during religious festivals. In cities, there were public dining rooms, and several are known in Athens. Some of the most elaborate *androns,* however, have been found in private houses. Mosaic floors, made of pebbles in this period, are a prominent feature of these, and a particularly fine example was found recently at Eretria in Euboea. A mosaic floor, while being decorative, would also have been easy to keep clean. For once a symposium got under way, there would have been quite a lot of refuse. There are even mosaic representations at a later period of "unswept floors," strewn with discarded bones and shells. To these we might have to add spilt wine and worse, and this is probably why the *andron* was regularly equipped with a drain out to the street. The word *andron* in fact means "men's room," which tells us that the Greek symposium was intended for men's amusement; any women servants, flute girls, acrobats, and so on, were there for the men's entertainment, and only incidentally for their own. It was indeed, even for men, a mark of distinction to *recline* at dinner rather than to sit; we are told by Atheneans that in fourth-century Macedonia a man could not recline at dinner unless he had killed a boar outside the net. We do not know whether this rule was enforced in fifth-century Athens, but even there it was probably only the gentry who regularly indulged in symposia.

Many literary accounts of Greek dinners are unbelievably exaggerated; the nearest we get to a plausible description is an account of what happened at Naucratis:

"In Naucratis, the people dine in the town hall on feast days, all appearing in white robes.... After reclining they rise again, and kneeling, join in pouring a libation, while the herald, acting as priest, recites the traditional prayers. After this they recline, and all receive a pint of wine excepting the priests of Pythian Apollo and Dionysus: for to each of these the wine is given in double quantity, as well as the proportions of everything else. Thereupon each diner is served with a loaf of fine wheat bread molded flat, upon which lies another loaf which they call oven bread; also a piece of swine's flesh, a small bowl of barley gruel or of some vegetable in season, two eggs, a bit of fresh cheese, some dried figs, a flat-cake, and a wreath.... But on all other days of the year any diner who wishes may go up to the town hall and eat, after preparing at home for his own use a green or leguminous vegetable, some salt or fresh fish and a very small piece of pork; sharing these he receives half a pint of wine. No woman may enter the town hall except the flute-girl. Nor is it allowed to bring a chamber-pot into the townhall either."

These fairly modest but adequate food allowances probably represent the dietary norm, at least for a citizen of average means. His slaves would get the leftovers.

The chief business of a private symposium

The drinking of wine was the principal activity at a Greek symposium (the word actually means "drinking together"), but the wine, which was probably rendered extremely intoxicating by the addition of herbs, was always diluted in a mixing bowl ("crater") such as the one seen on this cup.

seems to have been the drinking of wine. Greek wine was notoriously powerful, and it must have contained additional intoxicant herbs and opiates, for it was nearly always drunk diluted with several parts of water. Amphictyon, the legendary king of Athens, is supposed to have learned from Dionysus

Left: A maenad, one of the mythical devotees of the wine god, Dionysus, whirls in a frenzy on an Attic red-figure vase.

The fresco panel shown above was found on the wall of a tomb in Paestum (founded as the Greek colony Poseidonia). Symposiasts recline on their couches, talking and singing. The drinking vessel below was made in Boeotia in the fourth century with a false bottom. A practical joker would give it, apparently full, to his victim; one mouthful and it would be empty.

Far right: A silver drinking cup of the late fifth century B.C. found in a tomb at Nymphaeum in southern Russia. It well illustrates the degree to which even non-Greeks had taken to Greek dining customs.

The young aristocrat Philippus, in the scene at right, rejects the advances of the flute girl Callisto whose pipes he has taken from her. Professional flute girls would turn up at a symposium in the hope of employment. The one who came to Plato's *Symposium* was shown the door.

the art of mixing wine: "So it was that men came to stand upright, drinking wine mixed, whereas before they were bent double by the use of unmixed." There was an awareness, moreover, of the power of drink: in a play by Eubulus, Dionysus is made to say:

"Three bowls only do I mix for the temperate—one to health which they empty first, the second to love and pleasure, the third to sleep. When this is drunk up wise guests go home. The fourth is ours no longer, but belongs to violence; the fifth to uproar, and sixth to drunken revel, the seventh to black eyes. The eighth is the policeman's, the ninth belongs to vomiting, and the tenth to madness and hurling the furniture."

The usual entertainment, apart from conversation, was musical. Flute girls seem to have come along to a symposium in the hope of employment. Their equipment was of the simplest: a double flute carried in a bag. The lyre was another instrument that figured prominently at symposia, and just as every Jane Austen heroine played the pianoforte, so too young men of respectable families learned to play the lyre as part of their education. One reason why Themistocles was not acceptable in the "right circles" was that he did not possess this skill, and this fact in turn suggests that secular symposium scenes on vases only show upper-class conviviality, and no matter how reprehensible

the subject matter, they should not be interpreted as vignettes of low life.

The lyre of course was the regular accompaniment to Greek lyric poetry—poems which were composed to be sung at symposia, and which were collected in order to provide symposiasts with something to sing when their own invention failed to rise to

186

the occasion. Each symposiast would take a turn to sing either a composition of his own or to sing or recite some passage from a famous poet. There was also a form of banquet song which must have put quite a strain on the inventiveness of those taking

part, in which the leader started by singing a short verse on a subject and in a meter of his own device. This would have to be topped by the next singer, and so on round the room.

A favorite after-dinner game was kottabos. There were several versions, but all involved flicking a small amount of wine from a drinking cup at a target. In the most elementary form of the game the target was simply a cup held up by a neighbor. In another version, the targets might be small dishes floating in a bowl and the object here

was to sink as many as possible. A character in Sophocles' *Salmoneus* is made to say, "There are ticklings and the smack of kisses; there are the prizes set up for the one who best shoots the kottabos," and it has been suggested that the stake in the game was the servant—male or female—who served the drinks.

The symposium had its origins in the kind of banquet held to honor Homeric heroes. It is clear from the poets that the symposium continued to be an important institution in the life of the rich throughout the archaic period. Attic drinking songs composed in the late sixth and early fifth century, moreover, give us an insight into the political

nature of the clubs who met in such convivial surroundings. The tyrannicides figure prominently: "I will wear my sword in a spray of myrtle like Harmodius and Aristogiton when they killed the usurper and made Athens be once again a city where all are free."

Another fresco slab from the Paestan tomb. The couple on the right are clearly tied up in one another and are attracting the attention of the men in the center. The main interest for us, however, is the game of kottabos being played by the symposiasts on the left. One holds up his cup as a target for the other to hit with wine flicked from his cup.

Far left: A tipsy reveler who has clearly taken too literally the kind of injunction painted on the outside of the cup to left: "Rejoice and drink well!" Below, a discomfited symposiast receives tender loving care from his girl.

CLASSICAL DRAMA

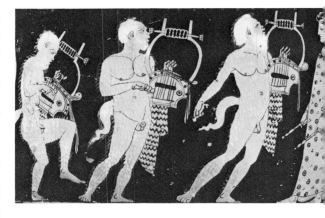

The Athenian public regularly enjoyed dramatic festivals which were held in the theater of Dionysus. The major event was the City Dionysia to which people would flock from the city and the surrounding countryside. On three successive days they would attend religious ceremonies in honor of the god soon after dawn, and then listen to three tragedies, a satyr play, and a comedy performed in quick succession. It used to be thought that the performances lasted all day, but it has recently been estimated, more realistically, that everything would have been over by midafternoon.

The festivals were organized by the state, but the production of the plays was sponsored by wealthy individuals as a public service or "liturgy." Unlike the contemporary theater which is largely a middle-class affair, ancient plays were performed for a

shared the comic stage with others. These, however, are the playwrights of the classical period (together with the anonymous author of the *Prometheus Bound* which used to be attributed to Aeschylus) whose works have come down to us in the form of complete plays.

The origins of the drama are obscure. Its association with Dionysus has made some look for its beginnings in rustic ritual, perhaps in the question and answer of a traditional poetic genre, the dithyramb; others prefer to see them in recitations by rhapsodes of the Homeric epics. But whatever its origins, the drama was fully developed by 472 B.C. when *The Persians,* the earliest of Aeschylus' six extant plays, was staged. There is relatively little action in the play, but this is compensated for by the graphic descriptions of the Battle of Salamis in long messenger speeches. In this respect

Below: A detail from a calyx-crater which shows satyrs lighting their torches from the fire which Prometheus stole from the gods and gave to mankind—an act for which he was to be punished by Zeus. The scene has been connected with a revival in about 440 of Aeschylus' satyr-play *Prometheus the Firelighter* which was first performed in 472 as a companion piece to the trilogy of which the *Persians* was part. Other vases show the chorus for satyr-plays kitted out with special loin-cloths which support an erect phallus and a tail. There are no loin-cloths visible here, and so it

is quite possible that this scene is not directly derived from the stage. The elderly satyr chorus at upper right, however, are certainly dressed for the stage. They are all wearing tights to which their tails are attached.

mass audience. Their reaction will inevitably have influenced the decisions of the judges whose task it was to award a prize to the best dramatist. Aeschylus, Sophocles, and Euripides were the most successful tragedians in the fifth century, though they were by no means the only ones; likewise Aristophanes

Right: An Attic red-figure bell-crater showing a scene which may be derived from Aeschylus' lost play the *Toxotides.* In the center Actaeon is being torn to pieces by his hounds which are being driven on by Lyssa. On the left, Zeus looks on; on the right, Artemis stands with a flaming torch in her right hand, a bow in her left, and a quiver over her shoulder. *Far right:* A graphic representation of a lost fourth-century production by an unknown playwright of the *Medea.* Creon stands in his palace trying to support his daughter who is already dying from the poisoned robe and tiara she has put on. Medea can be seen dressed in oriental costume about to murder one of her children. These are but two details of a melodramatic rendering of a melodramatic play.

Greek tragedy might perhaps be thought of as being closer to radio than television drama.

The Persians was obviously intended to refer to specific historical events, and the fact that the central theme of the play was the naval battle of 480 B.C. may have had something to do with attempts to remind the Athenian public of the contribution to Greek victory made by Themistocles, the architect of the Athenian navy, but whose political fortunes were on the wane in 472.

The historical relevance of Aeschylus' second play, *Seven against Thebes,* is less obvious but would have been equally apparent to the Athenian audience which saw it performed in 468. They would have recognized in the constant references to the fortifications of

the city in which the play is set (always called "the city of Cadmus," never "Thebes," and thus given a mythological distance from the contemporary city which had medized in 480–479) a reference to Cimon's current policy of fortifying the Athenian Acropolis whose "wooden walls" had proved so vulnerable in 480. Vivid verbal images will have brought back to the audience the memory of those days: "Great and grievous are the sufferings when a city is overcome. Man seizes man, makes prisoner, or slays. Yonder he carries fire and all the town grows foul with smoke."

According to Aristotle, tragedy achieves *catharsis* through pity and fear. The precise technical meaning of *catharsis* is a matter of debate. Scholars disagree as to whether it is that the spectator learns through pity and fear to avoid the destructive emotions expressed by the tragic hero, or whether by expending pity and fear the spectator's own emotional conflicts are resolved for the moment. In any event, the theme of fear pervades the first half of the *Seven.* Fear, or its synonyms, recurs very often indeed and is as prominent a feature as the descriptions of the shield blazons of the seven Argive heroes who are preparing to attack. (It is perhaps significant that the enemy is Argive, for Argos remained neutral in the Persian Wars.)

Aeschylus' *Seven against Thebes* is extremely carefully constructed on both the small scale and the large. The list of deities invoked by the chorus of women, fearful of what the enemy might do if they succeeded in taking the city, numbers seven—the same as the number of Theban gates under attack—and culminates in the name of Hera, the patroness of Argos. The descriptions of the fearsome shields of the Seven, and of some of

Left: It was customary for the actors in Greek tragedies to wear special masks, rather than make-up. Here we see an actor on a fragment of an Apulian red-figure vase standing with his mask in his hand. There is a great contrast between the noble features, perhaps those of a king, of the mask and the flabby and unshaven face of the actor himself.

A greatly simplified scene of an actor and his audience on an Attic red-figure vase of ca. 420 B.C. The performance appears to be a comic parody of Sophocles' *Andromeda.* The actor is wearing tights and has his artificial phallus looped up. He plays the part of Perseus and carries the curved knife with which he will cut off Medusa's head, and the bag into which he will put it. This is the

only representation we have of a stage on an Attic vase: it is approached by a short flight of steps which leads up from the orchestra. The audience (who may be the *choregus,* or producer, and the playwright) are seated on wooden chairs of a kind which were reproduced in marble in the fourth-century refurbishment of the Theater of Dionysus at Athens.

Far left: A rare representation of the Alcestis myth on an Apulian funerary vase of the third quarter of the fourth century B.C. Euripides staged a play with the same theme at Athens about a century earlier, in 438 B.C.
Left: Oedipus and the sphinx, a theme treated in Sophocles' great tragedy.

Portraits, of Roman date, of the fifth-century dramatists Aeschylus, Sophocles, and Aristophanes. Bronze statues of the three major Attic tragedians were set up in the Theater of Dionysus in 340–336; there are no recorded ancient portraits of the comic writer Aristophanes, but the portrait type on the right has been associated with him.

Sons and daughters of Thebes, behold: this was Oedipus, greatest of men; he held the key to the deepest mysteries; was envied by all his fellow-men for his great prosperity; Behold, what a full tide of misfortune swept over his head. Then learn that mortal man must always look to his ending. And none can be called happy until that day when he carries his happiness down to the grave in peace.

From Sophocles' Oedipus Rex

Euripides, the tragic poet, is seated on a *klismos* (chair) and receives a tragic mask from a female personification of the dramatic arts appropriately named Scene who holds a scroll in her right hand. To the right, a statue of Dionysus with a wine-cup in his hand looks on. The major dramatic festival at Athens was held in honor of Dionysus.

Right: The Theater of Dionysus at Athens. It used to be the case that scholars were undecided as to whether the marble seating, including the stately *klismoi* in the front row, was of fourth-century Greek or of Roman date. Now, however, as a result of a comparison of the trace elements in the lead into which the metal clamps are set with those of known dates, a fourth-century B.C. date is certain.

the defending champions, culminate in an account of that of Polynices whose "shield, true round, is new of build, with twofold emblem fixed cunningly upon it. A work of gold displays a man full-armed, and a woman leads him with sober guidance. 'Justice,' it seems, she calls herself, according to the letters...." These lines come at the very center of the play, and it is a striking fact that they are expressed in pictorial terms as two figures, one of them captioned, within a circular frame. One cannot help thinking in terms of the tondo of a Greek drinking cup, and it may not be too far-fetched to think of Aeschylus actually having such a cup (probably a metal one; such

do exist) in mind when he composed the *Seven.*

Not all Greek tragedies are as contrived as this, of course, but all must have a political or social "message" in addition to their plot. When it comes to deciding what that message might be, however, different scholars argue for different interpretations. Thus, for example, Hegel saw in Creon and Antigone of Sophocles' play of 442 B.C. representations of the polis on one hand and family and religion on the other; whereas V. Ehrenberg has maintained that Creon, whose tyrannical and self-righteous attitude provides such a contrast to Antigone's gentleness, was a reflection of certain aspects of Pericles' character and regime. Any such interpretations are, however, bound to be subjective; some scholars have reacted against the notion of historical references in much of fifth-century literature and argued instead for its universal application.

It is in comedy that the political and social references implicit in tragedy are made plain, whether it be in Aristophanes' stance in favor of peace or against intellectuals, or whether it be simple observations made almost in passing which the audience will have recognized with a guffaw or a belly laugh: in Aristophanes' *Clouds* for example, the would-be philosopher Strepsiades is shown a map of the world and has the city of Athens pointed out to him. His reply is "Don't be ridiculous, that can't be Athens, for I can't see even a single law court in session"—a pointed reference to some Athenians' love of litigation.

THE GREAT PHILOSOPHERS

SOCRATES

PLATO

Philosophy in the modern sense began in the East Greek world in the sixth century B.C. *The first philosopher of whom we know was Thales of Miletus. He and his followers Anaximenes and Anaximander sought the single moving force behind the universe: the first found it in "water," the second in "air," and the third in "the Infinite." Their speculations were based on*

the observation of natural phenomena; we can imagine teachers and students such as the birdwatchers on this Attic red-figure vase perhaps drawing similar conclusions about the world in which they lived from what they saw in nature. Such speculation inevitably led to a turning away from mythological concepts of the cosmos, and when teachers began propagating such a questioning attitude toward traditional beliefs, they and their pupils incurred accusations of impiety.

Said to have been the son of a sculptor and a midwife, but of a prosperous enough background to have served as a hoplite. Won praise for his courage in war (he fought at Potidaea, Delium, and Amphipolis) and peace (he defied the Thirty Tyrants by refusing to arrest a certain Leon, and risked death himself thereby). Trained as a scientific philosopher, he turned later in life to the search for truth, beauty, and justice. His method (the "Socratic method") was to ask questions of his listeners in order to make them realize the fundamental weakness of many of their assumptions. This did not win him general popularity, but he did become the "guru" of Athens' gilded

"Death is one of two things. Either it is annihilation, and the dead have no consciousness of anything; or, as we are told, it is really a change: a migration of the soul from this place to another."

"For no man but an utter fool or a coward is afraid of death itself, but he is afraid of doing wrong. For to go to the world below having one's soul full of injustice is the last and worst of all evils."

youth. He was mercilessly lampooned in Aristophanes' *Clouds*, a fact which contributed to his conviction on a charge of impiety in 399. He was condemned and died from a draught of hemlock.

Born of a prominent Athenian family in about 427 B.C., he met Socrates in ca. 407 and was part of his circle until the latter's trial and death in 399. It is to Plato that we owe most of our knowledge of Socrates' teaching and personality. Plato traveled to Italy and Sicily and associated with Pythagorean philosophers and Sicilian tyrants, but with these last he eventually became disillusioned. In 386 he founded his philosophical school, the

"...Virtue is shown as coming to us, whenever it comes, by divine dispensation; but we shall only know the truth about this clearly when, before enquiring in what way virtue comes to mankind, we first try to search out what virtue is in itself."

"There can be no end to the troubles of states, or indeed...of humanity itself, till philosophers become kings in this world, or till those we now call kings and rulers really and truly become philosophers."

Academy, in the outer suburbs of Athens beyond the Ceramicus. He lived to the age of eighty having taught and written for more than forty years. His learning encompassed the fields of geometry, arithmetic, astronomy, geography, natural history, and politics, and his works which were frequently written in the form of Socratic dialogues include the *Republic*, whose main theme concerns the rule of right by which a man should regulate his life, and the *Laws*, which deals with ethics, education, and jurisprudence.

DIOGENES

Diogenes the Cynic (414–323 B.C.) was born at Sinope on the Black Sea but was sent into exile when he, or his father, was accused of adulterating the currency. He came to Athens, made a virtue out of his poverty, and lived as simply as he possibly could, acquiring no little notoriety thereby. He was called "the dog" (in Greek *kuon*) by his contemporaries; hence Cynic. He lived for a time in a large

Diogenes called himself "a citizen of the world," "a governor of men," and led a life of great austerity, living, according to legend, in a tub. He reportedly walked about in daytime with a lantern "in search of an honest man."

Diogenes was once masturbating in the Agora. "Would that it were as easy," he said, "to relieve hunger by rubbing an empty stomach."

earthenware tub in the Metroon in the Athenian Agora, but traveled around Greece too. It was at Corinth that Alexander the Great came and stood next to him and said he would grant any favor Diogenes cared to ask: "Get out of my light!" came the reply.

ARISTOTLE

Aristotle was born at Stagirus in Chalcidice in northern Greece in 384, and as a young man went to Athens to join Plato's Academy. He excelled in the observation of natural phenomena, a gift which gave his work a more practical and down-to-earth character than Plato's. In 342–341 he accepted an invitation to become the tutor of Alexander the Great at Pella in Macedonia, a post he held until 335–334 when he returned to Athens to found his own school at the Lyceum situated just to the east of the

"It is characteristic of the great-souled man...to be haughty toward men of position and fortune, but courteous toward those of moderate station, because it is difficult and distinguished to be superior to the great, but easy to outdo the lowly, and to adopt a high manner with the former is not ill-bred, but it is vulgar to lord it over humble people: it is like putting forth one's strength against the weak."

"Let this then be agreed upon at the start: to each man there comes just so much happiness as he has of moral and intellectual goodness and of performance of actions dependent thereon. God himself is an indication of the truth of this."

ancient city of Athens—in fact close to the present Syntagma Square. Students of the Lyceum came to be called Peripatetics, either because of the portico *(peripatos)* which ran around a courtyard there, or because Aristotle walked up and down during his lectures. He created an important library and encouraged research in many fields. He died in Euboea as a political exile from Athens in 322.

ZENO

Zeno (333/331–264/261 B.C.) was born at Citium in Cyprus but was shipwrecked near Athens about 301. He went up to the city and in a bookshop began reading a life of Socrates. He was favorably impressed and asked where such men could be found. The Cynic philosopher Crates was pointed out to him, and Zeno became his disciple, although he eschewed some of the more extreme aspects of his master's philosophy. In about 280 he set up his own school which met in the Stoa Poikile in the Athenian Agora. He would walk up and down, his object being, it is said, to keep the place free of loungers. His pupils were given the name Stoics, and their philoso-

Zeno's words have survived only in fragmentary quotations. His teachings tended to be curt, dogmatic, and prophetic rather than discursive and analytical. He saw ethics as central to all philosophy. His criterion for truth was the "indubitable impression" made on the mind by an idea or utterance.

Zeno's epitaph: "Here lies great Zeno, dear to Citium, who scaled high Olympus, though he piled not Pelion on Ossa, nor toiled at the labors of Heracles, but this was the path he found out to the stars—the way of temperance alone."

phy Stoicism. In his old age, the Athenians granted him honors because "he has for many years been devoted to philosophy in the city, and has continued to be a man of worth in all other respects, exhorting to virtue and temperance those of the youth who come to him to be taught."

EPICURUS

Epicurus (341–271 B.C.) was probably born on Samos where his father had been an expatriate Athenian schoolmaster. He developed a taste for philosophy at the age of fourteen and studied in Samos before he went to Athens in 323. There he taught himself, successfully enough to open his own philosophical school at Mytilene on the island of Lesbos in 310.

"We declare pleasure to be the beginning and end of the blessed life; for we recognize this to be our first and natural good, and from this we start in every choice and avoidance; and this we make our goal, using feeling as the canon by which we judge every good."

"When we say, then, that pleasure is the end and aim, we do not mean the pleasures of the prodigal or the pleasures of sensuality, as we are understood to do by some through ignorance, prejudice, or willful misrepresentation. By pleasure we mean the absence of pain in the body and of trouble in the soul."

The school moved to Athens in 306 and Epicurus spent the next thirty-six years there teaching and writing surrounded by his devoted pupils. He was the first philosopher to allow women and slaves to attend his lectures. He taught that the end of life was pleasure—interpreted by him as freedom from bodily pain coupled with tranquillity of mind. The simple life was the ideal to be aimed at, for it enables men to meet all the necessities of existence, and to face changes of fortune with equanimity.

THE PELOPONNESIAN WAR

Thucydides the Athenian wrote the history of the war fought between Athens and Sparta, beginning the account at the very outbreak of the war, in the belief that it was going to be a great war and more worth writing about than any of those which had taken place in the past.

The writings of the Athenian Thucydides are far and away the most important source for the history of the Peloponnesian War. He was born about 460 B.C. and died around 400. He probably served in the earlier campaigns of the war, but fell ill of the plague in 430 or 427. While serving as general in 424 he failed in an attempt to relieve the siege of Amphipolis, was censured as a result, and spent twenty years in exile. It was then that he wrote the bulk of his work which was partly based on his own experience, but mostly on the reports of others.

Right: An Athenian warrior setting out for war would pour a libation to the gods against his safe return. Hoplites are frequently represented taking leave of their families on fifth-century Attic vases.

When the Spartan forces under their king Archidamus invaded Attica in 431 B.C., they were following the example of the Persian invaders of 480. The successive, almost annual, invasions of Attic soil which characterized the so-called Archidamian War, which lasted until the Peace of Nicias in 421, were aimed at damaging one of the mainstays of the Athenian economy, namely the olive oil industry. Just as the Persians had destroyed the olive groves on which the wealth of the Athenian aristocracy in large part depended—destruction from which it took a decade or more to recover—so the Spartans doubtless hoped to force the Athenians gently to exert the requisite political pressure to bring about a quick end to the war. Such a strategy was, however, a misjudged one, for power at Athens, at both the political and military levels, now lay with the *demos*. The navy, moreover, was the favored service, and it was generally felt that Athens could win a war with Sparta and her Peloponnesian allies so long as she retained the mastery of the seas and had sufficient wealth in her coffers to enable her to buy foodstuffs from abroad. The existence of the Long Walls and the silver stored on the Acropolis created the necessary mood of confidence, and Athenian counterattacks on the Peloponnese from the sea meant that both sides sustained equivalent losses.

But why should the Spartans have gone to war with Athens at all? There had been a growing rift ever since the 460s, which the misnamed Thirty Years Peace of 446 did little to narrow. The fact was that the Athenians were felt to be interfering overmuch in Peloponnesian affairs, especially those of Corinth whose control of western (i.e., south Italian and Sicilian) grain supplies and markets they were threatening. Conflict in 432–431 between Athens and Corinth over the latter's recalcitrant colony of Corcyra was not in itself sufficient to bring about an end to the peace, nor was a clash over Corinth's colony of Potidaea in Chalcidice; both incidents, however, brought formal hostilities between the Peloponnesians and Athens and her allies closer. The last stage in the escalation was the failure of increasingly bitter representations made to Athens by the Spartans on behalf of the small but strategically crucial city of Megara which had been arbitrarily excluded from markets that the Athenians controlled. Athens was unexpectedly debilitated early in

I began my history at the very outbreak of the war, in the belief that it was going to be a great war and more worth writing about than any of those which had taken place in the past.

My belief was based on the fact that the two sides were at the very height of their power and preparedness, and I saw, too, that the rest of the Hellenic world was committed to one side or the other; even those who were not immediately engaged were deliberating on the courses they were to take later. This was the greatest disturbance in the history of the Hellenes, affecting also a large part of the non-Hellenic world, and indeed, I might almost say, the whole of mankind.

Thucydides, Book I, Chapter 1

the hostilities. Plague, which broke out in both 430–429 and again in 427–426, carried off nearly a third of the men of military age, and probably an even greater proportion of the rest of the population. Pericles was among the dead, and the historian Thucydides among the afflicted; afterward, he was to write some of the most harrowing passages in the literature of war: "The bodies of the dying were heaped on top of one another, and half-dead creatures could be

194

The scene of some of the most prolonged fighting in the first part of the Peloponnesian War was Amphipolis, which lies in northern Greece on the River Strymon (visible in the background). It had been founded from Athens in 436 and quickly flourished, acting as a market for timber, furs, cereals, and minerals from the Thraceward area. During the war Amphipolis became a focus of anti-Athenian activity in the north, and in 424 it was taken by the Spartan general Brasidas just before Thucydides arrived to relieve the siege.

seen staggering around in the streets or flocking around the fountains in their desire for water."

There was naturally a desire for peace in some quarters, especially among the propertied families who, in addition to having their lands raided, were subjected to increasingly heavy taxes. Their feelings were expressed by Aristophanes in his comedy *The Acharnians* of 425 in the person of the old farmer Dicaeopolis who complains not so much of the destructive nature of war as of the petty inconveniences it brings in its train. Aristophanes was to support the peace party again in the last phase of the Peloponnesian War when the heroine of his audacious *Lysistrata* is made to organize a sex strike in order to force the menfolk of Greece to lay down their arms.

Against all the odds, Athens gained the upper hand in the Archidamian War. For in 425 some 292 crack Spartan troops were taken captive on the island of Sphacteria (in the bay of Pylos/Navarino) and held as hostages against further Spartan incursions into Attica. The main theater of war thenceforth moved to Amphipolis in the north where Athens suffered a serious defeat in 422. Athens' resources were overstretched, but the Spartans were now too preoccupied with their main Peloponnesian rival Argos to exploit this advantage. For in 421 a thirty years' peace with Argos was due to come to an end, and Sparta needed peace with Athens in order to be ready to face the new threat. A fifty years' treaty was drawn up between Athens and Sparta, but it was not to last. The Athenians overreached themselves in Sicily in 415–413, and their faction-ridden city could not withstand a Sparta reemergent as a naval power (in fact secretly financed by the King of Persia) in 407–405. The war ended with Athens' total defeat in 404.

A helmet of Corinthian type found at Olympia bearing an inscription that states it to have been dedicated to Zeus by Argives, who had won it in battle.

In this battle scene from an Athenian grave stele, a naked warrior, holding a shield, is about to be slain by a mounted soldier. Dating to some years after the Peloponnesian War, the relief gives an idea of some of the fighting methods of the time.

MAGNA GRAECIA

Sow then some seed of fame about the isle which Zeus, the lord of Olympus, gave to Persephone, and shook his locks in token to her that, as queen of the teeming earth, the fertile land of Sicily would be raised to renown by the wealth of her glorious cities; and the son of Cronus granted that the host of armed horsemen...would often be wedded with the golden leaves of Olympia's olive.

With such words Pindar praised the Sicilian winner of the chariot race at one of the pan-Hellenic games. He acknowledges that the land of Sicily was especially blest agriculturally, and that its sons were expected to win frequent Olympic victories. It was Sicily's wealth which attracted the Theban poet to Sicilian patrons in the hope that he might gain well-paid commissions, and it was the prospect of enjoying similar wealth which had made colonizing merchants, farmers, and adventurers leave Greece for Sicily and southern Italy in the first place. Between approximately 750 and 550 B.C. colonists from Corinth, Megara, Euboea, Rhodes, Crete, and elsewhere made their way westward to make their fortunes.

also the landless rich—younger sons with no hope of an inheritance at home, but who wished to possess their own estates. There were also merchants attracted by the hope of trade; indeed, the earliest settlements in the west seem to have been trading posts, although later on some clearly derived most of their wealth from agriculture.

The Greek cities of Sicily had to compete with their Carthaginian neighbors at the western end of the island, and twice in the fifth century there was open conflict. In 480 the Carthaginians were defeated at Himera, but in 409–404 they sacked most of the Greek cities before they were finally defeated by Dionysius I of Syracuse.

SEGESTA

GELA

LEONTINI

AETNA

MESSANA

The coins of Sicily and southern Italy are among the most splendid ever made. Segesta was not in fact a Greek city, but its inhabitants adopted many of the outward signs of Greek culture and built a temple and a theater, and struck coins closely modeled on those of their Greek neighbors. The coins of Gela show the personification of the local river (also called Gela), who appears as a man-headed bull being crowned with a wreath by a local nymph. The coins of Leontini bear a punning type, a common characteristic of Greek coins. The Greek for lion is *leon,* hence the presence here of a lion's head. Aetna's coins have fine images of satyrs, who are perhaps intended to refer to rich vineyards on the slopes of the nearby mountain. A lively hare can be seen on some coins of Messana, founded on the site of Zancle, both important cities in their time, for they dominated the straits between Sicily and Italy.

The reasons why so many should have left Greece in this way are complex. There were the landless poor, of course, but there were

Cumae
Neapolis
Poseido
Ele
Py

Zancle/Messar
Panormus
Segesta
Himera
Motya
Mt. Etna ▲ Nax
Selinus
SICILY
Catana
Heraclea Minoa
Acragas
Leontini
Palici
Gela
Syrac
Camarina

Of the Greek colonies founded around the coast of southern Italy, only three, Neapolis, Rhegium, and Taras, can be regarded as having been successful in the long term, for not only have they continued in existence, but they have become major cities: Naples, Reggio Calabria, and Taranto. The others have come down in the world and are small towns at best. Sybaris, indeed, was annihilated by its neighbor Croton in 511/510, though its reputation for dissolute ("sybarite") living has survived.

Metapontum

Taras

Heraclea

Laus

Sybaris-Thurii

Thurii, unusually, was an Athenian colony and was founded near or on the site of Sybaris in 443 B.C. Its coins bear the inscription *Thourion* and a bull, which is probably another punning device (the Greek for bull is *tauros*). Rhegium had frontal lions' heads on its coins. This device was imitated in the Middle Ages on the coins of Norman kings of Sicily. Cumae (*kuma* = Greek "wave") has a suitably billowy seamonster on its coins, and Heraclea its eponymous hero dispatching the Nemean lion.

Paestum (*above*) is the best preserved of all classical Greek sites with the possible exception of the Athenian Acropolis. The fact that it has survived more or less intact in its ancient form, however, is more a sign of its failure as a city than its success. Founded as Poseidonia in ca. 600 B.C., it was initially very prosperous and temples were built there in the sixth and fifth centuries. As early as the time of Augustus it was notorious for its malarial situation, and the city remained deserted and forgotten after it was sacked by the Saracens in the ninth century.

Croton

Terina

Caulonia

Locri Epizephyrii

egium

THURII

RHEGIUM

CUMAE

HERACLEA

A row of temples occupy the southernmost part of the city of Acragas, once famous for its chariot horses, or rather their owners, whose victories were sung by Pindar.

Elea, famous for its school of Eleatic philosophers, was founded in about 536 B.C. from Alalia in Corsica, which in turn had been established by Greeks from Phocaea in Asia Minor.

Croton was an Achaean colony founded in 710 B.C. It was famous in antiquity for its medical school and its successful athletes. Pythagoras remodeled its constitution about 530 B.C.

GELA: A GREEK COLONY

We are particularly well informed concerning the archaeology of the Greek city of Gela, founded on the southern coast of Sicily in 689 B.C. by colonists from Rhodes and Crete. The site is now occupied by a busy and expanding town, but in the nineteenth century there was but a village there surrounded on the landward side by a large ancient necropolis which was a rich and constant source of ancient vases and terracottas. Some of these were dug up for profit by local entrepreneurs, but there were also excavations of a semi-official nature conducted at different times on behalf of the British Museum and the Ashmolean Museum, Oxford, by G.T. Dennis and Sir Arthur Evans.

The story goes that Dennis' wife would sit all day by the excavations in the shade of a parasol and put away the Attic vases beneath her crinoline as they were found. Evans worked in Sicily long before he was interested in Crete, and although his main con-

Right: A view over the fertile plain of Gela which stretches for several kilometers inland from the coastal city. The existence of this plain was the reason why Greeks settled here in the first place, and explains how some of its inhabitants, at least, became extremely wealthy.

One of the favorite activities of Gela's aristocracy was chariot racing. A highly relevant scene appears on an Attic wine-mixing bowl of the sixth century B.C. found at Gela by Sir Arthur Evans in about 1890.

The Victory on this Attic vase found at Gela by Evans may refer to the Greeks' triumph over the Carthaginians at Himera in 480. W. B. Yeats enthused over it: "I recall a Nike at the Ashmolean Museum with a natural unsystematized beauty, like that before Raphael...."

cern was with the coinage of the Greek colonies in Sicily, he spent some time excavating the cemeteries at Gela and thus acquired some remarkable vases and bronzes for the Oxford collection. Italian archaeologists have naturally done most of the work on the site, and Gela boasts one of the richest and most fascinating museums in Sicily.

The earliest fortifications were built, so Thucydides informs us, in a part of the city which the colonists called Lindii, and which in his day served as the acropolis. This must be the low prominence near the sea nowadays known as Molino a Vento or "Wind-

Triptolemus on an Attic red-figure vase found at Gela. He is supposed to have been sent out from Eleusis in Attica to spread the benefits of agriculture to mankind. He was the favorite of Demeter whose cult was, not surprisingly, very popular at Gela.

A bronze statuette of the wine-god Dionysus dressed in a panther skin and a long chiton, found at Gela in the late nineteenth century.

mill Hill," and its ancient name will doubtless have been a reference to the colonists' Rhodian home (Lindos is a city on Rhodes). Foundations of two temples, one of the sixth and the other of the fifth century B.C., have been found there; the earlier one was lavishly adorned with polychrome terracotta revetments, many of which can now be seen in the Gela Museum.

The reason why Gela was colonized at all was because of its splendid situation on the coast with its rich hinterland eminently suitable for growing wheat. We hear of colonists leaving their native cities in Greece on account of both poor harvests and overpopulation, and the Geloan plain must have seemed to such settlers rather as did the rich prairies of Kansas and Oklahoma to nineteenth-century pioneers. The *Geloi campi* were proverbial by Virgil's day for their wealth, and it is scarcely surprising that among the Athenian vases that were exported to Gela were ones with scenes relating to the cult of Demeter, the Greek equivalent of the Roman Ceres, the goddess of agricultural plenty.

Rich Geloans could afford to keep stables of racehorses, and we hear of them competing for prizes, together with other members of the chariot-racing set, at pan-Hellenic festivals such as the Olympic or Pythian games. Chariot racing was the ancient equivalent of polo or show-jumping and attracted a simi-

larly cosmopolitan and exclusive following. The tyrant Gelon set up a statue at Olympia commemorating his victory of 488.

Gela was so successful that, a century after its foundation, a further colony was established at Acragas, some seventy or so kilometers along the coast to the west. The Geloans' authority was thus extended into an area which was within the sphere of influence of Carthage, which had established colonies of a similar nature to the Greek ones in the western part of the island. Conflict was inevitable, and the Carthaginians were utterly crushed by the combined Greek forces under Gelon at Himera in the north of Sicily in 480 B.C., on the same day, it was said, as the Battle of Salamis. Winged Nikai, or goddesses of Victory, exist in quantity on the Attic vases found at Gela, and their presence must in most cases refer to the Greeks' triumph over their oriental foes.

Gelon was tyrant of Gela until 485–484 when he gained power at Syracuse, but Gela continued in existence and was sufficiently attractive a place for Aeschylus, the Attic tragedian, to spend his last years there. The city was completely laid waste, however, when the Carthaginians went on the offensive again in 405 B.C., not to be reoccupied until 338. At this period it was given impressive fortifications of which the mudbrick walls are still preserved.

THE ATHENIAN DISASTER AT SYRACUSE

The main feature of the fortifications which Dionysus erected on the heights above Syracuse was the castle of Euryalus, built probably between 402 and 397 B.C. It was built at the point where the northern and southern fortifications converged at the west, and where a road linking Syracuse with the rest of the island entered the city. The castle was not merely defensive, but was capable of being used for offensive purposes.

Right: The nucleus of the ancient city of Syracuse was the island of Ortygia (= "bird island") connected to the mainland by a bridge. Near this point was situated the Doric Temple of Apollo, the earliest Greek temple in the city, erected in the early sixth century B.C. The form of the Greek theater *(far right)* may have been imposed in the third century B.C., but there may well have been an earlier theater on the site where Aeschylus' *Persians* was performed during one of his visits to Sicily.

It was clear to any member of the Athenian assembly which met early in 415 to discuss the proposed expedition to Sicily that the undertaking would be something of a gamble, but no one could have predicted how disastrous the outcome would be. Relations between Athens and Sparta had reached an impasse; neither side could win a decisive victory over the other. Athens' financial resources were low and, moreover, she badly needed to ensure a permanent supply of wheat for her citizenry. The appeal for help which she received from her old ally Segesta in 415 seemed to many to offer an ideal pretext for gaining a foothold in Sicily: there was the prospect of increased tribute as well as a secure food supply.

There was opposition to the project, too, and the mistake was made of appointing to the joint leadership of the expeditionary force generals who represented the different viewpoints expressed in the assembly: the headstrong Alcibiades, eager for success, but who was soon to desert the cause in order to escape prosecution for impiety; Nicias, his personal enemy, firmly opposed to the adventure, and whose ineffectual leadership was to be the major cause of the disaster that befell the force at Syracuse; and Lamachus, despised by the other two for his low birth, but probably a better general than either of them.

The call for help had come from Segesta against Selinus, but it was generally agreed that the real objective was Syracuse. Nicias, however, took a long time getting there, and spent the summer in indecisive campaigns in northern Sicily. By October, however, the Athenians were encamped within the Great Harbor at Syracuse, but instead of pressing home this advantage, Nicias waited for the spring. Walls and counterwalls were built on the heights of Epipolae to the north of the city, and the Syracusans were losing until Gylippus, a Spartan general, managed to enter the city with a small relief force. A second Athenian fleet arrived in 413 under Demosthenes. An attack by moonlight on Epipolae almost succeeded, but the Athenians were themselves put to flight. Demosthenes wanted the Athenians to return home, but Nicias was afraid of the reception they would receive at Athens and, superstitious man that he was, interpreted an eclipse of the moon as an indication that they should delay for "thrice nine days." This was a fatal mistake. The Syracusans were able to block the harbor mouth and to prevent the Athenians from slipping out unnoticed. A desperate sea battle within that harbor resulted in a total Syracusan victory and the remnants of the Athenian forces retreated in chaos. Demosthenes and Nicias were killed and seven thousand prisoners were taken. These were put into stone quarries where "they suffered everything which one could imagine might be suffered by men imprisoned in such a place."

There was a democratic revolution at Syracuse after the Athenian disaster and their best general, Hermocrates, was sent away to fight in Asia Minor against the Athenians there, on the ground that he was considered to be a potential tyrant. The Carthaginians, moreover, were determined both to reduce Greek influence on the island and to avenge their humiliating defeat in 480 when Hamil-

Hermocrates then reappeared on the scene, determined to try to deal with the Carthaginian threat himself. He landed at Messana with one thousand men, rushed to western Sicily, and attacked the Carthaginian towns. He refortified Selinus and at Himera buried the bones of the Greek dead. The Syracusans, however, still refused to recall him. Foolishly, he tried to get into the city by night with some of his associates, but was set upon by a mob who put nearly all of them to death. One of those who survived was a certain Dionysius, rescued by friends. Dionysius had been eager for power from his earliest youth, and after Hermocrates' failure began to employ various populist devices to gain effective control at Syracuse with the backing of the *demos* so that he could lead what he felt to be the necessary resistance against the Carthaginians. Events at Acragas in 406 played into his hands. The Syracusan generals who had been sent to aid

Three huge ditches cut into the rock to the west of the Euryalus fort prevented a frontal attack with artillery. Behind the innermost ditch there were built five immense square towers *(left)* originally some fifteen meters high on which catapults were mounted to attack any enemy that attempted a siege. There were steps and passages cut into the rock which

car, a member of their ruling family, had been killed beneath the walls of Himera. Again it was the Segestans who were the immediate cause of conflict: in 409 they invited Hannibal to help them against Selinus, a city the Carthaginians hated. Selinus fell, followed quickly by Himera, where three thousand citizens were sacrificed to the spirit of Hamilcar.

The Syracusans rushed to help the two endangered cities, but were not quick enough; in any case they were also trying to guard the approaches to their own city against a surprise attack from Hamilcar.

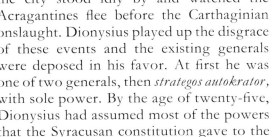

the city stood idly by and watched the Acragantines flee before the Carthaginian onslaught. Dionysius played up the disgrace of these events and the existing generals were deposed in his favor. At first he was one of two generals, then *strategos autokrator,* with sole power. By the age of twenty-five, Dionysius had assumed most of the powers that the Syracusan constitution gave to the people.

In 405, Dionysius persuaded the people of Gela and Camarina to retreat to Syracuse, where they would be protected from the Carthaginians by the fortifications he

linked one defensive ditch with another; one tunnel was even excavated along the outside of the walls for a distance of about 175 meters so that the defenders could appear behind an attacker and pin him against the walls of the fort. Euryalus is one of the most stupendous of all classical sites.

planned to build; it was clearly the case that the more hands there were, the more quickly Syracuse could be protected. Dionysius' intention was to make the city safe from attack from both land and sea. A lesson that had been learnt from 415–413 B.C. was that an enemy occupying the heights of Epipolae seriously threatened Syracuse itself. Dionysius therefore decided to prevent a repetition by building a huge fort at Euryalus at the westernmost tip of the large wedge-shaped plateau (Euryalus means "broad nail" in Greek) and to erect an imposing wall for some 27 kilometers (18 miles) along the cliff edge between this fort and the sea. One stretch 5 kilometers (3 miles) long was put up in 402 in only 20 days. Sixty

The new fortifications, now put to the test for the first time, were a complete success. Plague and boredom affected the besiegers. Dionysius attacked them by night, taking two strongholds and destroying or capturing part of their fleet. The Carthaginian commander then sought peace and agreed to pay an indemnity. The walls had proved their worth and the Greeks were saved. Dionysius was to remain ruler of Syracuse until 367 B.C., and succeeded in creating the first of the empires of the kind which Alexander the Great and his successors were to establish later in the fourth century in the eastern Mediterranean. Ortygia, the island on which the urban part of Syracuse was situated, had early become a palace fortress

Below: The temple at Segesta, the city whose request to Athens for aid led to the Athenian expeditionary force being sent to Sicily. The inhabitants of Segesta were Elymians, not Greeks; they were descended, so the story went, from Trojans who, like Aeneas, escaped their city's destruction to find new homes in the west. At all events they probably came from the eastern Mediterranean.

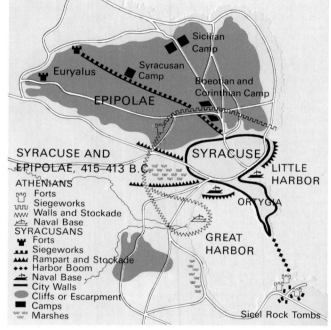

SYRACUSE AND EPIPOLAE, 415–413 B.C.
ATHENIANS
Forts
Siegeworks
Walls and Stockade
Naval Base
SYRACUSANS
Forts
Siegeworks
Rampart and Stockade
Harbor Boom
Naval Base
City Walls
Cliffs or Escarpment
Camps
Marshes

Right: The details of the campaign at Syracuse in 415–413 are notoriously difficult to reconstruct. All plans are based to a large extent on Thucydides' narrative, but since this is open to several interpretations, each one is different, and walls sometimes occur in the most unexpected places. A crucial point seems to be the extent of the landward part of Syracuse, and especially the suburb of Achradina, which probably lay below the heights of Epipolae, rather than on them.

thousand workmen with 6,000 carts were employed to build the whole northern stretch. Dionysius himself joined in the building operations. The citizenry were armed as the result of a highly organized manufacturing effort. Within a few months 140,000 shields and as many swords and helmets were made. The fleet was put into a state of readiness and 300 warships were made operative.

The inevitable Carthaginian attack was provoked by a Syracusan incursion at Motya at the other end of Sicily. A Carthaginian expeditionary force began to move on Syracuse, defeated the Syracusan navy, and then encamped to the number of 300,000 men on the plain below the south wall of Euryalus.

for Dionysius and his personal guard of 10,000 mercenaries. By 390 Sicily was divided into Syracusan and Carthaginian "empires," and victories in southern Italy meant that Dionysius effectively controlled most of Magna Graecia. He felt strong enough to declare war on Carthage in 382, but suffered a serious defeat in about 375 which meant relinquishing some Sicilian territory.

The court of Dionysius II, the son and successor of the savior of Syracuse, was the scene of Plato's attempt to make Dionysius a practical example of his theory of constitutional monarchy. But the scheme was bedeviled by court factions, and despite two visits and several letters, Plato retired disillusioned from his task.

The Athenian prisoners taken after their failure in the Syracusan campaign of 415–413 were placed in a stone quarry somewhat like this one (the actual quarry, the Latomia dei Cappuccini, is to be found near the Villa Politi in the northeastern part of the city). Thucydides tells us of the intolerable conditions under which they were kept: crowded together without any shelter for months on end; disease rampant, and the stink of unburied bodies; hunger and thirst (they had a daily allowance of a pint of grain and half a pint of water).

The tombstone of the Athenian marine Democlides son of Demetrius of the early fourth century expresses the pathos of death in war. The Athenian artist has chosen to show a small figure, probably the deceased, seated at the prow of his ship, bareheaded, his elbow resting on his knee and his head on his hand. Behind him rest his shield and a Corinthian helmet.

203

THE RISE
OF MACEDON

Euripides left Athens in 408 and died, aged more than seventy, in 407–406 in Macedonia whither he had been invited by King Archelaus, who was eager to import high culture to his unsophisticated kingdom. Archelaus had built a theater at Dion and established a festival of Zeus and the Muses (who, according to legend, had actually been born in the locality). On Euripides' death the manuscript of the *Bacchae* was found among his papers, and the play was put on at Athens where it won first prize. Euripides may well have been inspired by his Macedonian surroundings to write what is one of the most powerful Greek tragedies that have come down to us.

Archelaus also moved his palace from Aegae to Pella where, by the late fourth or early third century, a regularly planned city had been laid out. The houses were extremely lavish, with courtyards surrounded by colonnades, and the rooms decorated with polychrome mosaics, some geometric, others pictorial. It was only when roof tiles bearing the stamped inscription *Pelles* were found in 1957 that archaeologists were certain that this was in fact the famous Macedonian capital where Philip held court and Aristotle tutored Alexander.

The most graphic account of the condition of Macedonia before the mid-fourth century comes from a speech put into the mouth of Alexander the Great when he was addressing mutinous Macedonian troops at Opis in Babylonia in 324: "When Philip took you over you were nomadic and poor, the majority of you clad in skins and grazing sparse herds on the mountains, putting up a poor fight for them against Illyrians, Triballians and the neighboring Thracians. He gave you cloaks to wear in place of skins. He brought you down the mountains to the plains, making you a match in battle for the neighboring barbarians, trusting for your salvation no longer in the natural strength of places so much as in your own courage. He made you dwellers in cities and graced your lives with good laws and customs. As to those very barbarians by whom previously you had been constantly plundered and pillaged, both your possessions and your persons, from being slaves and subjects he made you their leaders and he added most of Thrace to Macedon. Seizing the best-situated places on the sea-board, he opened up the land to trade, and he made it possible to work the land without fear."

The archaeological record of the area of Macedonia (which stretched from beyond Lake Ochrid in the west to the River Strymon in the east, and from the River Haliacmon northward to the upper reaches of the Vardar) bears out Alexander's statement concerning the simple way of life of the early Macedonians. Numerous small bronze pendants, beads, fibulae, bracelets, and hair ornaments have been found all over this area in contexts which seem to date from the tenth to the fifth or even fourth century. They are similar in many respects to the kind of objects which in Greece itself are usually classified as Geometric, and are often mis-

takenly dated by reference to the Geometric period at Athens. The fact is, however, that a Geometric or sub-Geometric culture persisted in the north long after oriental modes of decoration had supplanted Geometric in the south. Thus, there is scarcely a break between the primitive beads and bangles of the skin-clad, nomadic, and poverty stricken herdsmen who had clearly existed within living memory in Alexander's day, and the lavish, hyper-Hellenic luxury goods which were imported by Macedonian nabobs in the fourth century. Recently discovered Royal tombs at Vergina near the original Macedonian capital of Aegae contain golden caskets containing golden fabrics, and silver jugs and alabaster. The most elaborate vessel to be found in Macedonia, however, is the bronze volute crater from Dherveni near Thessalonika. This masterpiece of fourth-

century metal work, with intricate figures beaten out from the body of the vase, shows the sacred marriage of Dionysus with Ariadne and a Bacchic procession.

This is the background against which the

rôle, and by generously rewarding loyal service. This, coupled with the introduction of new fighting methods, gave Macedon a strength it had never before possessed, but it also meant that the army had to be kept active; this factor, it has been plausibly suggested, almost alone explains Philip's career of conquest surpassed only by his son's.

Ancient historians believed that Philip's new army, handed down to Alexander, helped account for the son's victorious campaigns. Diodorus Siculus, for example (on the basis of sources now lost to us), placed great emphasis on Philip's innovations:

"*. . . Having reformed the military formations to give greater strength and equipped them with the weapons suitable for these*

Some of the mosaic floors at Pella are very striking. This one was signed by the artist: "Gnosis made [me]" and shows two young men on the point of killing a frightened deer which their hound has cornered. Hunting played an important role in Macedonian society, hence, no doubt, the prominence of such scenes on the floors of courtiers' houses. All the mosaics at Pella were made of river pebbles, not *tesserae* (cubes of stone) as mosaics were to be later.

Another pebble mosaic from Pella shows the rape of Helen by Theseus. Phorbas waits in the getaway chariot which is shown in an interesting three-quarter view. The scene is again probably taken from a lost mural painting, the main features of which had found their way into mosaicists' pattern books by about 300 B.C.

Philip II's conquests in Thrace brought the gold mines of Mount Pangaeus. These brought him in an annual income of 1,000 talents, equivalent to the wages for 6 million working days. Both gold and silver coinage was issued. This is a silver tetradrachm struck between 359 and 336 with a type of a horse and rider.

achievement of Philip II of Macedon must be judged. His was the guiding hand which transformed his country from provincial to great power status. He had spent some years as hostage at Thebes before succeeding to the Macedonian throne in 359. In the past, Macedonia had been unable to meet either domestic or foreign challenges through a lack of unity. Philip solved this problem partly by demographic engineering and by insisting that the teenage sons of the aristocracy should attend his court, but mostly by giving the army a national rather than a local

formations, he was constantly parading and training them for combat. He devised both the close array of the phalanx and its equipment, in imitation of the close shield formation of the heroes before Troy, and he was the first to put together the Macedonian phalanx."

THE SUBJECTION OF GREECE

Philip of Macedon *(right)* was the first to unify this relatively backward country. As in many an emerging nation today, the army was the principal means by which unity was achieved. The army, moreover, once created had to be kept occupied; hence Philip's career of conquest.

Olynthus was a city in Chalcidice laid out on up-to-date lines probably in 432. It stood in the way of Philip's policies, and it fell to him after a siege in 348. Many arrowheads bearing Philip's name were found there.

Philip had already possessed himself of the rich mineral resources of Thrace (in particular the gold mines of Mount Pangaeus) before he looked south to Greece. He saw a region which was, in the words of Xenophon, "in confusion and disorder." The Spartans had won the Peloponnesian War with Persian aid, and managed, fitfully, to preserve their control over Greece until they were not only defeated at Leuctra in 371, but invaded and reduced to insignificance by Epaminondas of Thebes. It was during the years that Thebes was dominant in Greek affairs that Philip lived there as a youthful hostage; the experience will doubtless have proved a valuable one. Thebes, however, lost her preeminent position with her defeat

at Mantinea in the Peloponnese in 362. Athens was quick to use the situation to recover lost ground, made an alliance with the Thessalian confederacy, and began to think of regaining lost territories in the Thraceward areas.

Thessaly and Thrace were, however, the regions which Philip needed to control before he could even consider further conquests. It is still the subject of great scholarly dispute the extent to which Philip had specific aims of conquest, and if so, how early he developed them. While certain answers cannot be given to these questions,

it had been plausibly argued that Philip's conquests have an underlying pattern to them. Some areas, those to the west and north of Macedonia, were simply buffer states whose internal policies Philip did relatively little to influence. It was otherwise with Thessaly and Thrace, whose governments he carefully manipulated and eventually completely overhauled to his liking. The reason for this interest was that these were in effect "transit" states, control of which left Philip's options open.

The military machine which he began to build from the moment of his accession in

359 depended for its effectiveness on an extremely high degree of physical fitness on the part of both officers and men, coupled with an effective and flexible use of each branch of the army: the cavalry, archers, lightarmed troops, and above all, the phalanx. This was a greatly improved version of the hoplite method of fighting: that tended to degenerate into a series of personal combats along the line of battle. The phalanx instead consisted of a group of men whose strength lay in their unity. Their armor was light, which enabled them to wield their long, pike-like spears the more skillfully and effectively. Protection was provided by other parts of the army. To this new tactical device can be attributed not just

such an extent, I say, that, instead of paying tribute to the Athenians and being at the beck and call of the Thebans, they have to depend on us for their security. He went to the Peloponnese and set things in order there, and was appointed Leader with full authority for the campaign against the Persians. By this he brought as great glory on the Macedonian state as on himself."

Damned as a Hitler, or hailed as a proto-Bismarck, Philip has enjoyed a reputation which depends as much as anything on critics' estimation of Demosthenes, his principal Athenian opponent. But no matter how admirably and strongly felt Demosthenes' desire for freedom may have been, the fact is that his opposition was neither as

The victory which led to Philip's unchallenged overlordship of Greece was that at Chaeronea in 338. This lion was set up shortly afterward, perhaps to mark the grave of the Theban elite troops, though opinions vary. It was broken into small pieces in 1818 by a misguided Greek patriot who hoped to find gold in it, but was restored in 1904.

Belligerent as the hoplite on this sixth-century cup tondo may appear, his was an outmoded way of fighting by the fourth century. Heavily armed hoplites were replaced by Philip with phalangites, troops whose principal weapon was the long *sarissa*, and whose formation could be quickly varied according to the situation.

"Those who were at war against the peace of the city welcomed [Demosthenes] to the speaker's platform, naming him as the only person in the city who had never taken a bribe. He would step forward and present them with the causes of war and confusion.... And he brought things to such a pass that if Philip did not send ambassadors he said that he despised Athens, but that if he did send them, he said that Philip was sending spies, not ambassadors."

Aeschines

When Demosthenes heard the news of Philip of Macedon's assassination in 336, he is said to have put off mourning for his recently deceased daughter so that he could rejoice at the death of his enemy: such was the depth of Demosthenes' antipathy toward Philip.

This statue of Demosthenes is a Roman copy of one that was set up in the center of the Athenian Agora. Another, lost, copy has been shown to have been used by the Venetian artist Giovanni Bellini as a model for apostle figures.

Philip's military success, but also that of his son Alexander.

Alexander's panegyric of his father at Opis tells in brief how the conquest of Greece went from a Macedonian standpoint: "[Philip] made you rulers of the Thessalians —you were once scared to death of them —and by humbling the Phocian people he made the way into Greece for you broad and easy instead of narrow and difficult. The Athenians and the Thebans, who used constantly to look for any chance against Macedon, he humbled to such an extent (and by now he had me to share in his efforts)—to

wise nor effective as it might have been. Philip, moreover, did not abuse his power over the Greek states after the battle of Chaeronea in 338, but rather imposed an extremely mild and easy settlement; so much for Demosthenes' doom-laden prophecies. With Greece no longer a thorn in Macedon's side, Philip was free to turn his attention eastward, toward the Persian empire.

ALEXANDER

It was Alexander the Great who was to conquer the East with the powerful military machine his father Philip had created. For Philip was assassinated in 336 during a festival at Aegae to which representatives of all his new Greek allies had been invited. There was one major absentee: Olympias, Alexander's mother and Philip's sixth wife whose position at court had recently been challenged not merely by the existence of a seventh wife, but by the latter's fecundity: Eurydice had given birth to a daughter and had become pregnant again within a year. It has been suggested, but cannot be proved, that Olympias was behind the assassination

suaded to return to his native climes by the promise of a rich salary. Among other things, Aristotle encouraged in his pupil a devotion to the works of Homer, especially the *Iliad* to whose hero Achilles Alexander was constantly to compare himself. He was always to travel with a copy of the *Iliad* that had been prepared with Aristotle's help and slept with it as a pillow. One of Alexander's first acts on landing in Asia on the campaign which was to last for the rest of his life was to visit the site of Troy and to run naked around the tomb of his hero. He took from the temple of Athena some armor and weapons which were thought to date back

Olympias, Alexander's mother, was out of favor at the Macedonian court at the time of Philip's assassination and her son's succession in the summer of 336 B.C. She was a violent and headstrong woman, a fact that is exemplified by the way in which she reasserted her position and that of her son by means of a few judicious murders of people who might stand in their way.

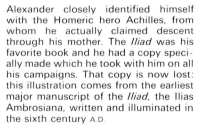

Alexander closely identified himself with the Homeric hero Achilles, from whom he actually claimed descent through his mother. The *Iliad* was his favorite book and he had a copy specially made which he took with him on all his campaigns. That copy is now lost: this illustration comes from the earliest major manuscript of the *Iliad*, the Ilias Ambrosiana, written and illuminated in the sixth century A.D.

in order to protect Alexander's interests. At all events, she and her son were the prime beneficiaries of the murder.

The kingdom of Macedon, moreover, survived the upheaval. There was a round of executions of people who might have presented a challenge to the twenty-year-old king, including Eurydice's children and her uncle Attalus who was abroad as one of the commanders of a preliminary task force in Asia sent by Philip and the alliance of Greek states subject to him. The eastern campaign was postponed until Alexander had first tried to persuade, then actually forced the Greeks to come to heel. The destruction of Thebes (only the house that had been Pindar's was left standing) was a salutary warning to other Greek states to concur with Alexander's policies.

No expense had been spared on Alexander's education. His tutor was Aristotle, per-

Aristotle was employed for some years as Alexander's tutor. He figures largely in the legends which grew up around Alexander and which were told for centuries from Central Europe to India. A group of fourth-century A.D. statues belonging to a building in Thessalonica in Macedonia, the so-called Incantadas, were said to have been members of Alexander's court turned to stone "by his conjurer, Aristotle."

Alexander wanted people to believe that he was descended from Zeus, and portraits often show him gazing upward as though to emphasize his divinity. In his lifetime only three artists were allowed to portray him: Lysippus the sculptor, Apelles the painter, and Pyrgoteles the gem-cutter. This splendidly leonine head was made at Pergamum long after Alexander's death.

Alexander's horse Bucephalas was bought from a Thessalian breeder for the unparalleled sum of thirteen talents. The animal was at first thought to be uncontrollable, but the twelve-year-old Alexander saw that it was shying at its own shadow, calmed the horse down, and mounted it. A gold medallion of a later period found at Aboukir in Egypt shows a heroically nude Alexander seated next to the horse that was his mount for twenty years.

to the time of the Trojan War. This was an obvious evocation of the fact that Achilles had been presented with divine armor before he fought with Hector, the Trojan hero. According to Herodotus, whose work was also well known to Alexander, the Trojan War culminating in the sack of an Asiatic city by a European foe was regarded by the Persians as one of the underlying causes of the war they conducted with the Greeks in 490 and 480/479 B.C. Alexander clearly regarded his own remarkable invasion of Asia as yet another stage in the perennial conflict between East and West. After victories in Asia Minor (at the Granicus and the Issus), and the capture of Tyre and the foundation in Egypt of the first of his many Alexandrias, he went on to capture Persepolis in 330, the ceremonial center of the Persian Empire, which he destroyed by fire because "he wished to take revenge on the Persians for invading Greece, for razing Athens and burning her temples."

It was about this time that the story began to be told that the reason why Alexander had visited the shrine of Zeus Ammon in the Egyptian desert some twenty months earlier was that "Perseus and Heracles had been there before him." It was not simply that Perseus and Heracles were sons of Zeus and that Alexander wished to emulate them, but that Perseus was both an Argive hero (the Macedonian ruling house was supposed to be descended from Argives) and the eponymous ancestor of the Persians. The tale must be connected with the integration Alexander was now trying to achieve between his Macedonian supporters and his new Persian subjects.

Alexander's conquest did not end with his capture of Persepolis and the subsequent death of the last Great King Darius III. The

Persian empire was only half-won, and although Alexander's troops were talking of returning home, he persuaded them with promises of future victories and attendant riches to press on eastward to India. Already he had begun to adopt some of the appurtenances of the Persian king: he collected tribute from his new subjects whom he administered for the most part still with oriental officials, he enrolled Asiatics in his army; he began to wear a diadem as a sign of royal authority, and he even toyed with the practice of *proskynesis*, kissing the hand as a gesture of respect, among his own Macedonian courtiers. He was eager that in Asia at least Greek and oriental should be assimilated. In 327 he married the Iranian Roxane, said to be the most beautiful in all of Asia, and in imitation of his father Philip's intro-

duction of royal pages to Pella from elsewhere in Macedonia, he ordered thirty thousand Iranian boys to be enrolled as military cadets, to be trained—in Greek—in Macedonian fighting methods.

This was but one of the devices Alexander adopted in order to Hellenize his new empire; another was urbanization. The art of town-planning in Greece had reached a high degree of professionalism in the fifth and fourth centuries B.C. New foundations would be laid out on a grid pattern with the usual institutions of a Greek city—agoras, temples, theaters, and stadia—carefully disposed within it according to the principles established by Hippodamus of Miletus. The best-known example (to us) of such planning is actually to be found in northern Greece, at Olynthus in Chalcidice, but since

A silver tetradrachm issued by the mint at Alexandria, the capital of the Ptolemies, a couple of decades after Alexander's death. It shows him idealized, with large staring eyes, and wearing an elephant-skin hat—an indication of the fact that Alexandria was an African city.

One of the highest titles that a member of the Macedonian court could possess was that of Companion. Alexander began to bestow it on especially favored oriental subjects such as the king of Sidon, a detail of whose sarcophagus is illustrated here. Alexander is shown at the Battle of the Issus wearing a lionskin hat. This identifies him as a second Heracles, who in addition to his warlike qualities was also a son of Zeus, a claim that Alexander made for himself.

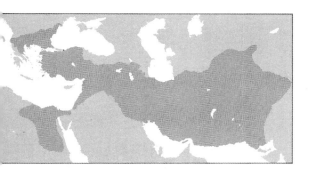

A map to show the fullest extent of Alexander's empire at the time of his death at Babylon in 323. It comprised nearly all of the Persian empire and extra territories besides, in particular parts of the Northwest Frontier of India.

One of the wonders of the ancient world was the Pharos, the Lighthouse, at Alexandria. It stood on the outer edge of the harbor and its fire could be seen for miles around. It survived until the early fifteenth century when it fell down in an earthquake. The site is now occupied by a fortress (below, left).

Olynthus had been razed to the ground by Philip II in 348 B.C., it is unlikely to have itself been the pattern for the numerous cities founded by Alexander and his Hellenistic Successors in both Macedonia and the Near East. These settlements were created partly as a means of Hellenization and partly as a way of rewarding veteran soldiers.

of, for example, the Seleucid foundations of Damascus, Aleppo, or Latakiyah in Syria can still be detected today underlying those of the modern cities. The principal reasons for such continuity are partly that it is easier to re-use the foundations of an existing house than to make new ones, and partly that there was a Byzantine law to the effect

One of Alexander's most skillfully executed battles was the one he won against King Porus at the River Jhelum in northwest India. Porus was encamped on one side of the river in a very strong position, the stronger for the fact that he had two hundred elephants which in the words of a Greek observer "stood along the bank and when carefully goaded, they wearied the ear with their hideous trumpeting."
Alexander therefore made sham attacks and tricked Porus into believing that a crossing would be attempted at the spot that was being defended. In fact,

Regularly planned cities were well suited for the latter purpose, for the veterans would draw lots, and it prevented acrimonious recriminations if one allotment was as similar to another as possible. Despite Olynthus' destruction, indeed because of it, we are better able than we might be to envisage how the new cities originally appeared before they were built over in subsequent centuries. At Olynthus each block in the grid contained ten houses, five along one side and five on the other. All faced south. Another, related plan has been found at Pella, the Macedonian capital, where the streets are likewise laid out on a grid pattern. The courtiers' houses there, however, sometimes occupy whole blocks.
Any attempt to reconstruct the original plan of Alexandria in Egypt is bound to be largely speculative, but the Hellenistic plans

that no one could change the course of a street without the permission of the local authority.
Alexander's principal legacy was the Hellenization of the eastern Mediterranean. Sadly, the longterm effects of his attempts to westernize Iran were less successful. The western kingdoms which arose in the western part of Alexander's empire were gradually taken over by Rome as she too adopted the forms of a Hellenistic state. Macedon fell first in 196, and Greece in 167. Pergamum was actually bequeathed to Rome by its last ruler in 133, and the romantic story which lies behind Rome's conquest of Cleopatra's Egypt beguiles theater- and cinemagoers even today.

Alexander made a crossing several miles upriver and took the enemy by surprise. Sadly, his horse, Bucephalas, died in the battle, and Alexander founded two cities to commemorate his triumph: one, Bucephalas, after his horse, and the other, Nicaea, after the goddess of Victory. Both these subjects are featured prominently on a decadrachm struck at Babylon soon afterward: on one side Bucephalas bravely attacks an elephant and on the other Alexander is crowned by Nike.

Overleaf: The Alexander mosaic found at Pompeii in the House of the Faun where it was probably laid in the second century B.C. It is probably a painstaking copy of a major wall painting of the fourth century B.C. and shows the confrontation at the Battle of the Issus between Alexander (on the left of this detail) and the Great King of Persia. The sarissae of the Macedonians are very much in evidence, and Darius' very unGreek chariot is decorated with numerous oriental lions. The execution of the mêlée is brilliant; it is unfortunate that we cannot be sure of the artist's name.

In the preceding pages we have seen the Greeks and their achievements revealed by every possible means: their art and architecture recovered by archaeology, their deeds and thoughts recorded for posterity by themselves. Their great material legacy to European civilization provided the inspiration both for the Roman Empire that followed them, and the European Renaissance which gave structure to the world in which we still live. But even more important than the material legacy is the spiritual and intellectual one. It thus seems fitting to leave the last word to the Greeks themselves.

But I claim there will be some who remember us when we are gone.

Sappho

Socrates in my opinion stated an important principle of architecture when he said that a practical house was also a beautiful one.... Putting it in a nutshell, a house where a man can find the most agreeable shelter for himself and the safest repository for his possessions all the year round may reasonably be regarded as the most agreeable and the most beautiful dwelling place. Paintings and decorations detract from the cheerfulness of the place more than they contribute to it.

Xenophon, *Memorabilia*

"Nothing to excess" and "Know thyself" are among the traditional sayings attributed to ancient Greek wise men; these and other aphorisms are said to have been engraved on the walls of the Temple of Apollo at Delphi.

So much for very early training of children: the next stage up to five years old, which is not yet suited to any formal learning or compulsory effort, if their growth is not to be impeded, nevertheless needs sufficient exercise to avoid physical sloth: this should be provided by various means, particularly play.

Aristotle, *Politics*

As to the study of music there might be dispute. Most people nowadays take part in it for pleasure; but others originally established it in education because human nature itself seeks, as I have often said, not merely to work rightly but to be able to use our leisure well.

Aristotle, *Politics*

All the laws we are now discussing are those commonly known as unwritten laws and in fact all hereditary customs come under this head. And we were quite right in making our recent proviso that we should neither call them laws nor on the other hand leave them unmentioned, for they are the bonds of every society, linking together all written laws past, present, and future—hereditary and utterly ancient customs, which, if they are soundly established, hold together in a mantle of absolute security all subsequent written laws; but, if they go away, like joiners' supports in buildings when they give way from the middle, bring everything else to the ground with them on top of each other and there they lie, both themselves and later additions however well built, because the original supports have collapsed.

Plato, *Laws*

I will make nothing better by crying,
I will make nothing worse
by giving myself
what entertainment I can

Archilochus

Socrates to Lamprocles: "You surely don't suppose that it is sexual desire alone which leads men to beget children, when the streets and brothels afford ample opportunities for gratifying that. It is clear that we consider what sort of women would give us the best children, and then unite with them to produce children."

Xenophon, *Memorabilia*

γνῶθι σαυτόν

know thyself

Was it the jealous search for wealth to exalt their home that drove their sails racing before the wind, that plashed their pinewood oars, two wings as one, to bring home riches over the wide waters? such hope is sweet to men: though it bring sorrow, it is not satisfied. They wander over the waves, visit strange cities, seeking a world of wealth, all alike sure of achievement, yet one man's aim misses the lucky moment, another finds fortune in his lap.... Welcome justice! Yet—o dearest news of all—if some ship from Hellas came to free me from this weary slavery! O my land, my father's home! even in dream to see you now! there to taste, as long ago, ecstasy of singing, rich and poor together!

Euripides, *Iphigenia*

.War is sweet to those who have not tried it. The experienced man is frightened at the heart to see it advancing.

Pindar

In Polygnotus' painting near the man who injured his father and is for that reason suffering torment in Hades, a man who has pillaged sanctuaries is punished. The woman who is punishing him is expert in drugs, especially ones painful to people. People were, you understand, still immensely devoted to religion, as the Athenians showed when they captured a sanctuary of Olympian Zeus at Syracuse, without disturbing any of the dedications, and leaving the Syracusan priest to look after them.... Thus at that time everyone held the gods in honor, and on that basis Polygnotus painted the section relating to the temple-robber.

Pausanias

There are ten thousand things wrong in Greece, but none is worse than the race of athletes...for who has ever helped his native city by winning a prize for wrestling or running fast or throwing a discus or hitting someone squarely on the chin? Will they fight the enemy discus in hand, or kick them out of the country like so many footballs?

Euripides, *Autolycus*

Things never come into being or are destroyed, but they are compounded of existing matter, and dissolved into them.

Anaxagoras

What is more there is no correspondence, they say, between what is naturally admirable and what is conventionally so. As for natural morality, there is no such thing, but morality is a matter of constant argument and change. Any change is sovereign for the moment, resulting as it does from contrivance and conventions and no natural cause. All this, my friends, is the creed of clever men, whether laymen or poets, presented to the young—a claim that morality is whatever a man can make prevail by force; and so you find all sorts of irreverence besetting the young, on the grounds that the gods in whom the law enjoins belief do not exist, and the result is division in society because they are pressurized toward the "naturally" correct life, namely a life of dominance over others rather than "servility" to one's fellows under the law.

Plato, *Laws*

In these short quotations, ranging from serious political philosophy to frivolous comment, from Sappho's concern with posterity to Anaxagoras' adumbration of our own views on the fundamental indestructibility of matter, the Greeks here record their views on matters of importance to themselves. That the problems they address seem familiar and their conclusions relevant to ourselves, is a measure both of their concern with the universalities of human behavior, and of the extent to which we are their spiritual and intellectual heirs.

Overleaf: In the depiction of their divinities, the classical Greeks raised the human form to an ideal. Two splendid examples are seen here: a bronze head of Apollo *(left)*, dated 470–460 B.C.; and a bronze head of Aphrodite said to be by Praxiteles, fourth century B.C.

SELECTED BIBLIOGRAPHY

GENERAL

Arias, P.E., and Hirmer, M. *A History of Greek Vase Painting*. London, 1962.

Berve, H., Gruben, G., Hirmer, M. *Greek Temples, Theaters and Shrines*. London, 1963.

Boardman, J. *Greek Art*. London and New York, 1964.

— Dörig, J., Fuchs, W., Hirmer, M. *The Art and Architecture of Ancient Greece*. London, 1967.

Burg, J.B. *A History of Greece to the Death of Alexander the Great*. 3rd ed. London, 1967.

Cook, R.M. *Greek Painted Pottery*. London, 1972.

— *The Greeks until Alexander*. London and New York, 1962.

Dinsmoor, W.B. *The Architecture of Ancient Greece*. 3rd ed. London, 1950.

Finley, M.I. *The Ancient Greeks*. London, 1963.

Frost, F.J. *Greek Society*. Lexington, Mass., 1971.

Grant, M. *Ancient History Atlas*. New York, 1972.

Hammond, N.G.L. *A History of Greece to 322 B.C.* 2nd ed. Oxford, 1967.

Hatzfeld, J. *History of Ancient Greece*. London, 1966.

Kitto, H.D.F. *The Greeks*. Harmondsworth, 1957.

Kraay, C.M., and Hirmer, M. *Greek Coins*. London and New York, 1966.

Kurtz, D.C., and Boardman, J. *Greek Burial Customs*. London, 1971.

Lesky, A. *A History of Greek Literature*. London, 1966.

Lévêque, P. *The Greek Adventure*. London, 1968.

Lloyd-Jones, H. *The Greeks*. London, 1962.

Mackendrick, P. *The Greek Stones Speak*. London, 1962.

Nilsson, M.P. *A History of Greek Religion*. 2nd rev. ed. London, 1962.

Richter, G.M.A. *A Handbook of Greek Art*. London, 1959.

Robertson, D.S. *Greek and Roman Architecture*. 2nd ed. Cambridge, 1945.

Robertson, M. *Greek Painting*. Geneva, 1959.

Seltman, C. *Greek Coins*. 2nd ed. London, 1955.

Webster, T.B.L. *Hellenistic Poetry and Art*. London, 1964.

Whitehouse, D. and R. *Archaeological Atlas of the World*. London, 1975.

Wycherley, R.E. *How the Greeks Built Cities*. 2nd ed. London, 1967.

KINGS OF THE SEA

Alexiov, S., Platon, N., Guanella, H., von Matt, L. *Ancient Crete*. London, 1968.

Barnett, R.D. *The Sea Peoples*. Cambridge, 1969.

Branigan, K. *The Foundations of Palatial Crete*. London, 1970.

— *The Tombs of Mesara*. London, 1970.

Caskey, J.L. *Greece, Crete, and the Aegean Islands in the Early Bronze Age*. Cambridge, 1966.

Evans, Sir Arthur. *The Palace of Minos at Knossos*. Vols. 1–4. London, 1921–1935. Index Volume, 1936. Repr. New York, 1963.

Graham, J.W. *The Palaces of Crete*. Princeton, N.J., 1962. Repr. 1969.

Higgins, R.A. *Minoan and Mycenaean Art*. London and New York, 1967.

Hood, S. *The Home of the Heroes: The Aegean before the Greeks*. London, 1967.

— *The Minoans*. London, 1971.

Hutchinson, R.W. *Prehistoric Crete*. Harmondsworth, 1962.

Luce, J.V. *Lost Atlantis*. London, 1969.

Marinatos, S., and Hirmer, M. *Crete and Mycenae*. London and New York, 1960.

Matz, F. *Minoan Civilization: Maturity and Zenith*. Cambridge, 1962.

Pendlebury, J.D.S. *The Archaeology of Crete*. London, 1939. Repr. New York, 1965.

Renfrew, C. *The Emergence of Civilization: The Cyclades and the Aegean in the Third Millennium B.C.* London, 1972.

von Matt, L. *Ancient Crete*. London, 1968.

Zervos, C. *L'Art de la Crète néolithique et minoenne*. Paris, 1956.

HEROES AND MEN

Blegen, C.W. *Troy*. Cambridge, 1964.

— *Troy and the Trojans*. London, 1963.

Carpenter, R. *Discontinuity in Greek Civilization*. Cambridge, 1966.

Desborough, V.R. d'A. *The End of Mycenaean Civilization and the Dark Age*. Cambridge, 1962.

— *The Greek Dark Ages*. London, 1972.

Finley, M.I. *The World of Odysseus*. London, 1956.

Higgins, R. *Minoan and Mycenaean Art*. London and New York, 1967.

Marinatos, S., and Hirmer, M. *Crete and Mycenae*. London, 1960.

Mylonas, G. *Ancient Mycenae*. London, 1957.

— *Mycenae and the Mycenaean Age*. Princeton, N.J., 1966.

Nilsson, M.P. *The Minoan-Mycenaean Religion and its Survival in Greek Religion*. 2nd ed. Lund, 1950.

Samuel, A.E. *The Mycenaeans in History*. Englewood Cliffs, N.J., 1966.

Snodgrass, A. *The Dark Age of Greece*. Edinburgh, 1971.

Stubbings, F.H. *The Expansion of Mycenaean Civilization*. Cambridge, 1965.

— *The Recession of Mycenaean Civilization*. Cambridge, 1965.

— *The Rise of Mycenaean Civilization*. Cambridge, 1963.

Taylour, W. *The Mycenaeans*. London, 1964.

Ventris, M., and Chadwick, J. *Documents in Greek*. Cambridge, 1973.

Vermeule, E. *Greece in the Bronze Age*. Chicago, 1964.

Wace, A.J.B. *Mycenae: An Archaeological History and Guide*. Princeton, N.J., 1949.

THE AGE OF IRON

Boardman, J. *The Greeks Overseas*. Harmondsworth, England, 1964.

Charbonneaux, J., Martin, R., Villard, R. *Archaic Greek Art, 620–480 B.C.* London, 1971.

Cook, J.M. *Greek Settlement in the Eastern Aegean and Asia Minor*. Cambridge, 1961.

— *The Greeks in Ionia and the East*. London, 1962.

Forrest, W.G. *The Emergence of Greek Democracy: The Character of Greek Politics, 800–400 B.C.* London, 1966.

Graham, A.J. *Colony and Mother City in Ancient Greece*. New York, 1964.

Starr, C.G. *The Origins of Greek Civilization, 1100–650 B.C.* London, 1962.

Webster, T.B.L. *Greek Art and Literature 700–530 B.C.* London, 1959.

Woodhead, A.G. *The Greeks in the West*. London, 1962.

THE RULE OF ATHENS

Andrews, K. *Athens*. London, 1967.

Bowra, C.M. *Periclean Athens*. London, 1971.

Burn, A.R. *Alexander the Great and the Hellenistic World*. New York, 1962.

— *Pericles and Athens*. New York, 1949.

— *Persia and the Greeks*. London, 1962.

Charbonneaux, J., Martin, R., Villard, F. *Classical Greek Art, 480–330 B.C.* London, 1973.

Ehrenberg, V. *Sophocles and Pericles*. Oxford, 1954.

Flacelière, R. *Daily Life in Greece at the Time of Pericles*. London, 1965.

Ghirshman, R. *Persia: From the Origins to Alexander the Great*. London, 1964.

Green, P. *Alexander the Great*. London, 1970.

— *Armada from Athens: The Failure of the Sicilian Expedition, 415–413 B.C.* London, 1971.

— *The Year of Salamis: 480–479 B.C.* London, 1970.

Hignett, C. *Xerxes' Invasion of Greece*. Oxford, 1963.

Hopper, R.J. *The Acropolis*. London, 1971.

Kagan, D. *The Outbreak of the Peloponnesian War*. Cornell, 1969.

Laistner, M.L.W. *A History of the Greek World, 479–323 B.C.* London, 1936. 3rd ed., 1957.

Lang, M. *The Athenian Citizen*. Princeton, N.J., 1960.

Lewis, N. *Greek Historical Documents: The Fifth Century B.C.* Toronto, 1971.

Milns, R.D. *Alexander the Great*. London, 1968.

Sainte Croix, G.E.M. de. *The Origins of the Peloponnesian War*. London, 1972.

Tarn, W.W. *Alexander the Great*. 2 vols. Cambridge, 1948.

Travlos, J. *Pictorial Dictionary of Ancient Athens*. London and New York, 1971.

Wilcken, U. *Alexander the Great*. New York, 1967.

Zimmern, A.E. *The Greek Commonwealth: Politics and Economics in Fifth-Century Athens*. 5th ed. Oxford, 1931.

LIST OF ILLUSTRATIONS AND PHOTO CREDITS

Abbreviations

c.: Century
P: Photo
AM: Archaeological Museum
NAM: National Archaeological Museum

Front of jacket: Head of Apollo. From Temple of Zeus, Olympia, ca. 470–465 B.C. AM, Olympia. P: Ekdotike Athenon S.A., Athens.

Back of jacket: Head of Kore no. 674. From the Acropolis, ca. 500 B.C. Acropolis Museum, Athens. P: Ekdotike Athenon S.A., Athens.

2 Head of Zeus. Bronze. Olympia, early 5th c. B.C. NAM, Athens. P: Ekdotike Athenon S.A., Athens.

4 *Left:* Ionic column. Xanthus (Turkey). 420 B.C. British Museum. P: Michael Holford, Loughton.
Right, above: Woman's head, "La Parisienne." Fresco from the Palace of Knossos. ca. 1500 B.C. AM, Heraklion. P: Leonard von Matt, Buochs.
Right, below: Head of the "Rampin Horseman." Marble. From the Acropolis. Mid-6th c. B.C. Acropolis Museum, Athens. P: Ekdotike Athenon S.A., Athens.

5 *Above:* Head of a warrior. Ivory with boar's tusk helmet. Mycenae. 13th c. B.C. NAM, Athens. P: Hirmer Fotoarchiv, Munich.
Below: Head of a woman. Marble. From the Heraion, Argos. Late 5th c. B.C. NAM, Athens.

6 Matala, Crete. P: Leonard von Matt, Buochs.

8 *Left to right:*
Clay statuette of a worshipper, from Petsofa. ca. 1950 B.C. AM, Heraklion. P: Ekdotike Athenon S.A., Athens.
Copper statuette of a worshipper. ca. 1600 B.C. British Museum.
Biton. Marble kouros by Polymedes. Apollo Sanctuary, Delphi. ca. 590 B.C. AM, Delphi. P: Jean Mazenod, from *L'Art Grec*, Editions d'Art Lucien Mazenod, Paris, 1972.
Flute player. Bronze. From Samos. Later 6th c. B.C. NAM, Athens. P: Jean Mazenod, from *L'Art Grec*.
Apollo. Bronze kouros from Piraeus. 525 B.C. NAM, Athens. P: Scala, Florence.

9 *Left to right:*
"The Charioteer." Bronze statue from the Apollo Sanctuary, Delphi. ca. 475 B.C. AM, Delphi. P: Ekdotike Athenon S.A., Athens.
Doryphoros. Marble copy (bronze original by Polycletos, 400 B.C.). NAM, Naples.
Apoxyomenos. Marble copy (original by Lysippos, ca. 320 B.C.). Vatican Museums, Rome.
Agias. Marble contemporary copy (original by Lysippos, ca. 336 B.C.). AM, Delphi. P: Alinari, Florence.

10–11 Map of Greece and Asia Minor. With permission of the Atlas delegation of the Conference of Educational Directors, from Imhof, ed., *Schweizerischer Mittelschulatlas*, printed by Orell Füssli AG, Zurich.

12 *Left, above and below:* Taras riding a dolphin; rider holding a torch. Silver didrachmon from Taras (Italy), 272–235 B.C. Staatliche Münzsammlung, Munich.
Center: Battle scene between Greeks and Trojans. End 5th c. A.D. Greek Ms.F.205 Inf., Biblioteca Ambrosiana, Milan.
Right: Venus of Milo. Marble. ca. 150 B.C. Louvre, Paris.

13 *Left:* Concordia Temple, Agrigento, Italy. Mid-5th c. B.C. P: Leonard von Matt, Buochs.
Right: Votive stele from Epidaurus. AM, Epidaurus.

14 *Top left:* Dr. Heinrich Schliemann (1822–1890). P: The Bettmann Archive, New York.
Top right: Mrs. Schliemann wearing "Priam's Treasury" from Troy. From C. Schuchardt, *Schliemann's Excavations*, 1891.
Center left: "Mask of Agamemnon." Gold. From Grave V of Grave Circle A, Mycenae. 16th c. B.C. NAM, Athens. P: Dimitrios Harissiadis, Athens.
Center right: View of the Shaft Grave Circle A, Mycenae. P: Georges Viollon/ Rapho, Paris.
Below, left to right:
Three photographs, Ekdotike Athenon S.A., Athens:
Hexagonal wooden pyxis with golden plates. From Grave V of Grave Circle A, Mycenae. 16th c. B.C. NAM, Athens.
Golden signet-ring from Tiryns. See page 85.
Male figure in combat with a lion. Golden seal stone. From Grave Circle A, Mycenae. 16th c. B.C. NAM, Athens.

15 *Top:* Wild goat nursing her young. Cow with her calf. Faience plaques found in the repositories of the Palace of Knossos. 1600 B.C. AM, Heraklion. P: Ekdotike Athenon S.A., Athens.
Center left: Palace of Knossos. West wing. P: Leonard von Matt, Buochs.
Center right: Sir Arthur John Evans (1851–1941). P: Ashmolean Museum, Oxford.
Bottom: Excavation, Palace of Knossos. P: Ashmolean Museum.

16 *Above left:* Excavation at Olympia. First campaign, 1875/1876. P: Deutsches Archäologisches Institut, Athens.

16–17 *Top:* Model reconstruction of Olympia.
Center: Ruins of the Temple of Zeus at Olympia. 5th c. B.C.
Bottom row, left to right: Plan of Olympia, 1829; 1877; 1878; 1879; 1881.
All courtesy Deutsches Archäologisches Institut, Athens.

17 *Top right:* Sprinter at start. Bronze statuette. Argive, ca. 480 B.C. AM, Olympia. P: Deutsches Archäologisches Institut, Athens.
Center right: Ruins of columns at Olympia. P: Peter Grunauer, Munich.

18–19 Altis Sanctuary, Olympia. P: Kodansha Ltd., Tokyo.

20 *Top:* Excavations at Akrotiri. P: Robert Tobler, Lucerne.
Bottom left: Excavation of the bronze breastplate at Olympia. P: Deutsches Archäologisches Institut, Athens.
Bottom right: Bronze breastplate from a hoplite's armor. From Olympia. Early 6th c. B.C. AM, Olympia. P: Ekdotike Athenon S.A., Athens.

21 *Top left:* Marble Kouros and Kore. *In situ.* Found near Merenda, Attica. 6th c. B.C. P: Nikos Kontos, Athens.
Right: Clay vessels. Akrotiri. P: Robert Tobler, Lucerne.
Bottom right: Burial urn in the process of excavation. P: C. Bérard, Lausanne.

22–23 Ship. Detail of the Fresco of the Naval Campaign. Room 5 of the West House, Akrotiri. ca. 1500 B.C. NAM, Athens. P: Hannibal, Athens.

24 *Left:* Reconstruction of the fortified settlement at Dimini. From Jacquetta Hawkes, *Atlas of Ancient Archaeology*, Rainbird Reference Books Ltd., London, 1974.
Right: Red-polished neolithic bowl from Sesklo. ca. 3000 B.C. NAM, Athens.

25 *Top left:* Neolithic idol from Knossos. Terracotta. ca. 3000 B.C. AM, Heraklion. P: Ekdotike Athenon S.A., Athens.
Center: Juglet in the form of a bird from Koumasa. ca. 2500 B.C. AM, Heraklion. P: Arts Faculty Photo Unit, University of Sheffield.
Right: Cult hearth from Lerna. ca. 2500 B.C. AM, Argos. P: Dimitrios Harissiadis, Athens.

26 View of the Thessalian plain. P: Ekdotike Athenon S.A., Athens.
27 Landscape of the Cyclades. P: Robert Tobler, Lucerne.
28 *Left:* Clay sealing from the "House of the Tiles," Lerna. ca. 2200 B.C. Corinth Museum.
Right: View from the northwest of the House of the Tiles, Lerna. ca. 2200 B.C.
Both P: American School of Classical Studies at Athens, Courtesy Prof. John L. Caskey, University of Cincinnati.
29 *Left:* Underside of a terracotta dish with spiral motifs. From Syros. 2800–2200 B.C.
Right: Marble figure of a flute player. From Keros. 2800–2200 B.C.
Both NAM, Athens. P: Ekdotike Athenon S.A., Athens.
30 Marble figure of a harpist. From Keros. 2800–2200 B.C. NAM, Athens. P: Elsevier International Projects, Amsterdam.
31 Hedgehog-shaped vase. Painted clay. From Chalandriani, Syros. ca. 2300–2100 B.C. NAM, Athens. P: Erich Lessing/Magnum, Paris.
32 *Top right:* Gold pendant in the form of a bull's head. From Zakro. ca. 1450 B.C. AM, Heraklion. P: Leonard von Matt, Buochs.
Bottom, left to right:
Snake Goddess. Ivory and gold. From Crete. ca. 1600–1500 B.C. Museum of Fine Arts, Boston.
View of the bay of Kato Zakro. P: Leonard von Matt, Buochs.
View of the pillared hall and end of the central court, Palace of Mallia. P: Hirmer Fotoarchiv, Munich.
33 *Left:* West façade, Palace of Phaistos. P: Leonard von Matt, Buochs.
Right: General view of the Palace of Knossos. P: Ekdotike Athenon S.A., Athens.
34 *Left:* The "Royal Road," Palace of Knossos. P: Leonard von Matt, Buochs.
Right: Reconstruction drawing of the west wing, Palace of Knossos. P: Ekdotike Athenon S.A., Athens.
35 *Left:* The sacred horns of a bull. Symbol crowning the palace walls at Knossos. P: Erich Lessing/Magnum, Paris.
Right: North entrance to the Palace of Knossos. P: Ekdotike Athenon S.A., Athens.
36 "The Priest-King." Restored relief fresco from the Palace of Knossos. ca. 1500 B.C. AM, Heraklion. P: Ekdotike Athenon S.A., Athens.
37 Main staircase, east wing of the Palace of Knossos. Reconstructed by Evans. P: Leonard von Matt, Buochs.
38 *Top:* Engraved double axe, north wall of the Palace of Zakro. P: Leonard von Matt, Buochs.
From Palace of Knossos:
Center above: Snake Goddess. Faience statuette. ca. 1600 B.C. AM, Heraklion. P: Ekdotike Athenon S.A., Athens.
Center left: Vestibule to the Hall of the Double Axes, from outside. East wing.
Center right: Vestibule to the Hall of the Double Axes.
Both P: Hirmer Fotoarchiv, Munich.
Bottom left: Pithoi in the western magazines. P: Elsevier Publishing Projects, Lausanne.
Bottom right: "Throne of Minos." Throne room. P: Dimitrios Harissiadis, Athens.
38–39 *Above:* Plan of the Palace of Knossos. From von Matt/Alexiou/Platon/Guanella, *Das Antike Kreta,* NZN Buchverlag Zurich, 1967.
Below: Reconstruction drawing of the Palace of Knossos, from southeast. From Jacquetta Hawkes, *Atlas of Ancient Archaeology,* Rainbird Reference Books, London, 1974.
39 *Top left:* Water system. East gate, Palace of Knossos. P: Peter Clayton, Boxmoor.
Top right: Clay bathtub from Pachyammos near Gournia. ca. 1500 B.C. AM, Heraklion. P: Leonard von Matt, Buochs.
Center left: Pillared hall in the main staircase.
Center right: "Queen's Megaron" with pillared hall.
Both: Palace of Knossos. P: Hirmer Fotoarchiv, Munich.
Bottom, left to right:
Sardonyx seal stone from Knossos. P: Ekdotike Athenon S.A., Athens.
Amphora from the Palace of Knossos. P: Leonard von Matt, Buochs.
Both: AM, Heraklion.
Obsidian dolium shell chalice from Ayia Triadha. 1700–1450 B.C. P: Peter Warren, Bristol.
40 *Left:* Clay sealing with portrait of a Minoan king. From Knossos, 1800–1700 B.C. AM, Heraklion. P: Ekdotike Athenon S.A., Athens.
40–41 The Phaistos disk, side A. Terracotta. From the Palace of Phaistos, after 1600 B.C. AM, Heraklion. P: Hirmer Fotoarchiv, Munich.
41 *Above right:* The Phaistos disk, side B. See pages 40–41. P: Ekdotike Athenon S.A., Athens.
Bottom left and right: Linear A tablets from Ayia Triadha, 1450 B.C. AM, Heraklion. P: Ekdotike Athenon S.A., Athens.
42–43 Bull-Leaper fresco, Palace of Knossos. ca. 1500 B.C. AM, Heraklion. P: Erich Lessing/Magnum, Paris.
44 *Left:* Gold signet ring from a Cretan tomb. ca. 1500 B.C. AM, Heraklion. P: Hirmer Fotoarchiv, Munich.
Right: Faience Snake Goddess from the Treasury of the Central Sanctuary at Knossos. ca. 1500 B.C. AM, Heraklion. P: Leonard von Matt, Buochs.
45 *Top left:* So-called pillar crypt, Palace of Knossos. P: Hirmer Fotoarchiv, Munich.
Top right: Peak sanctuary with wild goats. Detail of a chlorite rhyton from the Palace of Zakro. ca. 1450 B.C. AM, Heraklion. P: Leonard von Matt, Buochs.
Bottom right: Bronze statuette of a worshipper. From Tylissos, ca. 1500 B.C. AM, Heraklion. P: Ekdotike Athenon S.A., Athens.
46 *Left:* Gold earring from Mavro Spelio near Knossos. ca. 1450 B.C. P: Leonard von Matt, Buochs.
Right: Steatite rhyton, Little Palace of Knossos. ca. 1450 B.C. P: Erich Lessing/Magnum, Paris.
Both: AM, Heraklion.
47 *Top:* Golden double axes, Arkalokhori. ca. 1500 B.C. P: Dimitrios Harissiadis, Athens.
Center: Religious representations, sarcophagus from Ayia Triadha. 1500–1400 B.C. P: Ekdotike Athenon S.A., Athens.
Both: AM, Heraklion.
48 *Top right:* Votive bowl from Palaikastro. 1900 B.C. AM, Heraklion. P: Leonard von Matt, Buochs.
Left: Detail of the "Harvester Vase." Villa of Ayia Triadha. ca. 1500 B.C. AM, Heraklion. P: Ekdotike Athenon S.A., Athens.
Bottom right: Olive press in the villa at Vathypetro. P: Hirmer Fotoarchiv, Munich.
49 *Top left:* The fisherman. Fresco from Room 5 of the West House, Akrotiri. ca. 1500 B.C. NAM, Athens. P: Hirmer Fotoarchiv, Munich.
Top right: Bronze bulls, cave on the Lassithi Plain. ca. 1600 B.C. AM, Heraklion. P: Leonard von Matt, Buochs.
Below right: Minoan farmhouse at Vathypetro. P: Ekdotike Athenon S.A., Athens.
Bottom: Pithoi from Akrotiri. P: Hannibal, Athens.
50 *Left:* Gold pendant. From Chryssolakkos at Mallia. ca. 2000 B.C. AM, Heraklion. P: Ekdotike Athenon S.A., Athens.
Center: Golden cup from Vaphio. 15th c. B.C. NAM, Athens.
Right: Kamares ware cup from Phaistos. ca. 1800 B.C. AM, Heraklion.
Both P: Dimitrios Harissiadis, Athens.
51 *Left:* Rock-crystal rhyton from the Palace of Zakro. ca. 1450 B.C. P: Leonard von Matt, Buochs.
Right, above: Haematite seal stone from Monastiriako at Knossos. Around 1400 B.C. P: Ekdotike Athenon S.A., Athens.
Right, below: Sard seal stone. P: Ekdotike Athenon S.A.
All: AM, Heraklion.
52 Faience plaques of Minoan house façades. From the Palace of Knossos. 1800–1700 B.C. AM, Heraklion. P: Leonard von Matt, Buochs.
53 *Left:* Plan of Gournia. From Jacquetta Hawkes, *Atlas of Ancient Archaeology,* Rainbird Reference Books Ltd. London, 1974.
Right, top to bottom: Carpenter's tools; oil press; drain pipe; statuette and cult vessel. All from excavations at Gournia. Artwork Franz Coray.
House model from Arkhanes. Artwork Franz Coray.
54 *Left:* Road. North part of the town of Gournia. P: Hirmer Fotoarchiv, Munich.
54–55 Port. Detail of the Fresco of the "Naval Campaign." From Room 5 of the West House, Thera. ca. 1500 B.C. NAM, Athens. P: Ekdotike Athenon S.A., Athens.
56 *Top right:* Golden cup from Vaphio. See page 50.
Center left: Egyptian scarab. Glazed steatite from the Royal Road area at Knossos. 1900–1800 B.C. AM, Heraklion. P: British School at Athens.
Center right: Keftiu in the tomb of Rekhmire, Thebes. From a painting by Mrs. N.de G. Davis. P: Courtesy of the Metropolitan Museum, New York.
Bottom left: Alabastron lid with cartouche of Pharaoh Khian from Knossos. AM, Heraklion.
Bottom right: Two-handled and spouted jug from a grave at Abydos, Egypt. Kamares style. AM, Oxford.
57 *Top, left to right:*
Two scenes from Mesopotamian cylinder seal. Black haematite from a tomb at Platanos. 19th–18th c. B.C. AM, Heraklion.
Syrian dagger from Platanos. P: Prof. K. Branigan.
Wingless sphinx. Impression of a signet-shaped seal of green jasper. 19th–18th c. B.C. AM, Oxford.
Bottom, left to right:
Shell inlay from Phaistos. Ashmolean Museum, Oxford.
Egyptian bowl of porphyritic rock and white crystals. Found in the Palace of Zakro. AM, Heraklion.
Egyptian cup found in Crete. Louvre, Paris.
58 *Left:* Nippled ewer with barley motif. From Room A 2 of Section A, Akrotiri ca. 1500 B.C.
Right: Detail of the fresco of Room 1 of the "House of the Ladies," Akrotiri. ca. 1500 B.C.
Both: NAM, Athens. P: Hannibal, Athens.
59 *Top, left to right:* Nippled ewer with swallow. Ewer with molded eyes. Ewer with reed motif. Ewer with molded eyes and dolphin.
All from Akrotiri, ca. 1500 B.C. NAM, Athens. P: Hannibal, Athens.
Center right: Frieze of antelopes. Akrotiri. ca. 1500 B.C. NAM, Athens. P: Hannibal, Athens.
60 *Left:* Entrance to the West House.
Right: Staircase. Both from Akrotiri. P: Hannibal, Athens.
61 Minoan port at Amnisos. P: Peter Clayton, Boxmoor.
62–63 "Mask of Agamemnon." See page 14.
64 *Top:* Gray Minyan pottery from Boeotia. Middle Bronze Age. NAM, Athens. P: Ekdotike Athenon S.A., Athens.
Left: Portrait of a man. Amethyst seal stone from Grave Γ of Grave Circle B, Mycenae 1600–1400 B.C. NAM, Athens. P: Hirmer Fotoarchiv, Munich.
65 *Top row, left to right:*
Theseus. Detail of a red-figure amphora by the Myson Painter. ca. 500 B.C. British Museum.
Menelaus. Detail of a red-figure cup by the Duris Painter. From Santa Maria in Capua Vetere, Italy. Early 5th c. B.C. Louvre, Paris. P: Maurice Chuzeville.
Cadmus. Detail of a black-figure cup. 6th c. B.C. Louvre. P: Giraudon, Paris.
Odysseus. Detail from a Lucanian krater. From Pistacci, Italy. British Museum. P: Michael Holford, Loughton.
Agamemnon. Detail from a Loutrophoros. British Museum. P: Michael Holford.
Center left: Heracles dressed in lion's skin. Detail of a Corinthian amphora. ca. 575 B.C. Louvre. P: Maurice Chuzeville.
Center right: Nestor. Detail of an Attic red-figure vase. 5th c. B.C. Collection Lynes 732, Bibliothèque Nationale, Paris.
Bottom: "Throne of Minos." See page 38.
66 Plan of a Middle Helladic apsidal house at Eutresis. Franz Coray after Gorringe.
67 *Left:* Rhyton in the shape of a bull's head. Silver and gold. From Grave IV of Grave Circle A, Mycenae. 16th c. B.C. NAM, Athens. P: Ekdotike Athenon S.A., Athens.
Right: Temple façade. Goldwork from the upper Grave Circle, Mycenae. 16th c. B.C. NAM, Athens. P: Hirmer Fotoarchiv, Munich.
68–69 Funerary masks from Mycenae. 16th c. B.C. NAM, Athens. P: Hirmer Fotoarchiv, Munich.
70–71 Acropolis of Mycenae. P: Dimitrios Harissiadis, Athens.
71 *Right:* "The Lion Gate," entrance to the acropolis at Mycenae. 13th c. B.C. P: Dimitrios Harissiadis, Athens.
72 *Center left:* Reconstruction drawing of Grave Circle A, Mycenae. Franz Coray after Barnard.
Bottom left: Golden breast shield. From upper Grave Circle, Mycenae. 16th c. B.C. NAM, Athens. P: Dimitrios Harissiadis, Athens.
72–73 *Top:* Grave Circle A, Mycenae. P: Dimitrios Harissiadis, Athens.
Center above: Bronze blade. From Grave V of Grave Circle A, Mycenae. NAM, Athens. P: Hirmer Fotoarchiv, Munich.
Center below: Bronze dagger blade. Gold, silver, and black niello. From Grave IV of Grave Circle A, Mycenae. 16th c. B.C. NAM, Athens. P: Hirmer Fotoarchiv, Munich.
Bottom row, left to right:
Drinking cups from Grave Circle A, Mycenae. 16th c. B.C. NAM, Athens. P: Hirmer Fotoarchiv, Munich.
73 *Top right:* Gold rhyton. From Grave IV of Grave Circle A, Mycenae. 16th c. B.C. NAM, Athens. P: Hirmer Fotoarchiv, Munich.
74 *Left:* "The Lion Gate." See page 71. P: Bruno Balestrini, Milan.
74–75 Mycenae. P: Ekdotike Athenon S.A., Athens.
75 *Right, top to bottom:*
Passageway to an underground spring, Mycenae. P: Bruno Balestrini, Milan.
View from the east, Mycenae. P: Hirmer Fotoarchiv, Munich.
Paved roadway and ramp. Mycenae. P: Boudot-Lamotte, Paris.
76 *Center left:* Telemachus and Nestor. Detail of a red-figure bowl from lower Italy. 4th c. B.C. Staatliche Museen, Berlin. P: Erich Lessing/Magnum, Paris.
Center right: Plan of the Palace of Nestor at Pylos. Franz Coray after Blegen.
Bottom right: Clay bathtub. From Room 43, Palace of Nestor, Pylos. From Carl W. Blegen et al., *The Palace of Nestor at Pylos in Western Messenia,* Vol. I, Part 2. © 1966 by Princeton University Press. Reprinted by permission of Princeton University Press and the University of Cincinnati.
76–77 *Top:* Tholos tomb at Koryphasion. P: Hirmer Fotoarchiv, Munich.
77 *Right:* Clay pithos with lid. From Archives Room, Palace of Nestor, Pylos.
Bottom left: Pots from Room 20, Palace of Nestor, Pylos.
Both from Carl W. Blegen et al., *The Palace of Nestor at Pylos in Western Messenia,* Vol. I, Part 2. © 1966 by Princeton University Press. Reprinted by permission of Princeton University Press and the University of Cincinnati.
78 *Left, center and below:*
Palace of Nestor, Pylos.
– The Court of the Megaron. Reconstruction drawing by Piet de Jong, 1956.
– General view along axis of main building from northwest. P: Alison Frantz.
From Carl W. Blegen et al., *The Palace of Nestor at Pylos in Western Messenia,* Vol. I, Part 2. © 1966 by Princeton University Press. Reprinted by permission of Princeton University Press and the University of Cincinnati.
78–79 The Throne Room of the Megaron. Palace of Nestor, Pylos. Reconstruction drawing by Piet de Jong, 1956. From Carl W. Blegen et al., *The Palace of Nestor at Pylos in Western Messenia,* Vol. I, Part 1. © 1966 by Princeton University Press. Reprinted by permission of Princeton University Press and the University of Cincinnati.
79 *Right, top:* Decorative ceiling of a limestone burial chamber at Orchomenos, ca. 1300 B.C. NAM, Athens. P: Hirmer Fotoarchiv, Munich.
Right, center: Griffin and lion fresco from Queen's Hall. Palace of Nestor, Pylos. Reconstruction drawing by Piet de Jong. From *The Palace of Nestor,* Vol. II, *The Frescoes* by Mabel L. Lang. © 1969 by Princeton University Press. Reprinted by permission of Princeton University Press and the University of Cincinnati.
Right, bottom: Painted decoration of stucco floor of Throne Room. Palace of Nestor, Pylos. Reconstruction drawing by Piet de Jong. From Carl W. Blegen et al., *The Palace of Nestor at Pylos in Western Messenia,* Vol. I, Part 2. © 1966 by Princeton University Press. Reprinted by permission of Princeton University Press and the University of Cincinnati.
80 *Top right:* Clay tablet with Linear B script. *Center left:* Pot.
From the Palace of Nestor, Pylos. P: Alison Frantz. From *A Guide to the Palace of Nestor at Pylos,* © 1962 The University of Cincinnati. Reprinted by permission of Princeton University Press and the University of Cincinnati.
Bottom left: Pot fragment with Linear B script. From the Palace of Knossos. After 1400 B.C. AM, Heraklion. P: Hirmer Fotoarchiv, Munich.
81 Clay tablet with Linear B script from Pylos. ca. 1250 B.C. AM, Heraklion. P: Ekdotike Athenon S.A., Athens.
82 *Top right:* Gold head of a silver pin. From Grave III of Grave Circle A, Mycenae. 16th c. B.C. NAM, Athens. P: Hirmer Fotoarchiv, Munich.
Bottom, left to right:
Goddess holding a spray of wheat. Fresco fragment from Mycenae. NAM, Athens. P: Ekdotike Athenon S.A., Athens.
Goddess wearing Minoan dress. Gold figurine. From Grave Circle A, Mycenae. 16th c. B.C. NAM, Athens. P: Dimitrios Harissiadis, Athens.
Mother goddess with child. From a chamber tomb, Mycenae. 13th c. B.C. NAM, Athens. P: Dimitrios Harissiadis, Athens.
Votive female figurine from Tiryns. 1400–1200 B.C. Louvre, Paris. P: Réunion des Musées Nationaux, Paris.
83 *Left:* "The Lady of Philakopi." Paint-

ed terracotta statuette. From Philakopi, around 1200 B.C. AM, Melos. P: Erich Lessing/Magnum, Paris.
Center: Horned god. Bronze statuette from a sanctuary at Enkomi, Cyprus. 12th c. B.C. Cyprus Museum, Nicosia. P: Ekdotike Athenon S.A., Athens.
Right: Ivory triad of figures. From Mycenae, 15th c. B.C. NAM, Athens. P: Hirmer Fotoarchiv, Munich.

84 *Center:* Ground plans of Mycenaean megaron (left) and archaic temple (right). Artwork Franz Coray.
Bottom left: Artemis. Detail of a handle of the "François-Vase," by the Kleitas Painter. From Chiusi, Italy, around 570 B.C. AM, Florence. P: Alinari, Florence.
Bottom right: Two priestesses. Golden signet ring from Mycenae. NAM, Athens. P: Hirmer Fotoarchiv, Munich.

85 Lion-headed demons. Golden signet-ring from Tiryns. 15th c. B.C. NAM, Athens. P: Hirmer Fotoarchiv, Munich.

86 *Top right:* Painted limestone head of a woman. Mycenae, 14th–13th c. B.C. NAM, Athens. P: Hirmer Fotoarchiv, Munich.
Center row, left to right:
1, 2, and 4: Heads of gold and niello. From Propylon and Ramp 59, Palace of Nestor, Pylos. NAM, Athens. P: Dimitrios Harissiadis, Athens.
3: Clay head from Asine. 12th c. B.C. AM, Nauplia. P: Dimitrios Harissiadis, Athens.
Bottom left: Lady from a fresco from Tiryns. Reconstruction. NAM, Athens. P: Ekdotike Athenon S.A., Athens.
Bottom center: Woman. Fresco fragment from the Palace of Tiryns. 13th c. B.C. NAM, Athens. P: Hirmer Fotoarchiv, Munich.
Bottom right: Two women on a veranda. Fresco fragment from Mycenae. 15th c. B.C. NAM, Athens. P: Hirmer Fotoarchiv, Munich.

87 *Left:* Ivory statuette of a woman. From a grave in Prosymna, near Mycenae. NAM, Athens. P: Dimitrios Harissiadis, Athens.
Right: Ivory head from a shrine of Mycenae. 13th c. B.C. P: Ekdotike Athenon S.A., Athens.

88 Rhyton. Terracotta. From Karphi, 1200–1000 B.C. AM, Heraklion. P: Dimitrios Harissiadis, Athens.

89 Olive trees. P: Leonard von Matt, Buochs.

90 *Top left:* Cypro-Mycenaean krater from Enkomi, Cyprus. Clay. 13th c. B.C. Cyprus Museum, Nicosia. Published by permission of the Director of Antiquities and the Cyprus Museum.
Top right: Ostrich-egg jar. From Grave Circle A, Mycenae. 16th c. B.C. NAM, Athens.
Below left: Cylindrical seal stone. 14th–13th c. B.C. P: The Pierpont Morgan Library, New York.
Bottom right: Odysseus and companions blinding the giant Cyclops. Argive vase. P: Mansell Collection, London.

91 *Top left:* Egyptian oinochoe. 15th c. B.C. Musée Borély, Marseille.
Top center: Carved lid of a pyxis. Ivory. From Ugarit, Syria, 14th–13th c. B.C. Louvre, Paris.
Top right: Jason. Red-figure kylix. Vatican Museums, Rome.
Bottom center: Odysseus. Detail of a stamnos by the Siren Painter. From Vulci, Italy, 490–480 B.C. British Museum. P: Michael Holford, Loughton.
Bottom right: Telemachus and Penelope. Attic skyphos from Chiusi, Italy. 460–450 B.C. Museo Civico, Chiusi.

92 *Bottom, left to right:*
Sardonyx seal stone from Vaphio. ca. 1500 B.C. NAM, Athens.
Head with boar's tusk helmet. See page 5.
Carved grave stele showing a chariot. From Grave V of Grave Circle A, Mycenae. NAM, Athens.
All P: Hirmer Fotoarchiv, Munich.

93 *Top:* Bearded soldiers. From the so-called Warrior Vase from Mycenae. Around 1200 B.C. NAM, Athens. P: Hirmer Fotoarchiv, Munich.
Bottom right: Bronze armor and boar's tusk helmet. From a chamber grave near Dendra-Mideia. 15th c. B.C. AM, Nauplia. P: Dimitrios Harissiadis, Athens.

94 *Top, left to right:*
Gold handle of a bronze sword. From Grave 36, Necropolis of Zapher Papura near Knossos. ca. 1450–1400 B.C. AM, Heraklion.
Gold handle of a sword. From Grave Δ of Grave Circle B, Mycenae. 16th c. B.C. NAM, Athens.
Both P: Hirmer Fotoarchiv, Munich.
Gold signet showing a battle scene. From Grave IV of Grave Circle A, Mycenae. ca. 1580–1500 B.C. NAM, Athens. P: Dr. Ingo Pini, Archiv des CMS, Marburg.
Bottom left: Painted shield from a wall painting at Mycenae. 13th c. B.C. P: Ekdotike Athenon S.A., Athens.
Bottom center: Gold shield from Pylos. NAM, Athens. P: Hirmer Fotoarchiv, Munich.
Bottom right: Duel. Gold signet from Grave III of Grave Circle A, Mycenae. ca. 1580–1500 B.C. NAM, Athens. P: Dr. Ingo Pini, Archiv des CMS, Marburg.

95 *Top row, left to right:*
Gold handle of a ceremonial sword from Staphylos. ca. 1500 B.C. P: Hirmer Fotoarchiv, Munich.
Gold handle of a bronze dagger. From Grave IV of Grave Circle A, Mycenae. 16th c. B.C. P: Dimitrios Harissiadis, Athens.
Dagger with gold handle and bronze blade. Pylos. ca. 1500 B.C. P: Hirmer Fotoarchiv, Munich.
Bronze dagger blade showing nautiluses. Pylos ca. 1500 B.C. P: Hirmer. These four from NAM, Athens.
Bottom left: Duel. Ametyhst seal stone B.C. AM, Pylos. P: Dr. Ingo Pini, Archiv des CMS, Marburg.
Bottom right: Detail of a bronze dagger blade. From Grave IV of Grave Circle A, Mycenae. ca. 1570–1550 B.C. NAM, Athens. P: Hirmer Fotoarchiv, Munich.

96 *Center left:* Approach to Gate VI S, Troy. From Carl W. Blegen et al., *Troy*, Vol. III, Part 2. © 1953 by Princeton University Press. Reprinted by permission of Princeton University Press and the University of Cincinnati.
Bottom left: Remains of a human skeleton found in Stratum 4 at Troy. From Carl W. Blegen et al., *Troy*, Vol. IV, Part 2. © 1958 by Princeton University Press. Reprinted by permission of Princeton University Press and the University of Cincinnati.

96–97 *Top:* Mound at Hissarlik, Turkey. P: Fulvio Roiter, Lido di Venezia.

97 *Center:* Plan of Troy. Franz Coray after W. Dörpfeld.
Bottom: House VII (Θ) of Troy VIIa. Floor at east end showing four pithoi *in situ*. From Carl W. Blegen et al., *Troy*, Vol. IV, Part 2. © 1958 by Princeton University Press. Reprinted by permission of Princeton University Press and the University of Cincinnati.

98 *Top row, left to right:*
Hephaestus at his smithy. From black-figure amphora. British Museum. P: Michael Holford, Loughton.
Athena. From a red-figure amphora by the Berlin Painter. From Etruria. Antikenmuseum, Basel. P: Claire Niggli.
Poseidon. From a black-figure amphora by the Amasis Painter. From Vulci, 540–530 B.C. Bibliothèque Nationale, Cabinet des Médailles, Paris. P: Giraudon, Paris.
Hera. From a krater. 5th c. B.C. Museo di Spina, Ferrara. P: Hirmer Fotoarchiv, Munich.
Center left: Judgment of Paris. From a red-figure pyxis by the Penthesilea Painter. From Cumae, Italy, 465–460 B.C. Metropolitan Museum, New York, Rogers Fund, 1907.
Center right: Fight between Trojans and Greeks. From a black-figure Psykter-amphora by the Inscription Painter. Chalcidian, ca. 540 B.C. Felton Bequest, 1956. National Gallery of Victoria, Melbourne.
Bottom left: Helen pours out a drink for Priam. From a red-figure plate. Museo Municipale, Tarquinia. P: Alinari, Florence.
Bottom center: Menelaus. See p. 65.
Bottom right: Achilles receiving Odysseus' and Ajax's legation in presence of Patroclus. Detail of a red-figure skyphos. Early 5th c. B.C. Louvre, Paris. P: Maurice Chuzeville.

99 *Top row, left to right:*
Zeus. Detail of a black-figure cup from Vulci. ca. 540–530 B.C. British Museum.
Apollo with Artemis. Detail of a red-figure amphora from Vulci. 510–500 B.C. British Museum.
Aphrodite on a goose. From a kylix by the Pistoxenos Painter. From Camirus, 460 B.C. British Museum. P: Michael Holford, Loughton.
Ares. From the "François Vase" by the Kleitas Painter. From Chiusi, Italy, ca. 570 B.C. AM, Florence. P: Scala, Antella.
Center left: Achilles bandaging the wounded Patroclus. From a cup by the Sosias Painter. From Vulci, ca. 500 B.C. Staatliche Museen, Berlin. P: Bildarchiv Preussischer Kulturbesitz, Berlin.
Center right: Achilles mourning Briseis' departure. From a red-figure kylix from Vulci. 480–470 B.C. British Museum.
Bottom center: Odysseus and Diomedes surprising Dolon. See page 65.
Bottom right: Menelaus and Hector fighting over the body of Euphorbus. Polychrome plate from Camirus. ca. 600 B.C. British Museum. P: Michael Holford, Loughton.

100 *Top left:* Arming of Hector. From a red-figure amphora. Signed by Euthymides. From Vulci, ca. 510–500 B.C. Staatliche Antikensammlungen und Glyptothek, Munich.
Top right: Battle between Achilles and Hector. From a cup. 5th c. B.C. Vatican Museums. P: Alinari, Florence.
Center row, left to right:
Achilles slaying Penthesilea. From a black-figure amphora by the Exekias Painter. From Vulci, ca. 540 B.C. British Museum. P: Michael Holford, Loughton.
Achilles carrying Penthesilea's body. From a black-figure hydria by the Painter A of the "Leagros-Group." From Vulci, 510–500 B.C. British Museum.
Anthilochus and Achilles fighting Memnon. From a black-figure vase. 6th c. B.C. British Museum.
Ajax carrying Achilles' body. From a black-figure cup by the Phrynos Painter. From Vulci, ca. 540 B.C. Vatican Museums, Rome.
Bottom left: Ajax commits suicide by throwing himself on his sword. From a red-figure vase from Vulci. British Museum.
Bottom center: Achilles' armor given by Odysseus to Neoptolemus. From a red-figure cup by the Duris Painter. From Caere, ca. 490 B.C. Kunsthistorisches Museum, Vienna.
Bottom right: The Trojan Horse. Wall painting from Pompeii, Italy. NAM, Naples. P: Alinari, Florence.

101 *Top left:* Pyre of Patroclus. From a red-figure crater by the Dareios Painter. From Canosa, Italy, ca. 340–330 B.C. NAM, Naples. P: Soprintendenza alle Antichità di Napoli.
Top center: Funeral games in honor of Patroclus. Fragment of a black-figure Dinos by the Sophilos Painter. From Pharsalos, ca. 580 B.C. NAM, Athens. P: Ekdotike Athenon S.A., Athens.
Top right: Priam and Achilles. From a red-figure skyphos by the Brygos Painter. From Caere. Kunsthistorisches Museum, Vienna.
Center left: Nereids mourning Achilles' death. From a black-figure hydria by the Damos Painter. From Caere, ca. 550 B.C. Louvre, Paris. P: Réunion des Musées Nationaux, Paris.
Center right: Draw of Achilles' armor. From a red-figure cup by the Duris Painter. ca. 490 B.C. Kunsthistorisches Museum, Vienna.
Bottom left: Death of Priam. From a black-figure amphora from Vulci, ca. 550 B.C. British Museum.
Bottom center: Cassandra and Ajax. From a red-figure hydria by the Kleophrades Painter. From Nola, Italy, ca. 480 B.C. NAM, Naples. P: Soprintendenza alle Antichità di Napoli.
Bottom right: Menelaus meeting Helen for the first time. From a red-figure vase. 4th c. B.C. British Museum.

102 *Left:* Drawing of the fortress at Tiryns as it probably appeared in the 13th c. B.C. From Jacquetta Hawkes, *Atlas of Ancient Archaeology*, Rainbird Reference Books Ltd., London, 1974.
Center: Part of the citadel gateway at Tiryns. P: Hirmer Fotoarchiv, Munich.
Right: Mycenaean warrior. Ivory, from Delos. 1400–1200 B.C. AM, Delos.

103 *Left:* Gallery in the south defense wall at Tiryns. P: Hirmer Fotoarchiv, Munich.
Right: Smashed pottery as found in the Palace of Nestor, Pylos. Photo Alison Frantz. From Carl W. Blegen et al., *The Palace of Nestor at Pylos in Western Messenia*, Vol. I, Part 2. © 1966 by Princeton University Press. Reprinted by permission of Princeton University Press and the University of Cincinnati.

104 *Top:* Graffiti. *Center:* Frieze of a seal stone.
Both from Enkomi, Cyprus. From Claude F.A. Schaeffer, *Enkomi-Alasia*, Paris 1952, Tome I.

105 *Center right:* Heracles fighting Geryon. From a black-figure amphora, ca. 530 B.C. Bibliothèque Nationale, Cabinet des Médailles, Paris.
Bottom left: Sherd from Tiryns showing two soldiers. P: Deutsches Archäologisches Institut, Athens.

106 *Top right:* Mycenaean jug from Enkomi. Cyprus Museum, Nicosia. Published by permission of the Director of Antiquities and the Cyprus Museum.
Center: Carved longside of an ivory box from Enkomi, Cyprus. 1300–1100 B.C. British Museum.

107 *Left:* Bronze statuette of the "Ingot-God" from Enkomi, Cyprus. 12th c. B.C. Cyprus Museum, Nicosia. Published by permission of the Director of Antiquities and the Cyprus Museum.
Center, top: Clay figurine of a goddess. From Karphi, ca. 1100–1000 B.C. AM, Heraklion. P: Hirmer Fotoarchiv, Munich.
Right: Two vultures. Upper part of a royal gold scepter from a tomb at Kourion. 11th c. B.C. Cyprus Museum, Nicosia. P: Ekdotike Athenon S.A., Athens.

108 *Left:* Drawing of a ship from the relief at Medinet Habu.

108–109 Colored reconstruction of the relief at Medinet Habu, Egypt, showing the naval battle between Egyptians and Philistines. XXth Dynasty (1192–1160 B.C.).
Both from Yigael Yadin, *Art of Warfare in Biblical Lands*, Vol. II, International Publishing Co. Ltd., 1963.

110 *Left:* Fibulae from Kerameikos. From Kraiker and Kübler, *Kerameikos: Ergebnisse der Ausgrabungen*, 1939.
Bottom right: Grave of young girl from the Agora. ca. 1000 B.C. Agora Museum, Athens. P: Edwin Smith, Saffron Walden.

111 *Top left:* Pins and fibulae from Athens. From *Hesperia*, Journal of the American School of Classical Studies at Athens.
Top right: Protogeometric toy horse from Athens. P: Courtesy of *Archaiologike Deltion*.
Bottom left: Protogeometric vase. 1000 B.C. British Museum. P: Michael Holford, Loughton.
Bottom right: Clay statuette of a centaur from Lefkandi. From *Annual of the British School at Athens*.

112–113 Harmodius and Aristogiton. Roman copy of the group by Kritios and Nesiotes. Marble. 477–476 B.C. NAM, Naples. P: G. Tomsich, Spectrum Color Library, London.

114 *Above:* Lions of Delos. P: Robert Tobler, Lucerne.
Bottom left: Jumping weights from Corinth. P: René Burri/Magnum, Paris.
Bottom center: Long jumping. From a neck-amphora, ca. 6th c. B.C. British Museum. P: Michael Holford, Loughton.
Bottom right: Runners. From a Panathenaic amphora. From a Panathenaic amphora by the Euphiletos Painter. 500 B.C. British Museum. P: Michael Holford, Loughton.

115 *Top:* View of the sanctuary at Samothrace. P: A. Kalogeropoulou, Athens.
Bottom left and center:
Athletes. From a prize vase by the Euphiletos Painter. From Vulci, 520 B.C. British Museum.
Boxers. From an amphora by the Leagros Group, 510–500 B.C. British Museum.
Both P: Michael Holford, Loughton.
Bottom right: Earliest intact prize amphora from the Panathenaic games. ca. 566–562 B.C. British Museum.

116 *Left, above:* Apollo pouring libations. Interior of a white kylix from Delphi. ca. 470 B.C. AM, Delphi. P: René Burri/Magnum, Paris.
Left, below: Sacred Way, Delphi. P: Ekdotike Athenon S.A., Athens.
Right, top: "The Charioteer." See page 9.
Right, center: Ruins of the great Temple of Apollo, Delphi. P: Ekdotike Athenon S.A.
Right, below: Athenian treasury at Delphi. P: Michael Vickers, Oxford.

117 Sanctuary at Delphi. P: Ekdotike Athenon S.A., Athens.

118 *Top:* Greek landscape. P: Henri Cartier-Bresson/Magnum, Paris.
Bottom left: Cadmus slaying the dragon. See page 65.
Bottom right: The "Municipal Laws" of Gortyn. P: Charles Harbutt/Magnum, Paris.

119 *Top:* Warrior in combat. Detail of an amphora from Melos. 625–620 B.C. NAM, Athens. P: Erich Lessing/Magnum, Paris.
Below left: Birth of Ericthonius. From a red-figure amphora. ca. 465 B.C. Staatliche Antikensammlung und Glyptothek, Munich. P: C.H. Krüger-Moessner.
Below right: View of Argos. P: H. Wagner, Heidelberg.

120 *Above:* A hammered gold bowl dedicated by the sons of Cypselus at Olympia. ca. 600 B.C.
Below: Harmodius and Aristogiton on a late red-figure oinochoe. 6th c. B.C.
Both Museum of Fine Arts, Boston.

121 The Electra Gate, Thebes. 8th c. B.C. P: Erich Lessing/Magnum, Paris.

122 *Top:* Marble bust of Solon. NAM, Naples. P: Anderson-Giraudon, Paris.
Center left: Reconstruction drawing of the Stoa Basileios, Athens. Franz Coray after W.B. Dinsmoor Jr.
Bottom right: Painted terracotta plaque showing clay miners. From Laurion, 7th–6th c. B.C. Staatliche Museen, East Berlin.

123 *Left:* Herdsman watching his flock. Black-figure Kyathos signed by Théozotos. 6th c. B.C. Louvre, Paris. P: Giraudon, Paris.
Right: Stone inscription of a Solonic text from the early 5th c. B.C. Epigraphic Museum, Athens. P: TAP Service, Athens.

124 *Left:* Perseus and the Minotaur. Attic

black-figure amphora. ca. 550–540 B.C. Ashmolean Museum, Oxford.
Right: The so-called "Man with three bodies." From the Old Temple of Athena, Athens. Acropolis Museum, Athens. P: Ekdotike Athenon S.A., Athens.
125 *Left:* Theseus and Antiope. Marble, from the Apollo Temple, Eretria. ca. 510 B.C. AM, Chalkis. P: Jean Mazenod, from *L'Art Grec,* Editions d'Art Lucien Mazenod, Paris, 1972.
Right: Athena mounting her chariot. From a black-figure amphora by the Priam Painter. From Cerveteri, Italy, late 6th c. B.C. Ashmolean Museum, Oxford.
126 *Above left:* Oinochoe with earliest Greek inscription. From a grave near Dipylon, ca. 740 B.C. NAM, Athens.
Bottom right: Decree of Salamis. 6th c. B.C. Epigraphical Museum, Athens.
Both P: Deutsches Archäologisches Institut, Athens.
127 *Top:* Greek rock inscription from Thera. 7th c. B.C. From H. Roehl, *Inscriptiones Graecae antiquissimae,* Berlin 1882.
Right: Cup from Pithecusae, Ischia. 720–710 B.C. P: Dr. Giorgio Buchner, Porto d'Ischia.
Bottom: Earliest extant example of a Greek chronological table. From the Arundel Collection presented by Lord Henry Howard, 1667. Ashmolean Museum, Oxford.
128 *Left:* Rhapsode. From a neck amphora by the Keophrades Painter. From Vulci, Italy, 490–480 B.C. British Museum. P: Michael Holford, Loughton.
Bottom: Girl picking apples. From a fragmentary cup by Sotades. From Athens, early 5th c. B.C. British Museum.
129 *Top:* Lion from the north frieze of the Siphnian Treasury, Delphi. ca. 525 B.C. AM, Delphi. P: Ekdotike Athenon S.A., Athens.
Center left: Fight on board a ship at sea. Detail of a funerary vase. 8th c. B.C. Metropolitan Museum of Art, Fletcher Fund, New York.
Center right: Zeus fighting Typhon. From a hydria from Vulci. 6th c. B.C. Museum Antiker Kleinkunst, Munich.
130 *Left to right:*
The Dipylon Head. Marble. 620–610 B.C. NAM, Athens.
Youth of the "Apollo type." Marble kouros. ca. 580 B.C. Metropolitan Museum of Art, Fletcher Fund, New York.
Marble kouros, called "Kroisos." From Anavyssos, ca. 525 B.C. NAM, Athens. P: Ekdotike Athenon S.A., Athens.
Marble kouros of Aristodikos. From Anavyssos, ca. 500 B.C. NAM, Athens. P: Deutsches Archäologisches Institut, Athens.
"Auxerre goddess." Limestone statuette, mid-7th c. B.C. Louvre, Paris. P: Réunion des Musées Nationaux, Paris.
The "Kore of Antenor." From the Acropolis, ca. 525 B.C. Acropolis Museum, Athens. P: Ekdotike Athenon S.A.
131 Head of the Kore no. 674. From the Acropolis, ca. 500 B.C. Acropolis Museum, Athens. P: Ekdotike Athenon S.A.
132 *Top left:* Imported Egyptian statuette. Bronze.
Top right: Imported Assyrian statuette. Bronze.
Both from the Heraion, Samos. ca. 700–630 B.C. AM, Samos. P: Deutsches Archäologisches Institut, Athens.
Center left: Bronze griffin from the sloping shoulder of a caldron. ca. 650 B.C. British Museum.
Bottom left: Geometric beetle from Olympia. Bronze, ca. 700 B.C. Ashmolean Museum, Oxford.
133 *Top left:* Fragment of a vase showing Silenus persecuting a woman. Terracotta by the Sophilos Painter. From the acropolis of Lindos. From Chr. Blinkenberg, *Lindos: Fouilles de l'Acropole 1902–1914.* Berlin 1931.
Top center: Detail of a black-figure krater by the Sophilos Painter. From Athens, ca. 570 B.C. British Museum.
Top right: Detail of a Geometric krater by the Analatos Painter. Early 7th c. B.C. Staatliche Antikensammlung und Glyptothek, Munich.
Center right: Winged sphinx from a Cretan pithos. 7th c. B.C. Ashmolean Museum, Oxford.
Center left: Bronze bowl of Syrian workmanship from Olympia. Late 8th c. B.C. Ashmolean Museum.
Bottom row, left to right:
Krater from the Dipylon cemetery. National Archaeological Museum, Athens. P: Deutsches Archäologisches Institut, Athens.
Proto-Corinthian aryballos. Late 7th c. B.C. Ashmolean Museum.
Transitional Corinthian olpe. 640–625 B.C. Ashmolean Museum.
Corinthian alabastron. ca. 625–600 B.C. Fitzwilliam Museum, Cambridge.
134 *Left:* Stag feeding. Electrum coin from Ephesus, ca. 600 B.C. British Museum. P: Michael Holford, Loughton.
Center: Lion's head. Electrum coin from Smyrna, ca. 575 B.C. British Museum. From G.K. Jenkins and H. Küthmann, *Münzen der Griechen,* Office du Livre, Fribourg, 1972.
Right: Lion devouring a bull. Tetradrachmon from Acanthus. British Museum. P: Michael Holford.
135 *Top left and right:* Obverse and reverse of a silver stater from Aegina showing a turtle and incuse pattern. ca. 560 B.C.
Top below: Reverse of an electrum stater from Halicarnassus. ca. 800 B.C.
All from Colin M. Kraay, *Archaic and Classical Greek Coins,* University of California Press, Berkeley and Los Angeles, 1976.
Below left: Heracles kneels stringing a bow. Coin from Thebes, Egypt. 446–426 B.C.
Below center: Lion's head. Didrachmo from Cnidus.
Below right: Parsley leaf. Didrachmon from Selinus.
These three: British Museum. P: Michael Holford, Loughton.
136 *Far left:* Small votive Hispano-Punic razor from Puig des Molins, Ibiza. 5th c. B.C. NAM, Madrid. P: E. Domínguez, Madrid.
Left below: Polychrome glass mask from Carthage. Museum of Carthage.
Center, top: Virile mask. Bronze, from Montsérié, France, 3rd–2nd c. B.C. Musée Massey, Tarbes. P: YAN, Toulouse.
Right, top: Bronze krater of Vix, France. Late 6th c. B.C. Musée Archéologique, Châtillon-sur-Seine. P: Lauros-Giraudon, Paris.
Right, below: The Northampton amphora from Castle Ashby. P: Courtesy of R.A. Wilkins, Institute of Archaeology, Oxford.
137 *Top:* Scythian bronze elk's head plaque from Nymphaeum. 5th c. B.C. Ashmolean Museum, Oxford.
Center right: Tribute bearers. Relief of the Palace wall at Persepolis. P: The Oriental Institute of the University of Chicago.
Bottom left: A sitting nymph. Tetradrachmon from Cyrene, 525–480 B.C. British Museum.
Bottom right: Neit and child Horus. Bronze, from Sais, Egypt. Late period. Ashmolean Museum, Oxford.
138 *Left above:* King Darius enthroned. Relief from the Palace at Persepolis. Late 6th–early 5th c. B.C.
Left below: King Darius hunting. Impression from a cylinder seal found in Thebes, Egypt. 6th c. B.C.
Both P: Holle Bildarchiv, Baden-Baden.
138–139 Audience hall of the Palace at Persepolis. Late 6th–early 5th c. B.C. P: Holle Bildarchiv, Baden-Baden.
139 *Right, above:* Fluted vase with ibex handles. Silver and gold.
Right, below: Gold phial. AM, Teheran.
Both P: Holle Bildarchiv, Baden-Baden.
140 *Center right:* A messenger reports a disaster to King Darius. Detail of a krater. From Apulia, Italy, ca. 350 B.C. NAM, Naples. P: Soprintendenza alle Antichità di Napoli.
Bottom left: Archaic kouros from Cyrene. P: Michael Vickers, Oxford.
141 *Center left:* Fight between a Greek and a Persian. From a kylix of the 5th c. B.C. The Royal Scottish Museum, Edinburgh.
Center right, above: A Corinthian helmet from Olympia. Bronze, 490 B.C. AM, Olympia. P: Ekdotike Athenon S.A., Athens.
Center right, below: Persian helmet from Olympia. Bronze, 490 B.C. AM, Olympia. P: Deutsches Archäologisches Institut, Athens.
Bottom left: Arms from Marathon. British Museum. P: Michael Holford, Loughton.
Bottom right: Mound at Marathon. P: Deutsches Archäologisches Institut, Athens.
142 Bronze statuette of a hoplite. From Dodona, late 6th c. B.C. Staatliche Museen, Berlin. P: Isolde Luckert.
143 Persian archers. Detail of the polychrome brick relief from the Darius Palace at Susa, Persia. 4th c. B.C. Louvre, Paris. P: Erich Lessing/Magnum, Paris.
144 *Left:* The site of the battle of Thermopylae. P: Henri Cartier-Bresson/Magnum, Paris.
Right: Hoplite wearing a cloak. Bronze statuette, ca. 490 B.C. Wadsworth Atheneum, Morgan Collection, Hartford.
145 *Center:* War ship. Detail of an Attic kylix. 540 B.C. British Museum. P: Michael Holford, Loughton.
Bottom right: Column drums from the earlier Parthenon, Athens. P: Elsevier Publishing Projects S.A., Lausanne.
146 *Top:* Themistocles. Marble bust, ca. 470 B.C. Museo Ostiense, Ostia.
Center left: Pythia, priestess of Apollo at Delphi. From a red-figure plate. Staatliche Museen, Berlin.
Center right: Warship. Tetradrachmon from Zancle, Italy, 493–489 B.C. British Museum. From G.K. Jenkins and H. Küthmann, *Münzen der Griechen,* Office du Livre, Fribourg, 1972.
147 *Left:* Part of the wall of Themistocles at Athens. P: NAM, Athens.
Center: Tribute bearers. See page 137.
Right: Ostraka. P: American School of Classical Studies, Athens.
148–149 Sacred owl of Athens. Silver tetradrachmon, ca. 460–450 B.C. British Museum. From G.K. Jenkins and H. Küthmann, *Münzen der Griechen,* Office du Livre, Fribourg, 1972.
150 *Left to right:*
Athena. Tetradrachmon from Athens, ca. 460–450 B.C. Cabinet des Médailles, Bibliothèque Nationale, Paris. P: Giraudon, Paris.
Lyre. Tetradrachmon of the Chalcidian League, ca. 410–400 B.C.
Head of Helios. Tetradrachmon from Rhodes, 408 B.C.
Ram's head. Stater from Melos, 420–416 B.C.
All British Museum. From G.H. Jenkins and H. Küthmann, *Münzen der Griechen,* Office du Livre, Fribourg, 1972.
151 *Top:* Aerial view of the harbor area of Delos. P: Rev. Prof. R. Schoder, S.J., Chicago.
Center row, left to right:
Torch. Tetradrachmon from Amphipolis, ca. 400 B.C.
Female head. 1/6 stater from Phocaea, ca. 460 B.C.
Ox. Tetradrachmon from Samos. 454 B.C.
All British Museum. From G.K. Jenkins and H. Küthmann, *Münzen der Griechen,* Office du Livre, Fribourg, 1972.
152 *Left:* Athena and Hera. Marble relief symbolizing treaty between Athens and Samos. From the Acropolis, 403–402 B.C. Acropolis Museum, Athens. P: Ekdotike Athenon S.A., Athens.
152–153 Cape Sunion. P: Kodansha Ltd., Tokyo.
154 *Center left:* Boy leading a pair of horses. Attic red-figure skyphos by Epiktetos. ca. 510–500 B.C. Ashmolean Museum, Oxford.
Below left: Drinking vessel in the shape of a dog's head. 5th c. B.C. Ashmolean Museum, Oxford.
Bottom right: Going to the market. Attic red-figure pelike by the Pig Painter. ca. 470–460 B.C. Fitzwilliam Museum, Cambridge.
155 *Top:* Olive-pressing. From a black-figure cup. Museum of Fine Arts, Boston.
Right: Reconstruction drawing of a silver-mining installation. Franz Coray after H.W. Catling.
Bottom: Jung hunter (Cephalus?). From a red-figure lekythos by the Pan Painter. From Gela, Italy, ca. 470 B.C. Museum of Fine Arts, Boston.
156 *Top:* Sheaf of wheat from a relief at Eleusis. P: Roger-Viollet, Paris.
Center left: Sacrifice. From an Attic red-figure krater. Museum für Vor- und Frühgeschichte, Frankfurt.
Center right: Artemis attended by devotees. Votive relief from the shrine of Artemis, Brauron. 4th c. B.C. P: Ekdotike Athenon S.A., Athens.
157 Parthenon of the shrine of Artemis, Brauron. P: Ekdotike Athenon S.A., Athens.
158 *Top left:* Herm of Aspasia. Found in Torre di Chiaruccia, Italy. Vatican Museums, Rome.
Top right: Bust of Pericles. Marble, 499–429 B.C. British Museum. P: Michael Holford, Loughton.
Center left: Aerial view of the harbor of Piraeus. P: Ekdotike Athenon S.A., Athens.
Bottom left: Plan of fortifications, Piraeus and Athens. Franz Coray after J. Travlos.
159 *Top:* Heracles. From the east pediment of the Parthenon, Athens. British Museum. P: Michael Holford, Loughton.
Right: Centaur treads down a lapith. Relief. Metope from the Parthenon, Athens. British Museum. P: Michael Holford, Loughton.
Bottom: Plan of Athens in Pericles' day. Franz Coray after J. Travlos.
160–161 Reconstruction drawing of the Acropolis in Athens ca. mid-5th c. B.C. Artwork Franz Coray.
160 *Below, left to right:*
General view of the Acropolis. P: Ekdotike Athenon S.A., Athens.
Head of Zeus. See page 2.
The Erechtheum, Athens. 421–409 B.C. P: Gerry Clyde/Michael Holford Library, Loughton.
Athena Promachos. Bronze statuette from the Acropolis. ca. 450 B.C. NAM, Athens. P: Ekdotike Athenon S.A., Athens.
161 *Below, left to right:*
The Parthenon, Athens. 447–432 B.C.
Artemis. Detail of a relief on the eastern side of the Acropolis.
Temple of Athena Nike, Athens. 5th c. B.C.
All three P: Ekdotike Athenon S.A., Athens.
The Propylaea, Athens. P: Hirmer Fotoarchiv, Munich.
162–163 The Acropolis seen from southwest with the theater of Herodes Atticus in the foreground. P: Ekdotike Athenon S.A., Athens.
164 *Left:* Priestess of Dionysus with attendants dispensing wine. From an Attic red-figure stamnos by the Villa Giulia Painter. From Gela, Italy, ca. 450 B.C. Ashmolean Museum, Oxford.
Right: Playing boys. From a red-figure oinochoe. 5th c. B.C. NAM, Athens. P: Ekdotike Athenon S.A., Athens.
165 *Left:* Dionysus. From a red-figure amphora from Vulci, ca. 500 B.C. Staatliche Antikensammlung und Glyptothek, Munich. P: Colorphoto Hans Hinz, Allschwil.
Center: Drunken Dionysus with two satyrs. From a red-figure oinochoe. 5th c. B.C. NAM, Athens. P: Ekdotike Athenon S.A., Athens.
Right: Woman and child folding the *peplos.* Marble relief from the Parthenon frieze. Late 5th c. B.C. British Museum. P: Michael Holford, Loughton.
166–167 Riders of the Panathenaic procession. Marble relief of the Parthenon frieze. 447–435 B.C. British Museum. P: Michael Holford, Loughton.
168 *Top right:* Birth of Athena. Red-figure pelike, ca. 450 B.C. British Museum.
Bottom: The twelve Olympians. Relief from Tarentum, Italy. P: F. Bruckmann KG Bildarchiv, Munich.
169 *Far left:* Athena. Marble. From the west pediment of the Temple of Aphaia. ca. 500–480 B.C. Staatliche Antikensammlung und Glyptothek, Munich. P: Jean Mazenod, from *L'Art Grec,* Editions d'Art Lucien Mazenod, Paris, 1972.
Top left: Athena flying her owl. Bronze figurine. 5th c. B.C. Metropolitan Museum of Art, Harris Brisbane Dick Fund, New York.
Top right: Mourning Athena. Marble relief from the Acropolis. ca. 460 B.C. Acropolis Museum, Athens. P: Ekdotike Athenon S.A., Athens.
Bottom left: Part of a relief. See page 168 bottom.
Bottom right: Athena. Detail of a red-figure hydria by the Meidias Painter. From Ruvo, Italy, ca. 420–410 B.C. Badisches Landesmuseum, Karlsruhe. P: Werner Mohrbach.
170 *Top left:* Plan of the Temple of Hephaestus, Agora, Athens.
Top right: Second Temple of Hera (so-called Temple of Neptune), Paestum, Italy. Mid-5th c. B.C. P: Leonard von Matt, Buochs.
Center left: Temple of Hera, Olympia. 6th c. B.C. P: Michael Vickers, Oxford.
Bottom left: Modern barn built of mud-brick. Arcadia. P: Michael Vickers, Oxford.
171 *Left row, top to bottom:*
Second Temple of Hera, Paestum, Italy. Detail. P: Leonard von Matt, Buochs.
Temple of Athena Nike, Athens. Detail. P: Michael Holford, Loughton.
Erechtheum, Athens. Detail.
Temple of Hephaestus, Athens. Detail.
Modern reconstruction of the Temple of the Great Gods, Samothrace.
Platform of the Temple of Apollo, Delphi. Late 6th c. B.C.
All P: Michael Vickers, Oxford.
Right, top to bottom:
Interior of Second Temple of Hera, Paestum, Italy. P: Leonard von Matt, Buochs.
Wall of Siphnian Treasury, Delphi. 6th c. B.C.
Detail of 5th century Temple at Eleusis.
Both P: Michael Vickers, Oxford.
172 *Left:* Northwest side of the Agora, Athens. P: Ekdotike Athenon S.A., Athens.
Top right: Nike. Marble. From the Agora, Athens. ca. 410–400 B.C. P: Jean Mazenod, from *L'Art Grec,* Editions d'Art Lucien Mazenod, Paris, 1972.
Center right: House of Simon. Artwork Franz Coray.
Bottom right: Boundary marker from the Agora, Athens. P: American School of Classical Studies, Athens.
172–173 Plan of the Agora, Athens. By J. Travlos. Courtesy American School of Classical Studies, Athens.
173 *Top:* Priest pouring a libation over an altar. From a red-figure cup by the Pan Painter. From Cerveteri. Ashmolean Museum, Oxford.
Center left: Metrological relief showing various standard measures. 5th c. B.C. Ashmolean Museum, Oxford.
Center right: Panathenaic way. Agora,

Athens. P: David Hurn/Magnum, Paris.
Below left: Stoa Basileios. See page 122.
Below right: Water clock. P: American School of Classical Studies, Athens.

174 *Top right:* Butcher. From a black-figure oinochoe. Late 6th c. B.C. Museum of Fine Arts, H.L. Pierce Fund, Boston.
Below left: Blacksmith's shop. From an Attic black-figure amphora. ca. 520–510 B.C. Museum of Fine Arts, H.L. Pierce Fund, Boston.
Below right: Carpenter. From an Attic red-figure hydria by the Gallatin Painter. From Gela, Italy, ca. 490 B.C. Museum of Fine Arts, Francis Bartlett Fund, Boston.

175 *Top:* School teaching. From a red-figure cup by the Duris Painter. From Cerveteri, Italy, ca. 480 B.C. Staatliche Museen, Berlin. P: Bildarchiv Preussischer Kulturbesitz, Berlin.
Center above, left: Armorer making a helmet. From an Attic red-figure cup by the Anthiphoa Painter. From Orvieto, Italy, ca. 480 B.C. Ashmolean Museum, Oxford.
Center above, right: Vase painters at work. From an Attic red-figure krater by the Komaris Painter. ca. 430–425 B.C. Ashmolean Museum, Oxford.
Center below, left: Men weighing merchandise. From a black-figure amphora. ca. 550–530 B.C. Metropolitan Museum of Art, New York.
Center below, right: Shoemaker at work. From a black-figure pelike by the Eucharides Painter. From Rhodes, early 5th c. B.C. Ashmolean Museum, Oxford.
Bottom: Sculptor at work. From a red-figure bowl. 5th c. B.C. National Museum, Copenhagen.

176 *Left and right:*
– Bronze foundry
– Bronze sculptors
From a red-figure drinking cup by the Foundry Painter. From Vulci, Italy, ca. 490–480 B.C. Staatliche Museen, Berlin. P: Bildarchiv Preussischer Kulturbesitz, Berlin.

177 *Left:* Apollo from Piraeus. See page 8.
Center: Mould for Archaic bronze statue. P: American School of Classical Studies, Athens.
Right above: Casting pit for a bronze statue. Drawing by Franz Coray after J. Travlos.
Right below: Casting pit for a bronze statue near the Temple of Apollo Patroos. 6th c. B.C. P: American School of Classical Studies, Athens.

178 *Center left:* Phidias' workshop. Outside and inside view. Model. P: Deutsches Archäologisches Institut, Athens.
Bottom, left to right:
– Marble feet
– Marble head
– Part of bronze wig
Fragments of an acrolithic statue. From Punta Alice, Italy, ca. 470 B.C. National Museum, Reggio Calabria. P: Leonard von Matt, Buochs.
Artist painting a statue. Fragment of a red-figure krater from Apulia, Italy, early 5th c. B.C. Metropolitan Museum of Art, Rogers Fund, New York.

179 *Top left:* Head of Zeus from Cyrene, Libya. Artwork by Franz Coray.
Top right: Phidias's Zeus on Roman coin of Elis. 2nd c. A.D. AM, Florence.
Center right: Reconstruction drawing of Phidias' workshop with statue of Zeus. Artwork Franz Coray after A. Nallwitz.
Bottom center: Bone chisels from Phidias' workshop. P: Deutsches Archäologisches Institut, Athens.
Bottom right: Base of an Athenian black cup with a graffito of the name of Phidias. From Olympia. Archaeological Museum, Olympia. P: Deutsches Archäologisches Institut, Athens.

180 *Left, above:* Vase fragment by the Achilles Painter. Mid-5th c. B.C.
Left, below: Vase fragment by the Pan Painter. Late 5th c. B.C.
Center: Youth carrying couch and table. From an Attic red-figure pelike by the Pan Painter. From Gela, Italy, ca. 480 B.C.
Right: Woman holding perfume vase and alabastron. A youth by a tomb. Attic white-ground lekythos by the Achilles Painter. From near Laurion, ca. 440 B.C.
All Ashmolean Museum, Oxford.

181 *Top:* Seated woman doing her hair. Older woman holding a cosmetic and a ribbon. Attic red-figure amphoriskos by the Eretria Painter. ca. 430 B.C.
Right: Vase fragment by the Eretria Painter. Mid-5th c. B.C.
Both Ashmolean Museum, Oxford.

182 *Left:* An "epinetron" by the Eretria Painter depicting Alcestis in her bridal chamber. ca. 425 B.C. NAM, Athens. P: Ekdotike Athenon S.A., Athens.
Bottom right: Women winding wool. White-ground pyixis from Attica. ca. 460–450 B.C. British Museum. P: Jean Mazenod, from *L'Art Grec,* Editions d'Art Lucien Mazenod, Paris, 1972.

183 *Top:* Toilet scene by the Eretria Painter.
Bottom center: Women at a fountain. From a black-figure hydria from Vulci. ca. 520 B.C.
Right, above: Baby feeder. Glazed terracotta.
Right, below: Child in a "potty chair" with a rattle. Vase painting. From the Agora, Athens.
All British Museum. P: Michael Holford, Loughton.

184 *Above:* Bronze banqueter, cast by the "lost-way" technique. Probably Peloponnesian, ca. 520 B.C. British Museum. P: Jean Mazenod, from *L'Art Grec,* Editions d'Art Lucien Mazenod, Paris, 1972.
Below: Floor mosaic in the house of Klosaia, Euboea. P: Pierre Ducrey, courtesy Ecole Suisse de Grèce, Lausanne.

185 *Left:* Dancing maenad. From an Attic hydria by the Meidias Painter. From Ruvo, Italy. ca. 420–410 B.C. Badisches Landesmuseum, Karlsruhe.
Right: Mixing wine. From a red-figure cup by a painter related to the Proto-Panaitian Group. From Gela, Italy, Ashmolean Museum, Oxford.

186–187 Greek dinner party. Fresco panel from the "Tomb of the Diver," Paestum, Italy. 480–470 B.C. NAM, Paestum. P: Jean Mazenod, from *L'Art Grec,* Editions d'Art Lucien Mazenod, Paris, 1972.

186 *Left:* Boeotian trick cup. 4th c. B.C. Ashmolean Museum, Oxford.
Center: Young aristocrat and flute girl. Interior of a red-figure cup by the Brygos Painter. British Museum. P: Peter Clayton, Boxmoor.
Right: Silver drinking cup. From Nymphaeum, Russia, late 5th c. B.C. Ashmolean Museum, Oxford.

187 *Left:* Tipsy reveler. From Attic red-figure cup potted by Hieron and painted by Makron. ca. 490 B.C. Ashmolean Museum, Oxford.
Center: Attic black-figure cup. 6th c. B.C. Ashmolean Museum.
Right: Symposiast with his girl. From a red-figure drinking cup by the Brygos Painter. From Vulci, ca. 490 B.C. Martin von Wagner-Museum der Universität Würzburg. P: Karl Oehrlein.

188 *Top right:* Satyr chorus playing zither. From a vase by the Polion Painter. Metropolitan Museum of Art, Fletcher Fund, New York.
Center left: Satyrs lighting their torches. From a red-figure calyx-krater. Ashmolean Museum, Oxford.
Bottom left: Scene from *Toxotides,* tragedy by Aeschylus. From an Attic red-figure bell-krater by the Lykaon Painter. 440 B.C. Museum of Fine Arts, Boston.
Bottom right: Scene of the *Medea.* From a vase in the Staatliche Antikensammlung und Glyptothek, Munich.

189 *Top left:* Tragedy actor. Fragment of a red-figure krater. From Taras, Italy, mid-4th c. B.C. Martin von Wagner Museum der Universität Würzburg.
Center right: Theater performance. From an Attic red-figure vase. ca. 420 B.C. NAM, Athens.
Bottom left: Scene of *Alcestis,* play by Euripides. From an Apulian loutrophoros by a forerunner of the Ganymede Painter, late 4th c. B.C. Antikenmuseum, Basel. P: Claire Niggli.
Bottom right: Oedipus and the sphinx. From a black-figure alabastron, probably 5th c. B.C. National Museum, Taranto.

190 *Top, left to right:*
Aischylos. Herm from the Farnese Collection. NAM, Naples.
Sophocles. Bust. NAM, Naples.
Aristophanes. Bust, said to be from Hadrian's Villa. Louvre, Paris.
Center: Euripides sitting on a klismos receiving a mask. Relief. AM, Istanbul.

191 Teater of Dionysus, Athens. Mid-4th c. B.C. P: Michael Vickers, Oxford.

192 *Top left:* Socrates. Bust from the Farnese Collection. NAM, Naples.
Top right: Plato. Herm in the Hall of Muses. Vatican Museums, Rome.
Center left: Discussion in the Academy. From a water jar. Museum of Fine Arts, Boston.

193 *Left to right:*
Diogenes. Large statuette in the Villa Albani, Rome. P: Alinari, Florence.
Aristotle. Kunsthistorisches Museum, Vienna.
Zeno. Herm from the Farnese Collection. NAM, Naples.
Epicurus. Head in the Stanza dei Filosofi. Capitoline Museum, Rome.

194 *Left:* Thucydides. Bust. Holkham Hall. From F. Poulsen, *Greek and Roman Portraits in English Country Houses,* 1923.
Bottom right: Setting-out of a hoplite. From an Attic red-figure stamnos. From Vulci, Italy, ca. 430 B.C. Staatliche Antikensammlung und Glyptothek, Munich. P: C.H. Krüger-Moessner.

195 *Top:* View of Amphipolis.
Bottom: Relief from the grave stele of Dexileos. Necropolis of Kerameikos, Athens. 394–393 B.C. Kerameikos Museum, Athens.
Both P: Ekdotike Athenon S.A., Athens.
Right: Corinthian helmet from Olympia. Bronze. British Museum. P: Michael Holford, Loughton.

196 *Left to right:*
Nymph Segesta. Tetradrachmon from Segesta, 410–400 B.C. British Museum.
River God Gelas with Sosipolis. Tetradrachmon from Gela, ca. 440 B.C. Collection Käppeli.
Lion's head. Tetradrachmon from Leontini, ca. 460 B.C. British Museum.
Head of Silen. Tetradrachmon from Aitna, ca. 470–465 B.C. De Hirsch, Brussels.
Running hare, below head of Pan. Tetradrachmon from Messana, ca. 425–420 B.C. Lloyd Collection, British Museum.
All From G.K. Jenkins and H. Küthmann, *Münzen der Griechen,* Office du Livre, Fribourg, 1972.

197 *Top right:* Second Temple of Hera and so-called Basilica, Paestum. P: Leonard von Matt, Buochs.
Center row, left to right:
Bull with bird and fish. Stater from Thurii, ca. 420 B.C.
Lion's mask. Tetradrachmon from Rhegium, ca. 435 B.C. Lloyd Collection.
Scylla, below shell. Stater from Cumae, ca. 430 B.C.
Heracles slaying lion with club. Stater from Heraclea, 410–400 B.C. Lloyd Collection.
All British Museum. From G.K. Jenkins and H. Küthmann, *Münzen der Griechen,* Office du Livre, Fribourg, 1972.
Bottom, left to right:
View over Acragas from the Temple of Juno. View over Elea from the acropolis. Column of the Temple of Hera Lacinia near Croton.
All P: Leonard von Matt, Buochs.

198 *Left:* Chariot racing. From an Attic black-figure krater by the Painter of Louvre F.G. From Gela, Italy, ca. 575–550 B.C.
Bottom right: Nike. Attic red-figure lekythos by the Pan Painter. From Gela, Italy, ca. 480 B.C.
Both Ashmolean Museum, Oxford.

198–199 View over the fertile plain of Gela, Italy. P: Leonard von Matt, Buochs.

199 *Top right:* Triptolemus. From an Attic red-figure lekythos by the Eucharides Painter. From Gela, Italy, ca. 490–480 B.C.
Bottom right: Dionysos. Bronze statuette from Gela, Italy, ca. 500 B.C.
Both Ashmolean Museum, Oxford.

200 *Left:* Ruins of fortification wall at Euryalus.
Bottom right: Ruins of the Temple of Apollo, Syracuse. ca. 565 B.C.
Both P: Leonard von Matt, Buochs.

201 *Top left:* Fort at Euryalus.
Center left and right: Underground gate and stairway of the fort at Euryalus.
Bottom left: Theater at Syracuse. Begun in the 5th c. B.C.
All P: Leonard von Matt, Buochs.

202 *Left:* Temple at Segesta, Italy. Inside. 425–409 B.C. P: Leonard von Matt, Buochs.
Right: Plan of the campaign at Syracuse. Franz Coray after Green.

203 *Left:* "Dionysius' Ear." Syracuse. P: Leonard von Matt.
Right: Funerary stele of Democlides. National Archaeological Museum, Athens. P: Jean Mazenod, from *L'Art Grec,* Editions d'Art Lucien Mazenod, Paris, 1972.

204 *Left:* Euripides. Herm from the Farnese Collection. NAM, Naples.
Bottom: View of the Royal Palace at Pella. P: Tombazi, Athens.

205 *Top:* Stag hunt. Floor mosaic from Pella. ca. 300 B.C. AM, Pella. P: Ekdotike Athenon S.A., Athens.
Center left: Rape of Helen by Theseus. Floor mosaic from Pella, ca. 300 B.C. AM, Pella. P: Hannibal, Athens.
Center right: Philip II. Silver tetradrachmon. 359–336 B.C. British Museum.

206 *Left:* Bronze arrowhead bearing the name of Philip II. Found at Olynthus. 348 B.C. British Museum.
Center: Marble head of Philip II. 4th c. B.C. Ny Carlsberg Glyptothek, Copenhagen.
Right: The marble Lion of Chaeronea. 338 B.C. P: Hirmer Fotoarchiv, Munich.

207 *Left:* Hoplite. 6th c. cup tondo. British Museum. P: Michael Holford, Loughton.
Right: Demosthenes. Marble statue. Braccio Nuovo, Vatican. P: Gabinetto Fotografico Nazionale, Rome.

208 *Above left:* Olympias, mother of Alexander. Silver medallion from Aboukir, Egypt. Staatliche Museen, East Berlin. P: Peter Clayton, Boxmoor.
Above right: Manuscript illustration. See page 12.
Bottom right: Aristotle. Bust. Bibliothèque Mazarine, Paris.

209 *Left:* Marble head of Alexander the Great. From Pergamum, Turkey, early 2nd c. B.C. AM, Istanbul. P: Peter Clayton, Boxmoor.
Right: Alexander the Great with his horse Bucephalus. Gold medallion from Aboukir, Egypt. Staatliche Museen, East Berlin.

210 *Left:* Alexander the Great. Portrait on a silver tetradrachmon. From Alexandria, Egypt. Auction Hess-Leu, Lucerne 1962. P: Leonard von Matt, Buochs.
Right: Alexander the Great in combat. Relief from a sarcophagus from Sidon, Lebanon, late 4th c. B.C. AM, Istanbul. P: Peter Clayton, Boxmoor.

211 *Center, left to right:*
Kairberg fortress, southside. Alexandria, Egypt.
Alexander the Great on horseback and King Porus on elephant. Silver ten drachma piece from Babylon, ca. 330 B.C. British Museum.
Nike flying to crown standing, armed figure of Alexander the Great. Silver ten drachma piece from Babylon, ca. 330 B.C. British Museum.
All P: Peter Clayton, Boxmoor.

212–213 Battle of Issus. Alexander Mosaic from the House of the Faun, Pompeii, Italy. 4th c. B.C. NAM, Naples. P: Leonard von Matt, Buochs.

216 Bronze head of Apollo. 470–460 B.C. British Museum. P: Michael Holford, Loughton.

217 Bronze head of Aphorodite by Praxiteles. 4th c. B.C. British Museum. P: Michael Holford, Loughton.

Acknowledgment

We gratefully acknowledge the kind permission of Professor A.R. Burn to quote (on pages 128–129) from his translation of Archilocus' works, first published in *The Lyric Age of Greece* (London, Edward Arnold Publishers, 1960).